THE SKY'S THE LIMIT

THE SKY'S THE LIMIT

A CENTURY OF CHICAGO SKYSCRAPERS

EDITED BY PAULINE A. SALIGA

INTRODUCTION BY JOHN ZUKOWSKY

CONTRIBUTIONS BY

JANE H. CLARKE

PAULINE A. SALIGA

JOHN ZUKOWSKY

RIZZOLI
NEW YORK

To the memory of my parents,
and to Dick, Trisha, Judy, and Rick
Jane Clarke

To John, Tom, and Nadia
Pauline Saliga

To Milli, Mom, and Dad
John Zukowsky

Frontispiece:
View of 190 South LaSalle Street (see no. 104)
with the Sears Tower (see no. 80) in the background.
Photograph courtesy the John Buck Company

First published in the United States of America
in 1990 by Rizzoli International Publications, Inc.,
300 Park Avenue South, New York, NY 10010
Copyright © 1990 Rizzoli International Publications, Inc.
Text © 1990 by Jane H. Clarke, Pauline A. Saliga, and John Zukowsky
All rights reserved
No part of this publication may be reproduced in any
manner whatsoever without permission in writing
from Rizzoli International Publications, Inc.

Library of Congress Cataloging-in-Publication Data

The Sky's the Limit: A Century of Chicago Skyscrapers /
    Introduction by John Zukowsky: edited by Pauline A. Saliga:
    contributions by Jane H. Clarke, Pauline A. Saliga, and John
    Zukowsky.
        p.   cm.
    Includes bibliographical references.
    ISBN 0-8478-1179-4
    1. Skyscrapers—Illinois—Chicago. 2. Architecture. Modern—19th
century—Illinois—Chicago. 3. Architecture. Modern—20th century—Illinois—Chicago. 4. Chicago (Ill.)—Buildings, structures, etc.
I. Zukowsky, John, 1948- . II. Saliga, Pauline A. III. Clarke,
Jane H
NA6232.S5   1990   89–43565
720′ 483′ 0977311—dc20   CIP

Edited by Jane Fluegel
Designed by Abigail Sturges
Composition by Rainsford Type, Danbury, Connecticut
Printed and bound in Japan by Dai Nippon Printing Company

Reprinted 1992.

Contents

Introduction
by John Zukowsky

1

CHICAGO! The city's name evokes countless images, from slaughterhouses and railroad yards to gin mills, jazz, and 1920s gangsters. But the image that has an even more powerful association with the city is that of the skyscraper. Indeed, Chicago is often credited with being the birthplace of that architectural form through the successful development in the 1880s of the fireproof steel frame and the safety elevator. The resulting "Chicago School" of commercial architecture of the late-nineteenth and early-twentieth centuries, with its characteristically unornamented skeletal façades and large windows, served as a major source of inspiration for European Modernists of the 1920s, some of whom emigrated to the United States a decade later. After the Second World War, they and their followers reshaped the American skyline, as did the succeeding generation of Postmodern architects of the 1980s. This book surveys that development in Chicago in more than a hundred extant skyscrapers built over the past century. But before touring those marvels, it is important to place them in a historical context and to consider the many significant high rises that were demolished as the city grew.

The city of Chicago was officially founded in 1837. It was a frontier settlement that had grown up around Fort Dearborn, a military outpost established in 1803. The site for this future metropolis of skyscrapers was, surprisingly enough, a marshy swamp whose name "Chicago" derives from *Chicagou,* or the wild onions that grew in this area adjacent to that great inland sea, Lake Michigan. Although this ground may not seem to be the best upon which to build a skyscraper city, it is actually easier to do so here than, say, on New York's Manhattan Island, where glacial deposits and sturdy bedrock must be dynamited. Some Chicago architects solved this marshy problem by laying rafts of concrete as foundations and embedding steel-and-iron railroad rails in them, much as medieval cathedral builders had used oak timbers and mortar centuries before.

The small city expanded rapidly during its first few decades, in part through the widespread use of the balloon frame, an 1832 innovation credited to Chicagoan George Snow. He had discovered that milled lumber could be quickly nailed together instead of being joined by the more laborious mortise-and-tenon method. Some likened the ease with which this building technique was executed to inflating a balloon. Before the end of the Civil War, in 1865, Chicago's stockyards were consolidated by the area's railroads, making it the meat-packing capital of America. The industry grew even faster after 1869, the year that marked both the first transcontinental railroad linkup and the introduction of the refrigerated railroad car. As a consequence, between the 1830s and the late 1860s, the population of Chicago grew from some 150 people to over 300,000! The city's destiny as a major metropolis and hub of the nation seemed certain (fig. 1). Then disaster struck. In 1871, a firestorm laid waste to nearly two thousand acres of the city between October 8 and 10 (fig. 2). It was a calamity of some magnitude, but it turned out in significant ways to be a blessing in disguise.

The entire population was galvanized by the disaster, working together to reconstruct the city to a level surpassing its condition before the Great Fire. In the effort talented architects were attracted to Chicago, such as Peter B. Wight, Louis H. Sullivan, and John Wellborn Root. The opportunity to rebuild the city also kept existing architectural firms in business during a time of economic recession, which turned into a full-scale depression by 1873. Finally, architects such as Wight and Sanford Loring developed and patented fireproofing systems in 1874 after first-hand inspection of the ruins of Chicago's holocaust of 1871.

The buildings constructed shortly after the fire were similar to their prefire predecessors in style and form. Most were four or five stories high (fig. 3), and had a sunken first floor for retail purposes. A mass of buildings rose in the 1870s, filling out the city's grid much as it had been before, although some undeveloped lots remained well after the fire. Architects and engineers in the next decade, however, were able to exploit the new technique of fireproof iron-and-steel construction and to take advantage of the newly developed electric safety elevator. The latter first came into use in Chicago in 1887, even though the hydraulic elevator had appeared in 1870 and earlier steam-driven examples dating back to 1857 were found in the Haughwout Building in New York and in Chicago's Charles B. Farwell Company Store of 1864. By 1895 there were more than three thousand elevators in high-rise buildings within the city.

In the 1880s the tall office buildings, or "skyscrapers," as contemporary writers called them, of ten to twenty stories were replacing the five-story buildings of a decade before. And, in this city noted for land speculation, the buildings of the 1880s and 1890s were in turn replaced by taller buildings in the twentieth century. One of the earliest such high rises was the Montauk Block, by Burnham and Root, from 1881–82 (fig. 4). Along with the smaller Borden Block of 1879–80 (demolished), by Adler and Sullivan, the Montauk was among the first in Chicago to use more than one elevator, thereby enhancing its marketability to tenants. Unlike most later skyscrapers, which had iron-and-steel skeletons, the Montauk was constructed with masonry bearing walls. Its severe, unornamented design and like construction made it similar to, though smaller than, Burnham and Root's renowned Monadnock Building of 1891 (see no. 8). Although some consider the ten-story Montauk to be the first tall office building in Chicago, many architectural historians give William Le Baron Jenney credit for designing the first fireproof, iron-frame skyscrapers.

2

3

4

Jenney's First Leiter Building of 1879, though originally
only five stories tall, incorporated iron pilasters to help
support the masonry piers, thus enabling him to design large
windows and a skeletal façade (fig. 5). Jenney's famed Home
Insurance Building of 1884–85 (fig. 6) was originally ten
stories high. Its side walls were of masonry bearing-wall
construction, but the façades on Adams and LaSalle streets
had masonry-reinforced iron frames. Other work of the same
scale by Burnham and Root from the mid- to late 1880s, such
as the Phoenix Building, Insurance Exchange (fig. 7), and
landmark Rookery (see no. 2), all combined masonry-
supported iron-and-steel framing in part of the building with
bearing-wall construction. The same may be said for buildings
by other architects of the period, including the Pullman
Building of 1884 by S. S. Beman (fig. 8) and even the
somewhat skeletal Tacoma Building of 1887–89 by Holabird
and Roche (fig. 9). It was not until the very late 1880s and the
early to mid-1890s that the full potential of masonry-clad and
fireproofed, rigid steel frames was realized by architects such
as Adler and Sullivan, Burnham and Root, and Holabird and
Roche. Unfortunately, some of the best of their buildings have
been destroyed.

Extant skyscrapers by Burnham and Root (and after Root's
death in 1891, by D. H. Burnham and Co.) include the
Monadnock, Reliance, and Fisher buildings (see nos. 5 and 8),
but two of their most famous office buildings have been
demolished: the Woman's Temple (fig. 10) and the massive
Masonic Temple (fig. 11), both from 1891–92. The latter
loomed over the city at twenty-two stories, or more than 300
feet high. It replaced Adler and Sullivan's 275-foot-high
Auditorium Building of 1889 (see no. 3) as the tallest building
in Chicago. By contrast, New York's tallest building in 1875
was Richard Morris Hunt's 260-foot-high Tribune Building. It
was superseded by George B. Post's Pulitzer Building of
1890, which topped out at more than 300 feet. But when put
into a larger context, these Chicago and New York structures
were not really that tall. For instance, the Washington
Monument when completed in 1885 reached a final height of
555 feet, whereas the Eiffel Tower of 1889 came to a height
of 984 feet when finished.

Even after Adler and Sullivan's Auditorium was no longer
the tallest building in Chicago, the firm actively continued to
build skyscrapers in this and other cities, ranging from the
well-known Wainwright Building of 1890–91 in St. Louis
through the slightly later but even more famous Guaranty
Building of 1894–96 in Buffalo. Two important Adler and
Sullivan buildings in Chicago that, sadly, have been
demolished, were the Schiller Building of 1891–92 (fig. 12)
and the Chicago Stock Exchange of 1893–94 (fig. 13). It was
in those buildings that Sullivan realized the design theory that
he later published in an 1896 essay titled "The Tall Office

Building Artistically Considered." This theory proposed that because skyscrapers were vertical forms, they should be designed as if they were "columns," with three distinct features: a pronounced base, a vertically accentuated shaft, and an elaborate capital. Unfortunately, all that survives of those two fine Chicago buildings are a number of architectural fragments, including the entrance arch to the Stock Exchange and the same building's Trading Room, both on permanent display at The Art Institute of Chicago. In addition to those executed buildings, Adler and Sullivan prepared a design intended to rival the Masonic Temple by Burnham and Root. It was called the Fraternity Temple in 1891 (fig. 14); planned to be thirty-two stories high with an observation deck, as in their Auditorium Building, it was in fact never built.

The work of Burnham and Root and of Adler and Sullivan was rich in ornamentation during the final two decades of the century (see the Rookery [no. 2], of 1885–88, by the former and the latter's Schlesinger and Mayer Store, now Carson Pirie Scott [no. 14], of 1899). Indeed some buildings designed by Holabird and Roche after their Tacoma Building were also ornate (see the Marquette Building, no. 11), but more often than not their structures were somewhat severe in character. Overt structural expression and triple-bayed Chicago windows (having a large, fixed central pane and double-hung side windows) typified buildings by the firm, such as the Gage Group, McClurg, Chicago Savings Bank, and Brooks buildings (see nos. 13, 15, 16, and 23), as well as the demolished Cable Building of 1899. Many of those structures, and many of their counterparts designed by Burnham and Root and by Adler and Sullivan, were speculative office buildings financed by New York and Boston developers. It has been observed with some truth that those investors, not being Chicago residents, did not wish to spend funds on unnecessary ornamentation. Hence, Chicago buildings of the era were on the whole less ornate than those of New York or Boston. Moreover, many elaborately ornamented New York buildings were corporate headquarters, which merited increased expenditures on decorations to promote the companies' images within the financial and business community. The era of the corporate headquarters built with advertising imagery in mind came somewhat later to Chicago, in the first two decades of the twentieth century. In the late-nineteenth and early-twentieth centuries architects, influenced by the classicism of the "White City" made popular by Chicago's World's Columbian Exposition of 1893, planned their skyscrapers much as they had before. Now, however, they frequently used limestone and white terra-cotta as their building materials and incorporated classical details instead of ornament based on Romanesque or Gothic styles. Specific examples include Edmund R. Krause's Majestic Building of 1905 (see no. 18); D. H. Burnham's Railway Exchange of

11

12

13

14

15

16

17

18

1903–04 (see no. 17), Peoples Gas of 1910–11 (also no. 17), and Conway Building of 1912–13 (see no. 27); as well as Holabird and Roche's minimally detailed McCormick Building of 1910–12 (see no. 22) and the now demolished Republic Building of 1905–09 (fig. 15). But the most famous Chicago-style building of this period is, ironically, in New York and not Chicago.

D. H. Burnham and Co., under the design direction of Frederick P. Dinkelberg, executed the Flatiron (Fuller) Building in 1902 (fig. 16). Planned as a series of stacked floors in the Chicago tradition, it departed from the usual New York skyscraper, which often had an ornamental tower rising from a lower, blocky mass. Charles Moore, in his monograph *Daniel H. Burnham* (1921), recounts that New York architect Charles McKim wrote Burnham on April 30, 1902, saying: "The only building higher than your Fifth Avenue and 23 Street building that I have ever heard of is the Tower of Babel. They are adding at a rate of about a story a day, and there are four more stories, they say, to go." This hints at the speed with which the fireproofed-steel skyscraper could be erected once the tentative construction systems of the 1880s had been perfected in the next decade. In fact, Louis Sullivan's Schlesinger and Mayer Store addition (see no. 14) was praised in *Fireproof* magazine (May 1903) for its speedy construction time of under fourteen weeks. But this quick construction also meant that high-rise records could be displaced rather easily. The twenty-three-story Flatiron was never really a contender.

Just three years before, in 1899, George B. Post had again secured the record for the tallest building in the world with his St. Paul Building, constructed in New York (but now demolished) near his Pulitzer Building of 1890. New York had a string of record-breakers for more than seventy-five years, with buildings such as Ernest Flagg's 612-foot-high Singer Tower, finished in 1908 (demolished); Cass Gilbert's Woolworth Building, of 1911–13, its terminus reached at 792 feet; the Bank of the Manhattan Company, of 1929, by H. Craig Severance, 927 feet high; William Van Alen's Chrysler Building, of 1929, which is 1,046 feet high; and the renowned Empire State Building, of 1931, by Shreve, Lamb and Harmon, which rose to the colossal level of 1,250 feet (fig. 17). It was not until 1974 that Chicago's Sears Tower (see no. 80), its 110 stories piled 1,454 feet high, topped New York's World Trade Center of 1970–71 as the record-holder by a bit more than 100 feet. Other Chicago buildings of the 1960s and early 1970s came close to this mark. The John Hancock Center of 1965–70 by Skidmore, Owings and Merrill has a hundred stories and Edward Durell Stone's Standard Oil Building of 1974 has eighty; both are more than 1,100 feet high (see nos. 75 and 77). In contrast with those Modernist megaliths, the Chicago skyscrapers built during the first three

Fig. 19. Graham, Anderson,
Probst and White. Preliminary
study for the National Life
Insurance Tower, c. 1921–22.
Pencil on tracing paper

Fig. 20. Andrew Rebori. Design
for a Michigan Avenue Tower,
1925

decades of the twentieth century rose to only half the height
of their tallest New York cousins.

The largest of these Chicago examples were designed by
Holabird and Root, the successor firm to Holabird and
Roche, and Graham, Anderson, Probst and White, one of the
successor firms to D. H. Burnham and Co. The Holabird
firm's buildings include the Chicago Temple Building of 1923,
556 feet high; 333 North Michigan Avenue of 1927–28, 435
feet high; the Palmolive Building of 1927–29, 468 feet high,
although its 150-foot-high Charles Lindbergh Beacon of two
billion candlepower could be seen some 500 miles away; the
LaSalle-Wacker Building of 1928–30, 491 feet high; and the
Chicago Board of Trade of 1930, at more than 600 feet high,
the tallest building in Chicago during this era (see nos. 30, 41,
45, 51, and 53). Graham, Anderson, Probst and White also
built comparably; their Wrigley Building of 1922/1925 is 398
feet high; the Pittsfield Building of 1927 is 557 feet high; the
Civic Opera of 1929 is 555 feet in height; and the Field
Building of 1934 is 535 feet high (see nos. 29, 44, 50, and 57).
In good part, the adoption of various zoning ordinances in
Chicago during the 1920s contributed to the overall
appearance and massing of those skyscrapers.

Prior to 1923, the law allowed a maximum building height
of 260 feet above grade. Any towers exceeding that limit, such
as the Wrigley and London Guarantee (see no. 31) buildings,
had to remain unoccupied. But in that year Chicago passed a
building ordinance based on New York's zoning law of 1916.
The catalyst for the New York law had been the construction
of a Chicagoan's office building in New York. Designed by
Ernest R. Graham, of Graham, Anderson, Probst and White,
the thirty-eight story Equitable Building of 1912–15 (fig. 18)
had been built as a series of large, stacked floors that cast a
shadow some four blocks long. Realtors and concerned
citizens of New York feared that continued building at this
scale would upset local land values and disrupt neighborhood
support systems. According to the new law of 1916, buildings
exceeding a height of 300 feet were required to be stepped
back in varying ratios, although a part of a building equal to
one-fourth of the lot's size could be built to any height.
Likewise, the 1923 Chicago law permitted additions if they
did not exceed one-sixth of the building's cubic volume and
complied with related setback requirements. Existing towers
that were taller than the 260 feet allowed by law could now
be occupied, and new towers could be designed for
occupancy.

The boom years of the 1920s witnessed a surge in building
and in projects for buildings that were never executed
(some—figs. 19, 20—reveal themselves by appearance alone as
dating from before or after the 1923 law). Several features of
the 1909 Plan of Chicago by Daniel H. Burnham and Edward
H. Bennett were realized, namely the widening of Michigan

19   20

Fig. 21. Eliel Saarinen. Project for
a lakefront development in
Chicago, from American
Architect, 1923

Fig. 22. Holabird and Root, with
Hood, Godley, and Fouilhoux,
and Voorhees, Gmelin, and
Walker. Model for Illinois
Central air-rights project:
Terminal Park, c. 1928

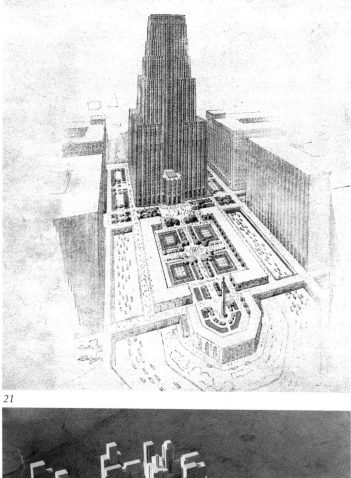

21

22

Avenue into a grand boulevard rivaling any found in Paris; the construction of the classically styled Michigan Avenue Bridge in 1918–20; the creation of Wacker Drive, a double-level street system built south of the bridge along the river; and the construction of Buckingham Fountain as the centerpiece of the city's lakefront Grant Park in 1925. Those years were also significant for another reason related to the 1923 ordinance and the establishment of Michigan Avenue as the grand stagefront boulevard of the city.

The 1922 international competition to design the *Chicago Tribune*'s new headquarters on Michigan Avenue, just north of the newly constructed bridge and almost directly opposite the new Wrigley Building, prompted 263 entries by architects from twenty-three countries. They each hoped to win the first prize of $50,000 and the opportunity to build this prestigious skyscraper. Although entries had to abide by the 260-foot height restriction in force prior to 1923, the new law enabled the premiated design by invited competitors John Mead Howells and Raymond M. Hood to be enlarged about ten stories to a total height of 462 feet in thirty-six stories (see no. 32). But the most prophetic design submitted to the competition was that of Finnish architect Eliel Saarinen, who was awarded second place. His project's overall appearance related to the zoning ordinances governing setbacks being developed in American cities at the time, and the project has been said to have influenced a number of later skyscrapers from coast to coast. Saarinen reused the design principles of this entry in his proposal to build a hotel and office complex, with underground parking, in Grant Park (fig. 21). This prefigured Terminal Park, the air-rights project on nearby Illinois Central land from the late 1920s (fig. 22). Although Terminal Park would eventually be realized in the Illinois Center of the 1960s (see no. 73), it was never built in its 1920s form because of the Stock Market Crash of October 29, 1929, and the resulting Great Depression, which ended many such dreams in Chicago and around the world.

The Depression of the 1930s and the Second World War that followed prevented most new construction on a skyscraper scale. At the war's end, the building industry geared up to satisfy returning servicemen's need for housing. As jobs became increasingly available in the late 1940s and early 1950s, new work places were needed. By that time, the German architect Ludwig Mies van der Rohe, who had arrived at Chicago's Armour Institute of Technology in 1938, and his émigré colleagues Ludwig Hilberseimer and Walter Peterhans had for almost a decade been training a new generation of architects, planners, and designers in the aesthetic philosophies of European Modernism. Among Mies's Chicago high rises his aesthetic is best seen in the 860–880 Lake Shore Drive apartments begun in 1948, the Federal Center begun in 1959, Illinois Center begun in 1967, and the

Fig. 23. Ludwig Mies van der
Rohe with Philip Johnson,
associate architect. Seagram
Building, 375 Park Avenue, New
York, 1954–58

Fig. 24. Ludwig Karl
Hilberseimer. Study for Near
North and West Loop Project,
c. 1960–65. Ink and pencil on
tracing paper

Fig. 25. Walter A. Netsch of
Skidmore, Owings and Merrill.
Administration Building of the
University of Illinois, Chicago
Circle Campus, 1960–65

Fig. 26. Harry Weese and
Associates. Proposed World Trade
Center, 210 stories high and
2,500 feet tall

IBM Building begun before his death in 1969 (see nos. 58, 61, 73, and 74). But many still cite, with good reason, the Seagram Building in New York from 1954–58 as the classic example of his design beliefs (fig. 23). Similar buildings were being done, with some variations, throughout Chicago in the 1950s and 1960s by firms such as Skidmore, Owings and Merrill and C. F. Murphy Associates. Moreover, a number of large urban-renewal schemes and multiuse complexes were designed (fig. 24) as well as implemented at this time (see Marina City [no. 64], of 1964–67, and McClurg Court Center [no. 76], of 1971).

Architectural historians as divergent as Sigfried Giedion (1941) and Carl W. Condit (1964) related the Modern movement works of figures such as Mies to the structural experiments of Chicago's skyscraper architects of the 1880s and 1890s, even terming some 1950s and 1960s buildings as examples of a "Second Chicago School" of architecture. But, as in the great diversity of design witnessed in the late nineteenth century, the 1960s and 1970s saw the more classically Modernist buildings of Mies and his aesthetic allies standing with individualist, Expressionist designs by Bertrand Goldberg, in his Marina City, Harry Weese in the Metropolitan Detention Center of 1975 (see William J. Campbell United States Courthouse Annex, no. 78), and Walter Netsch for Skidmore, Owings and Merrill, the University of Illinois Chicago Circle campus of 1965 (fig. 25). Comparable to these individualistic designs is the almost Gothic historicist work of Perkins and Will in office towers such as the United States Gypsum Building of 1963 (see no. 63). The structural experiments of the 1880s and 1890s were paralleled during the late 1960s and early 1970s by architect Bruce J. Graham and structural engineer Fazlur Khan, of Skidmore, Owings and Merrill. Their diagonally braced steel structure for the John Hancock Center of 1965–70 and the bundled-tube system of structural planning for the Sears Tower of 1968–74 and One Magnificent Mile of 1978–83 (see nos. 75, 80, and 92) enabled them to raise those buildings to enormous heights and yet maintain stability. Somewhat earlier, in 1956, the always adventurous Frank Lloyd Wright, who was well known for his structural experimentation on a residential scale, had proposed a Mile High Tower on the lakefront. Although it may seem farfetched, in 1982 both Bruce Graham and Harry Weese sent proposals to Chicago developer Stanley Raskow for buildings almost twice the height of the Sears Tower. In direct response to threats from New York developers to erect the world's tallest building, Raskow was proposing to secure the record for Chicago with a half-mile-high skyscraper (fig. 26). Only somewhat less ambitious was the 1989 proposal of Chicago developers Lee Miglin and J. Paul Beitler to top the Sears Tower's record with the 2,000-foot Miglin-Beitler Tower by Cesar Pelli (fig. 27).

23

25

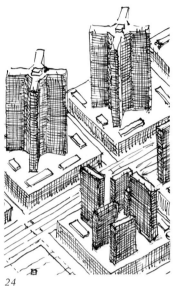

24

26

Fig. 27. Cesar Pelli and Associates. Proposed Miglin-Beitler Tower, which was intended to be the world's tallest building

Fig. 28. Fred Koetter. Late Entry to the Chicago Tribune Tower Competition, 1980. The entry lampoons Walter Gropius's submission to the 1922 competition

Fig. 29. Michael Janis with Tony Porto. Proposed Top for the Chicago Tribune Tower, 1983. Their proposal refers to the slant-topped Associates Center (see no. 89)

Fig. 30. Helmut Jahn of Murphy/ Jahn. Oakbrook Terrace Tower, 1986–88

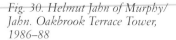

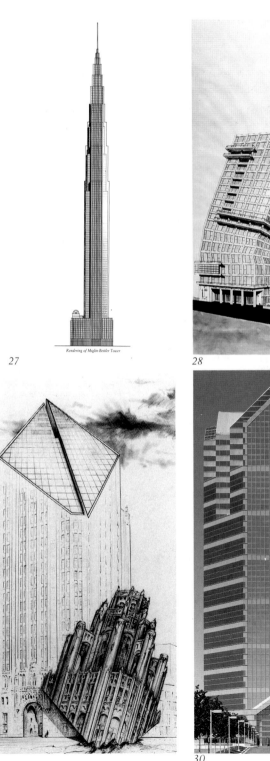

27 · *Rendering of Miglin-Beitler Tower*

28

29

30

Yet most architects and developers of the 1980s ignored this battle of the titans and searched for forms expressive of the American city of the present. New buildings were designed by Helmut Jahn of Murphy/Jahn; Ralph Johnson of Perkins and Will; Voy Lesnikowski of Loebl Schlossman and Hackl; Philip Johnson and John Burgee; William Pedersen of Kohn Pedersen Fox; and some of the younger design partners in Skidmore, Owings and Merrill, such as Adrian Smith, Diane Legge, and Joseph Gonzalez. They reached back into the urban imagery of Chicago's past for their new projects. This fascination with the city's architectural heritage was indicative of the widespread interest in architectural pluralism, classicism, and historicism that characterized what was termed Postmodernism in the early 1980s. In Chicago, exhibitions of the work of the Chicago Seven (architects Thomas Beeby, Laurence Booth, Stuart Cohen, James Freed, James Nagle, Stanley Tigerman, and Ben Weese, who took their appellation from the famous 1968 political activists) at Richard Gray Gallery in 1976–77, the revisionist traveling exhibition directed by Stuart Cohen and Stanley Tigerman entitled *Chicago Architects* from 1976, and the reestablishment of the Chicago Architectural Club in 1979 all contributed to a pluralistic interest in the city's architectural past as it has relevance to contemporary design. A theoretical project specifically geared to Chicago's role in skyscraper development was the traveling exhibition and book *Late Entries to the Chicago Tribune Tower Competition* organized by the Museum of Contemporary Art in Chicago in 1980. Directed by Stuart Cohen and Stanley Tigerman, the show was essentially a fantasy competiton with entries by renowned architects from around the globe. It provoked a variety of critical reactions, both negative and positive; but the show was significant in being a record of pluralistic design attitudes, not unlike the first competition, which attracted an eclectic array of proposals from architects in America and abroad. The *Late Entries* projects further reinforced interest in historic urban imagery and raised criticism of the previous generation of Modernists (fig. 28), finding their chaste responses to architecture somewhat limited. Because of the city's long-term link with the skyscraper, and the current interest in the decorative as well as technical aspects of that building type, the Chicago Architectural Club organized a similar competition called *Tops* in 1983. Entrants redesigned the tops of existing Chicago skyscrapers and, as with some of the "late entries" of 1980, provided humorous commentary (fig. 29) and references to famous skyscraper designs of the past.

In many ways, then, Chicago's skyscrapers of today are linked structurally and architecturally with their predecessors over the past century and before. Like those earlier buildings, the high rises since the 1950s have been commissioned to turn a profit for their investors. It is this entrepreneurial spirit that helped make building in Chicago a tangible expression of its business environment. But unlike the result in many other American cities, in Chicago developers and architects have given this flat yet dramatic site on Lake Michigan a spectacular skyline. It testifies to a continuing vitality of design. Although a number of historic skyscrapers that have been felled may be sorely missed, a great many important buildings have taken their places in the ranks, and a good number of high rises have been built outside the business district in Chicago's expanding suburban strips (fig. 30). The intention of this book is, however, to focus on the Loop and Near North Side and Streeterville areas, where most of the city's skyscrapers are located. The boundaries defined by the tracks of the Loop Elevated railroad in the 1890s, encompassing some thirty square blocks, stimulated ever taller building within their confines. The Chicago River to the west and north, Lake Michigan to the east, and the railroad yards to the south defined the essential limits of the city's business core during the late-nineteenth and early-twentieth centuries. The area called Streeterville and the Near North Side, located along the lakefront north of the Chicago River, was made increasingly desirable for high-rise development after the 1920 widening of Pine Street into North Michigan Avenue and the opening of the Michigan Avenue Bridge. This area blossomed in the 1970s and 1980s through an intensive real-estate promotion in which developers, resorting to hyperbole, termed Michigan Avenue the "Magnificent Mile."

The commercial real estate recession of the early 1990s impeded further skyscraper developments in Chicago and other cities, though office towers began to sprout throughout southeast Asia. Nevertheless, 1997 witnessed a turnaround for architectural construction in Chicago, even for high-rises. Blue Cross-Blue Shield opened their expandable skyscraper (see Epilogue), a high-rise hotel was under construction at McCormick Place, and developers planned apartment buildings northeast of the NBC Tower (see no. 102), along with the renovation, into condominiums, of venerable towers such as the Carbide and Carbon Building (no. 47) and the Trustees System Service Building (no. 54). Rising downtown real estate prices prompted one developer, in *Crain's Chicago Business* (August 11, 1997), to quip that new office buildings are "just around the corner" in this continuing saga of Chicago's legendary skyscrapers.

This survey of extant buildings concentrates on office buildings, hotels, and multiuse complexes. Although a few apartment buildings have made their way into the list, these are exceptions to the rule, based on either historic importance or location. The entries are arranged chronologically in most cases, and readers are encouraged not only to tour these buildings with us but also to experience the spaces and structures themselves through first-hand visits to these spectacular sites.

Selected Sources

Bach, Ira J. *Chicago on Foot,* 3d ed. Chicago: Rand McNally & Co., 1977.

————, ed. *Chicago's Famous Buildings: A Photographic Guide to the City's Architectural Landmarks and Other Famous Buildings,* 3d ed. Chicago and London: The University of Chicago Press, 1980.

The Chicago Architectural Journal. Vols. 1–9. Chicago: Rizzoli International Publications, 1981–90.

Cohen, Stuart, and Stanley Tigerman. *Chicago Architects.* Chicago: The Swallow Press, 1976.

————. *Late Entries to the Chicago Tribune Tower Competition.* New York: Rizzoli International Publications, 1980.

Condit, Carl W. *The Chicago School of Architecture: A History of Commercial and Public Buildings in the Chicago Area, 1875–1925.* Chicago: The University of Chicago Press, 1964.

————. *Chicago, 1910–29: Building, Planning, and Urban Technology.* Chicago and London: The University of Chicago Press, 1973.

————. *Chicago, 1930–70.* Chicago and London: The University of Chicago Press, 1974.

————. *The Rise of the Skyscraper.* Chicago: The University of Chicago Press, 1952.

Duis, Perry. "Yesterday's City," *Chicago History* 16, no. 2 (Summer 1987): 64–72.

Paul Gapp's Chicago. Chicago: Chicago Tribune, 1980.

Giedion, Sigfried. *Space, Time and Architecture;* 5th ed. Cambridge, Massachusetts: Harvard University Press, 1967. First edition 1941.

Goldberger, Paul. *The Skyscraper.* New York: Alfred A. Knopf, 1981.

Mayer, Harold M., and Richard C. Wade. *Chicago: Growth of a Metropolis.* Chicago: The University of Chicago Press, 1964.

Randall, Frank A. *History of the Development of Building Construction in Chicago.* Urbana: University of Illinois Press, 1949.

Tigerman, Stanley, ed. *Chicago Architecture. The New Zeitgeist: In Search of Closure.* Lisbon: The Gulbenkian Foundation, 1989.

Zukowsky, John, ed. *Chicago Architecture, 1872–1922: Birth of a Metropolis.* Chicago and Munich: The Art Institute of Chicago and Prestel Verlag, 1987.

————, Pauline Saliga, and Rebecca Rubin. *Chicago Architects Design.* Chicago and New York: The Art Institute of Chicago and Rizzoli International Publications, 1982.

I. BRIDGING TWO ERAS

*From Chicago School Pragmatism
to Classical Ornamentalism*

1. Studebaker Building, 1885

Now the Fine Arts Building
410 South Michigan Avenue
Solon Spencer Beman
Renovation: Solon Spencer Beman, 1896
Renovation of Studebaker Theater: Andrew N. Rebori, 1917
Wabash Avenue Annex: Andrew N. Rebori, 1924

Fig. 2. Studebaker Building, now the Fine Arts Building, after renovation by Solon Spencer Beman in 1896; the original top story was removed and three stories were added. To its right is the Studebaker Annex (later altered)

Painted inside each entrance to the Fine Arts Building, as the Studebaker is now known, are the words: "All passes—ART alone endures," a fitting motto for a building that has been home to artists, musicians, writers, and the theater for almost a century. Yet, as elegant and appropriately fitted for the arts as the building may be, it is an 1896 "adaptive reuse" of a wagon-and-carriage factory and showroom commissioned by the five Studebaker Brothers of South Bend, Indiana.

The Studebaker Building (fig. 1) and its 1896 renovation as the Fine Arts (fig. 2) were the work of the Chicago architect Solon Spencer Beman (1853–1914). Born in New York, Beman worked in the office of the prominent New York architect Richard Upjohn before opening his own practice in that city in 1877. Through his friend the landscape architect Nathan F. Barrett, Beman met railroad-sleeping-car-magnate George Pullman, who in 1879 invited the two men to design a now-renowned industrial community south of Chicago for his Pullman Palace Car Company. The Studebakers chose Beman to design their factory-showroom based on his creative planning for the industrial town and his design of a massive, Romanesque-style office building for Pullman on the southwest corner of Michigan Avenue and Adams Street (demolished 1956; see introduction, fig. 9).

Following the course set by the Chicago Pullman building, the original Studebaker was an eight-story, Romanesque-style structure with heavily rusticated red-granite and gray-limestone arches and piers, huge round arches defining the five bays of the façade, carved ornamental capitals, and conical roofs topping the end bays, with a curious row of three pyramidal roofs in between. Because the first four floors were used as showrooms, Beman incorporated large windows in the façade, a surprising accomplishment since it was a masonry, bearing-wall structure, not like the iron-and-steel frame structures of the later Chicago School buildings (see the Marquette, 1893–95, no. 11). This type of window, as John Zukowsky would note in an article titled "The First Chicago School and Chicago Architecture 1872–1909," in *Process Architecture* (no. 35, 1982), had its origins in the large display windows on the lower floors of commercial buildings from the 1870s and early 1880s, such as the triple bays of two now-demolished Adler and Sullivan buildings—the Rothschild Store (1881) and the Revell Building (1882–83). From such precedents there developed the three-part "Chicago window," a design in which a large, fixed, central pane of glass is flanked by double-hung, movable-sash windows on either side. The Chicago window as defined here first appeared in such buildings as Holabird and Roche's Tacoma Building (1887–89, demolished; see introduction, fig. 9) and would be used by Beman himself in his second Studebaker Building, at 623 South Wabash, in 1895–96 (fig. 3).

The upper floors of the 1885 Studebaker Building, where the

wagons and carriages were assembled, had groups of three much smaller windows. Beman's way of differentiating features of the façade to represent different functions in the building is an early example of the philosophy later codified by Louis Sullivan as "form follows function." Originally, the entrance to the building was in the center of the ground floor, while the round-arched opening at the south end of the façade was glazed and that at the north end was a driveway. The tightly composed façade had a sense of weight and massiveness characteristic of the Romanesque-revival style that swept the nation in the 1870s and 1880s.

In the late 1880s, the success of the Studebaker business demanded additional space, and a small, five-story annex was constructed immediately to the north. The Romanesque style of the annex harmonized with that of the original building. However, the annex did not solve the need for additional space, and in 1895, the Studebakers commissioned Beman to design the building for them at 623 South Wabash Avenue (extant, but greatly altered). The new building opened on June 1, 1896, while the Studebakers retained ownership of the Michigan Avenue structure for another seven years.

The driving force behind the conversion of the Studebaker into the Fine Arts Building (fig. 2) was Charles C. Curtiss, the son of a former mayor of Chicago, who had a successful career as a music publisher, owner of a piano factory, and developer of Weber Music Hall, purportedly the first building in Chicago designed with studios for musicians and artists. Beman designed the extensive renovation, which entailed changing the façade as well as the interior. The two arched openings on the first floor became doorways, with three storefronts in between. The conical and pyramidal roofs were removed, along with the attic and façade of the eighth floor, and three more floors were added. The interior was altered to accommodate two music halls on the first floor and soundproof studios, shops, and offices for artists, musicians, writers, and architects on the second through the tenth floors. The tenth floor had skylights and twenty-three-foot-high ceilings, which attracted prominent local painters such as portraitist Ralph Clarkson (1861–1943) and the city's leading sculptor, Lorado Taft (1860–1936). Beman also carved out a large interior light well, named the Venetian Court, running from the fourth floor to the roof.

From the time it opened in 1898 until the 1920s, the Fine Arts Building was very successful, housing two music schools, dozens of artists and musicians, and many cultural organizations, including the Municipal Art League and The Fortnightly, a literary club. After the turn of the century, the building became the local center of the women's suffrage movement, housing the offices of the Equal Suffrage Association and the Cook County Woman's Suffrage Party. In addition, it became an important center for the Arts and Crafts Movement in the Midwest and contained shops that sold silver, pottery, and the like. Frank Lloyd Wright, the most prominent figure in the movement, had an office on the tenth floor in 1908, and he designed a bookshop on the first floor and a gallery in the annex.

During the early years of the century, more changes were made to the building. In 1909, the annex to the north was remodeled, which included the removal of its Romanesque façade. In 1917 the architect Andrew Rebori (1886–1966) redesigned the Studebaker Theater, and in 1924 he built another annex, a narrow six-story building that faced Wabash Avenue. It was connected to the main building only at a fourth-floor bridge, but the real reason for its construction was to house the furnace for the main building, which until then had been warmed by the heating plant in what is today the Americana-Congress Hotel.

After 1920, the original art colony that had been centered in the Fine Arts Building began to disperse as tenants moved out. Ever since the 1930s, it has been subject to financial trouble as it passed through the hands of several successive owners. Despite that fact, the structure has remained virtually intact over the years, both in its appearance and in its appeal to artistic tenants. Today it still functions as a building devoted to the arts, from its small movie theaters on the first floor to its practice rooms for musicians above. The Fine Arts Building is a rare example of a nineteenth-century artists' colony that has survived to fulfill the same function in the twentieth century. —P.A.S.

2. Rookery, 1885–88

209 South LaSalle Street
Burnham and Root
Renovation of lobby: Frank Lloyd Wright, 1905;
William Drummond, 1931
Restoration: Hasbrouck-Hunderman, 1983–84;
Hasbrouck Peterson Associates, 1984–85 and 1989–90
Building renovation: Booth Hansen and Associates, begun 1985;
McClier Corporation, 1989–90; consulting architect:
Takayama and Associates, 1989–90

Fig. 1. Burnham and Root. Rookery, 209 South LaSalle Street, 1885–88

Figs. 2, 3. Entrance to the Rookery, 209 South LaSalle Street. Below, detail of ornamental jamb, with namesake rooks

When Daniel Hudson Burnham (1846–1912) and John Wellborn Root (1850–1891) formed their architectural partnership in 1873, the two young men were so poor they had between them, as Burnham put it, but "a full color box and one stick of India-ink." Eighteen years later, when their partnership ended with the untimely death of Root at age forty-one, they had 270 residences and commercial buildings to their credit, over forty in Chicago. Of their numerous skyscrapers in the Loop, only two survive, the Rookery (fig. 1) and the Monadnock Building (1892, see no. 8).

The theme of the Rookery is light. The large site is almost square (177 feet 8 inches by 167 feet 6 inches). Fronting on LaSalle and Adams streets to the west and north and on Rookery and Quincy courts to the east and south, the eleven-story building is situated so that air and light enter from all directions. At the ground level, two-story oriel windows face the two major streets, and flat panes of plate glass, separated by only the narrowest of mullions, face the more shadowed side courts. On the upper floors, tiers of double-hung windows are set between narrow columns. To bring light to the interior of the enormous commercial structure, the architects created an open light well and surrounded it with a ring of offices in a form that has been dubbed the doughnut.

The exterior is richly decorated with tourelles and Romanesque arches, as well as Islamic arabesques and other details of Moorish and Venetian origin (fig. 2). At the LaSalle Street entrance are two carved rooks (fig. 3), Root's whimsical allusion to the building's name, derived from the temporary City Hall that had occupied the site after the Great Fire of 1871. The dilapidated structure had attracted pigeons and presumably crows and so was derisively called The Rookery, an epithet that clung to the site despite the determined effort of one of the investors, Peter Brooks of Boston, to devise a more dignified name. Besides Brooks the other investors were his brother Shepherd, also a Bostonian, and the Chicagoan Owen Aldis; they were represented by E. C. Waller, who as a very young man had accompanied Burnham on a trip to the West to prospect for gold. Although they had not struck it rich, they remained friends all their lives and often did business together. It had been Waller who had secured a ninety-nine-year lease for the site at Adams and LaSalle from the City of Chicago and begun negotiations with the two Brooks Brothers for a large new building in the heart of the financial district.

Burnham, a masterful organizer of spaces, probably had a hand in the floor plan, but it was Root, the firm's chief designer, who enclosed the first two floors of the light well with a glass-and-iron roof, creating a light-filled interior court (figs. 4, 5). The stairs to the second floor were cantilevered into the space, but the flights to the upper floors were encased in an oriel tower located in the light well. The court, surrounded

by retail spaces and flooded with light, provided a lively center for the building. Light bounced off the innovative white-glazed brick walls of the light well, entering the inner offices above the court and filtering into the first-floor shops through the Luxfer-prism glass brick of the mezzanine floor.

This brilliantly organized design plan is a summation of what Burnham and Root had been working toward since their Chicago, Burlington and Quincy General Office Building of 1883 (demolished). The Burlington, with its rather awkward light court, was, according to Donald Hoffmann in *The Architecture of John Wellborn Root* (1973), "the first office building in Chicago in which a significant amount of space was sacrificed for lighting." Root's far more sophisticated design for the court of the Rookery transformed a functional space into an aesthetic masterpiece. As Meredith L. Clausen commented in *Chicago Architecture, 1872–1922* (1987), Root probably was inspired by the interiors of Bon Marché (1869–76) and Le Printemps (1881), the innovative French department stores he would have seen on a trip to Paris with his wife and daughter in 1886. However, the Rookery's dramatic, light-filled airy court was an imaginative design concept for the heart of an American commercial building.

The Rookery was a compendium of nineteenth-century technology in the transitional decade of the 1880s, when the metal-framed skyscraper was evolving and caissons—shafts driven down to a firm foundation and filled with concrete—had not yet come into common use as foundations. Supporting the enormous bulk of the Rookery on the marshy soil of Chicago may have seemed daunting to Root, but he solved the problem by using an improved form of the rail-grillage footings he had first employed in the Montauk Block (1881–82, demolished 1902). Also referred to as a floating foundation, this technical innovation was a raft of concrete reinforced with layers of steel rails that spread the load of a building. Carl W. Condit suggests in *The Chicago School of Architecture* (1964) that Root "thought of the raft as a steel foundation with a concrete envelope to prevent rusting." A century later, as the Rookery was undergoing restoration, virtually no settling was discovered.

Above ground the sides fronting on Rookery and Quincy courts are supported by iron frames, and those facing LaSalle and Adams streets, although resting on masonry piers at the base, also have, as Hoffmann states, "metal in the lintels, . . . beams within the masonry, . . . [and] hoop iron girding the fabric." A structurally independent iron frame, completely exposed and sheathed in glass at the court levels, encloses the light well. This skeleton made possible one of the earliest appearances of ribbon windows; they line the light well above the court, providing daylight for all the inner offices.

When completed in 1888, the eleven-story Rookery was hailed as the largest and finest office building in the country.

Fig. 5. Rookery, view of the original two-story interior light court, c. 1893

It quickly filled with prestigious clients, including the firm of Burnham and Root. In 1905 the owners commissioned the young architect Frank Lloyd Wright, who had at one time had an office in the building, to give the light court a more modern look, one in keeping with the new century (fig. 4). His treatment was sensitive to Root's design but radically altered the court's appearance, substituting white and gold for Root's wrought-iron tracery. Some twenty-five years later, in 1931, William Drummond made other alterations to the court and lobbies—and less sympathetic alterations followed. Among the glories of the original building were expansive, two-story lobbies facing Adams and LaSalle, which opened paths of light from the entrances into the central court. At some point they were divided to provide more rentable footage, their great second-floor windows were painted black, and the glass ceiling of the court was tarred over.

The Rookery was entered in the National Register of Historic Places in 1970 and designated a Chicago Landmark by the Chicago City Council in 1972. In 1982 the Continental Illinois National Bank and Trust Company bought the building and vacated it, intending to restore it and occupy all eleven floors. The exterior was cleaned and exploratory work began on the exterior. The current owner, Baldwin Development Company, commissioned McClier Corporation to complete the restoration as well as the renovation of the office floors.

The award-winning restoration, directed by Gunny Harboe, roofed the lightwell with glass to create a nine-story atrium (as in the Railway Exchange, see no. 17), which also protects the dramatic oriel stair from further deterioration. Although restoration of the interior court goes back to Wright, the removal of layers of tar from the glass roof and of floor tiles from the prismatic glass on the mezzanine level makes the court once more a source of natural light, as Root intended. The building has received "the bang-up job that it deserves," according to Tim Turner of the National Trust for Historic Preservation. —J.H.C.

3. Auditorium Building, 1887–89

Northwest corner of Michigan Avenue and Congress Parkway
Adler and Sullivan
Renovation of Hotel and Office Building: begun 1946
Demolition of Auditorium Bar and Hotel Café: 1952
Restoration of Auditorium Theater: Harry Weese and
Associates, 1967

*Figs. 3, 4. Auditorium Hotel,
views of the first-floor lobby,
c. 1889*

The Auditorium Building of Dankmar Adler (1844–1900) and
Louis H. Sullivan (1856–1924) is a tour de force of design
and engineering. Renowned for its beauty and ingenuity, the
building set numerous records in its time: At completion it
was the city's largest (63,500 square feet), tallest (seventeen
stories), and most expensive building ($3,200,000). And it was
also the heaviest structure in the world (110,000 tons). Of far
greater significance than these simple facts, however, was the
building's immediate recognition as the key symbol of
Chicago's cultural life in the late 1880s. Adler's engineering
innovations and Sullivan's incredibly beautiful interior
ornament elevated this building to the status of a work of art
and laid the groundwork for Adler and Sullivan's later success.

The Auditorium (figs. 1, 2), a ten-story building with a
seventeen-story tower, was originally a three-part structure
housing a 400-room, L-shaped hotel fronting on Michigan
Avenue and extending along Congress Parkway to the tower
(figs. 3–6); an office building of 136 individual offices located
on Wabash Avenue and in the tower; and a 7,000-seat theater
(fig. 7), the largest in America at the time. The theater was the
raison d'être of the structure, and the hotel and office block
were designed to support its activities. The building was
commissioned in 1886 by Ferdinand Peck and the Opera
Festival. Adler and Sullivan were well prepared to handle the
commission since they had already designed several highly
successful Chicago theaters (all since demolished), including
the Central Music Hall (1879), the Grand Opera House
(1879), the McVicker's Theater (1883), and a theater in the
Interstate Exposition Building (1885) that was renovated to
house the Chicago Opera Festival of 1885.

In order to construct the incredibly large building, whose
exterior walls were made of load-bearing masonry, Adler
employed all of the structural-engineering solutions known at
the time and then some. Among his innovations was an
ingenious raft foundation that equalized distribution of the
building's weight. To ensure that the building and tower
would settle evenly during construction in the Chicago mud
and clay, Adler artificially increased their weight at the outset
by adding enormous quantities of pig iron and brick in the
basement and lower stories. As the tower rose, the extra
weight was removed. Adler's method of artificial settling
proved successful, and in the end the building sank only
eighteen inches. Adler's other pioneering solutions to
engineering problems included providing the theater with a
hydraulically operated stage, an early system of air
conditioning, virtually unobstructed sight lines, nearly perfect
acoustics, and an ingenious partition system that allowed the
seating capacity to be decreased by 2,800 depending on the
size of the audience expected.

The exterior design of the ten-story building was based to a
large extent on the Marshall Field Wholesale Store (1885–87,

Figs. 5, 6. *Auditorium Hotel,*
views of the main dining room
and bar, c. 1889

Fig. 7. *Proscenium arch of the*
7,000-seat Auditorium Theater,
c. 1889

demolished 1930) of Henry Hobson Richardson. The massive store was one of the city's most influential buildings of the late nineteenth century owing to its enormous size and its successful transfer of the popular East Coast Romanesque-revival style to Chicago. Although the Auditorium's façade bears a strong resemblance to the Richardson building, Adler and Sullivan distinguished their effort from the earlier building by means of a seventeen-story tower located halfway down the Congress Parkway façade. An earlier scheme for the Auditorium provided for a tower of lesser height but with a conical roof and a much more complicated roofline, with smaller towers, mansards, and dormers (fig. 2). At the time of completion, the Auditorium tower was the tallest structure in Chicago and therefore housed an observatory and the United States Signal Service Station. It also contained prestigious office space and was the home of Adler and Sullivan's firm until it was dissolved in 1895; Sullivan himself kept an office there until the 1920s.

Probably the most remarkable feature of the building is its geometric and foliate interior ornament, some of Sullivan's finest. Exquisite murals and bands of painted patterning throughout the interior highlight the building's structure and various functions. The architect also incorporated elaborate carved oak, plaster, and leaded-glass details featuring interlocking geometric forms and curving stems of lush, spiky leaves. Sullivan's ornament from this period was intricate and sophisticated, with curving leaves, elegant arabesques, and intertwining geometric forms such as figure-eights and ribbon

patterns. His color scheme for the Auditorium of gold leaf laid over solid-colored backgrounds gave it an even more luxurious and ethereal appearance. Nowhere is that more evident than in the Auditorium Theater (fig. 7). Although the Auditorium Building's overall ornamental scheme was conceived by Sullivan, much of it was detailed by Frank Lloyd Wright, who had been hired by Sullivan as a draftsman to assist with the project.

The Auditorium played an extremely important role in Chicago's cultural life and helped change the image of the city from an isolated prairie town to a center of American culture that could compete with much older cities such as Boston and New York. The contemporary architect and critic Thomas E. Tallmadge, looking back at the time in his book *Architecture in Old Chicago* (1941), summed it up when he wrote: "Now magnificence and culture shone forth unmistakably where once the world fancied it saw only mud and pig sticking." When the Auditorium opened, it became the first home of the Chicago Opera Company, and until 1905, when Orchestra Hall was opened, also housed the Chicago Symphony Orchestra. However, by 1900, according to the *Inland Architect* (September–October 1989), the corporation that constructed the building would have preferred to demolish it and put up a steel-frame skyscraper in its place. In 1905, Sullivan himself presented a plan to eliminate the theater and construct an entirely separate building inside the present one. This scheme, calling for a structure of more than twenty stories, was killed by the prospect of lengthy legal battles with

the many landowners who leased the ground to the Auditorium Association. However, that did not put an end to the threats of demolition. In 1924, when architects Benjamin Marshall and Charles Fox were asked to assess the theater, they recommended that it be replaced with something "new and modern," and they particularly criticized the now revered Sullivan woodwork for being of "the old and antiquated type of design." In 1929 the onset of the Great Depression and the construction of the Civic Opera signaled the beginning of a long decline for the Auditorium Building. Considered architecturally obsolete and a financial failure, it was saved from demolition only by the enormous cost of razing the massive, expertly engineered structure. During the Second World War, it was used as a servicemen's center, and the theater's once magnificent stage was converted into bowling alleys.

After years of neglect and progressive deterioration, the building was purchased in 1946 by Roosevelt University, which had been established two years earlier. By 1947 hotel rooms and offices were converted into classrooms, faculty offices, and various other university facilities. When Congress Parkway was widened in 1952 as a feeder for expressways to the western suburbs, a part of the Auditorium Building was torn down to provide space for a sidewalk arcade. Beginning in 1953 the University undertook the restoration and renovation of many of the Auditorium's most important spaces, including the banquet hall and ballroom, which were converted into Ganz Memorial Recital Hall in 1957; the men's

smoking room on the second floor, which became the Spertus Faculty Lounge in 1960; and the tower itself, which would house the Walter E. Heller College of Business Administration and faculty offices from 1972 onward. Because restoration of the magnificent theater was beyond the resources of the University, the Auditorium Theater Council was established in 1960 to restore and operate it. Under the guidance of the architectural firm of Harry Weese and Associates, the theater was brought back to full splendor in 1967. The Auditorium Building was placed on the National Register of Historic Places in 1970, and in 1975 it was declared a National Historic Landmark by the United States Department of the Interior. In 1976 the renowned structure was designated a Chicago landmark.

In 1989 Roosevelt University celebrated the centennial of this important building. To commemorate its long and distinguished history, the Auditorium Building Centennial Archive was established and charged with recording the recollections and impressions of architects, historians, musicians, dancers, actors, students, faculty, and others who had come to know the beauty and majesty of the landmark. In 1995 architect Larry Booth completed the renovation of the Congress Parkway entrance to the theater and its lobby, using a design vocabulary that is sympathetic to the century-old structure. —P.A.S.

4. Pontiac Building, 1889–91

542 South Dearborn Street
Holabird and Roche
Renovation: Booth Hansen and Associates, 1985

The Pontiac Building is the earliest surviving skyscraper by William Holabird (1854–1923) and Martin Roche (1853–1927), and it follows the lead set by the architects in the Tacoma Building (1887–89, demolished 1929), their first important office-block commission and their first great achievement (see introduction, fig. 9). In the Tacoma, Holabird and Roche had incorporated numerous structural, technical, and design innovations, including a new system of wind bracing to increase the tall building's resistance to wind pressure and an L-shaped plan that gave all offices an outside exposure. In addition, the architects introduced the projecting window bay, running it in series from the second to the top floor to provide the offices with unprecedented amounts of light and air and to add greater interest to the façade. These innovations, including the projecting bay, reappeared in several of their subsequent buildings, among them the Pontiac and the southern addition to the Monadnock Building in 1893 (see no. 8).

Like the Tacoma, the fourteen-story Pontiac Building can be considered an early, unresolved form of the Chicago School skyscraper, for it does not yet exploit the steel frame to its full structural and aesthetic potential. The Pontiac's windows are the small, double-hung sash variety rather than the large Chicago windows introduced in later buildings, and its exterior is sheathed in solid brick, thus disguising its underlying steel structure. Two years later, however, Holabird and Roche would resolve these design issues in the Marquette Building (see no. 11), their first skyscraper that fully expresses the underlying steel frame.

The Pontiac Building was named after the Ottawa Indian chief who led the 1763 Indian uprising sometimes called the Pontiac War. Like so many Chicago skyscrapers of the late nineteenth century, the building was commissioned by the Boston real estate speculators Peter and Shepherd Brooks, who originally intended it to house printing plants and similar light-manufacturing businesses. Instead, as the building was nearing completion, they decided to lease it for offices. The Pontiac became the home of publishers of such popular journals as *Graphic* and *Western British-American* and such guidebooks and directories as the *Handbook to the World's Columbian Exposition* (1893) and the Banker's and Attorney's registers.

In 1979 the Pontiac was one of twenty-one buildings designated for inclusion in the Printing House Row Historic District by the Commission on Chicago Historical and Architectural Landmarks. All located in the South Loop, the buildings had been commissioned in the late nineteenth or early twentieth century to accommodate the printing industry (see also the Franklin Building, no. 25). As part of the renaissance of Printing House Row (or Printers Row as it has come to be called), the Pontiac was cleaned and renovated in 1985 by the firm of Booth Hansen and Associates. In recognition of the importance of this Chicago School skyscraper, its exterior features were maintained and the office space was simply updated to accommodate the needs of businesses in the 1980s. —P.A.S.

5. Reliance Building, 1890–91, 1894–95

32 North State Street
First and second floors: Burnham and Root, 1890–91
Upper floors: D. H. Burnham and Co., 1894–95

Fisher Building, 1895–96

343 South Dearborn Street
D. H. Burnham and Co.
Addition to the north: D. H. Burnham and Co., 1906

*Fig. 1. D. H. Burnham and Co.
Reliance Building, 32 North State
Street, 1895*

*Fig. 2. Reliance Building, detail
of the east façade, c. 1960. The
original cornice has been removed*

The Reliance Building of 1895 (fig. 1), boldly expressing its underlying metal-frame structure and sheathed almost entirely in glass, has been acclaimed by architectural historian Carl W. Condit and numerous critics as the direct precursor of the International Style skyscraper that was to emerge in Europe thirty years later. Although the historic impact of the Reliance Building is undeniable, the successive involvement of two different architects in its design, the novel method of its construction, and the material used for its cladding also contribute to the significance of this graceful tower.

As the Rookery (1888, see no. 2) had been a transitional building in Burnham and Root's understanding of metal framing, so the Reliance was transitional in the evolution of the firm. John Wellborn Root was the original designer of the Reliance Building. William Ellery Hale, a close friend of Burnham's, was the developer of the highly desirable site at the corner of State and Washington. He had purchased the corner lot and its four-story building in 1882, but his plans for a tall office block had to be postponed until tenant leases on the upper three floors expired on May 1, 1892. However, the lease on the ground floor and raised basement expired May 1, 1890. Under Root's direction, jackscrews were placed under the upper floors, and piers were sunk to support what would eventually be a fifteen-story structure. While tenants on the floors above went about business as usual, the first floor was demolished and a new, enlarged basement was excavated. The renovated first floor, designed for a retail store, was ready for its new occupant, Carson Pirie Scott and Company, on June 30, 1891, and the bronze and granite detailing of the façade, as well as the elaborate decorative work inside, was Root's design. However, he had not seen this phase of the work to completion; the young architect had died the previous January.

In April 1891, Burnham hired Charles B. Atwood (1840–1895) to replace Root as the firm's head designer. At the time, Burnham was chief of construction for the World's Columbian Exposition, scheduled to open in two years, and he named Atwood its designer in chief, as well. The first priority of the two men was the World's Fair, but there was also a commission for the Marshall Field and Company Store (see no. 9), an annex to be completed before the Fair's opening. Thus Atwood did not turn his attention to the Reliance until early in 1894, when according to Donald Hoffmann, in *The Architecture of John Wellborn Root* (1973), the *Chicago Times* reported that "new plans were drawn." Hoffmann further notes that no plans by Root exist for the upper stories of the Reliance, so it is impossible to know how the State Street skyscraper would have looked had he completed it.

Atwood's Beaux-Arts training was fully evident in his buildings at the 1893 Fair and in his Marshall Field Annex of

1892. However, the clearly articulated structure of the Reliance was a giant step in a different direction. The framing was a steel-and-iron skeleton that went up quickly—in just two weeks—above Root's 1891 base. In fact, Charles E. Jenkins, writing for the *Architectural Record* (1895), observed: "Seeing a tremendous building pushing up into the air while one can safely stand at its base and look into shop windows, crowded with the usual displays, is, to say the least, rather out of the usual."

The most remarkable feature for its time, and a forerunner of Modernist works by architects such as Ludwig Mies van der Rohe and Walter Gropius, was the glass curtain wall of the Reliance (fig. 2). On the State and Washington façades, columns of Chicago windows (a fixed center pane with a narrower double-hung window on either side) set almost flush with the surface alternate with protruding double bays divided by the narrowest of mullions. The bays, which added rhythm to the façade and provided the developer with greater floor space, were earlier used in Holabird and Roche's Tacoma Building (1887–89; see introduction, fig. 9). Atwood's use of delicate Gothic ornament on the spandrels has been both praised and damned, but it is consistent with the theory that the only precedent for the soaring height of the new skyscrapers was the Gothic cathedral. The transparency of the surface and the formula of the tall building as classical column, composed of base, shaft, and cornice, here yielded a building that was every inch a skyscraper.

Atwood retained Root's base of red Scotch granite, but the upper floors were entirely sheathed in a creamy-white-glazed terra-cotta. The dazzling surface elicited a great deal of comment, but for the chief designer of the 1893 World's Fair, where the major buildings were painted white, it was not such a surprising choice. Furthermore, Atwood had used creamy stone and terra-cotta in his first Chicago commission, the Marshall Field Annex.

The success of the Reliance Building led to an immediate offspring, the Fisher Building (1895–96, fig. 3), at 343 South Dearborn Street, also designed for D. H. Burnham and Co. by Charles Atwood. Three stories taller than the Reliance and with even more Gothic detailing, the Fisher is sheathed in a golden terra-cotta on its three visible façades and is equally transparent. An article about the building in the *Inland Architect* (May 1896) was titled: "A Building without Walls." Dolphin door handles and other aquatic ornament are a playful reference to the name of the owner, Lucius G. Fisher.

Atwood's brief career as a designer of skyscrapers ended with the Fisher Building, which he did not live to see completed. According to Ann Van Zanten, in *Chicago History* (Fall–Winter 1982), his mental and physical health deteriorated until his frequent absences from work led to his dismissal by Burnham in December 1895, and he died nine days later. Additions were made to the Fisher Building in 1906 by Peter J. Weber, who had been one of Burnham's original designers on the project. The building was renovated in the 1980s, although its rich interior furnishings of marble and mosaic have been much altered. Some of its bronze ornament may be seen at The Art Institute of Chicago in the installation "Fragments of Chicago's Past."

Unlike the Fisher, time did not treat the Reliance Building kindly; it narrowly escaped demolition in the 1960s, but was declared a Chicago landmark in 1975. Its salvation began in 1993 when the city bought it and agreed to fund exterior restoration, carried out by McClier Corporation. Its white terra-cotta surface cleaned, the glass skin repaired, and the cornice replaced, Atwood's tower is once more "gossamer gorgeous," wrote Blair Kamin in the *Chicago Tribune*. In 1998 the future of the building was secured when conversion of the interior into a hotel began by CCR McCaffrey Developments. —J.H.C.

6. Manhattan Building, 1889–91

431 South Dearborn Street
William Le Baron Jenney
Renovation: Hasbrouck-Hunderman, 1982

Fig. 1. *William Le Baron Jenney.*
Manhattan Building, 431 South
Dearborn Street, 1889–91. View
c. 1985

Fig. 2. *View of the Manhattan*
Building from the northwest,
c. 1891

For many years, the Home Insurance Building (1884–85, demolished 1931) by the Chicago engineer and architect William Le Baron Jenney (1832–1907) was credited with being the first skyscraper of skeletal construction, but recent scholarship has tended to diminish that role, considering it a synthesis of contemporary techniques rather than a revolutionary breakthrough. Although the Home Insurance had a skeleton of iron and even included steel girders on the top three floors, its piers were sheathed in masonry, which carried part of the load. However, Jenney's Manhattan Building (fig. 1), completed six years later, was one of the first skyscrapers to use skeletal construction throughout. At sixteen stories high, it briefly held the title of the city's tallest building. And for many years it was the only setback skyscraper in existence.

This startling innovation was noted at once by Louis Sullivan, in an essay called "The High Building Question" (*The Graphic,* December 1891), in which he proposed setbacks as the solution to the problems created by ever-taller buildings. According to Donald Hoffmann, in the *Journal of the Society of Architectural Historians* (May 1970), Sullivan illustrated the essay with his own drawing of a setback city and a rendering by William Bryce Mundie (later Jenney's partner) of the Manhattan Building, which was captioned: "The Inception of the Idea."

The Manhattan setback begins at the tenth floor, giving the building, as a contemporary critic noted, "shoulders like a grain elevator." Necessity was the mother of invention with regard to the setbacks. It was vital to withdraw loads from the party walls of the two far-smaller adjacent buildings (fig. 2; the one to the south has since been demolished). To shrink the Manhattan at the top by means of setbacks was one method, and to cantilever the foundations was another. According to Carl W. Condit in *The Chicago School of Architecture* (1964), the floors along the side elevations were carried "on cantilever beams anchored to the columns located on the second column line inside the plane of the party walls." The supports of the foundation were thus withdrawn from the property line.

The height and enormous weight of the Manhattan Building required still another innovation, wind bracing. To construct a stable building, the architect and his engineer employed both double diagonals to join the columns at the basement level and portal bracing, which had been developed earlier in the century to brace the end frames of truss bridges. Condit stated in *American Building* (second edition, 1982) that "in this simple but effective form [of bracing] rigidity is secured by riveting the deep girder to the column throughout the depth of the girder web." John Root also employed portal bracing in the Monadnock Building (see no. 8), which by the end of 1891 equaled the Manhattan in height.

Above a rusticated base, the Manhattan Building is decorated in rich terra-cotta ornament, which makes a striking contrast to the smooth, undulating surface of Root's tower, only two blocks north on Dearborn. Both architects made use of projecting bays, which add to the rentable floor space of a building and give a dynamic rhythm to the façade. The Manhattan is also notable for the variety of its window forms. Jenney's intention was to admit as much light as possible, and so the topmost windows above the setback are almost flush with the building's surface, to allow the sun's rays to penetrate the rooms more deeply.

The Manhattan Building has been renovated and converted to apartments with retail shops on the street level. The surrounding area, once a loft district known as Printers Row, has been renamed Burnham Park and offers housing, hotels, restaurants, office buildings, and an interior shopping court in the former Chicago and Western Indiana Railroad Station (designed by Cyrus L. Eidlitz in 1883–85), which dramatically caps Dearborn Street two blocks to the south. —J.H.C.

Fig. 1. William Le Baron Jenney.
Leiter Building, also called Second
Leiter Building, 403 South State
Street, 1891. View from the
southwest

7. Leiter Building, 1891

Now the Second Leiter Building
403 South State Street
William Le Baron Jenney

Fig. 2. Leiter Building, detail of the west façade, 1989

The Second Leiter Building (fig. 1), as it is known today, was commissioned by Levi Z. Leiter, one of Chicago's leading merchants of the late nineteenth century. Shortly after the Civil War, Leiter established a partnership with Marshall Field to form the Field and Leiter Store, a dry goods emporium that gained a reputation not only in Chicago but throughout the Midwest. In 1881 Leiter sold his share of the business to Field, who then established the great department store that bears his name. Leiter went on to develop real estate, and one of his most successful investments was the Second Leiter Building, designed by William Le Baron Jenney. Carl Condit described the building in *The Chicago School of Architecture* (1964) as "Jenney's triumph." Condit further wrote: "In its boldness, vigor, and originality it remains one of the most impressive works of commercial architecture in the empirical spirit that the nation can show. Jenney knew exactly what he was doing, and he never wavered in the execution of his plan."

The eight-story Second Leiter Building fronts on State Street, filling the entire block between Van Buren Street and Congress Parkway. It is the second building that bore Leiter's name; the first, a five-story structure (1879, now demolished) at the northwest corner of Wells and Monroe streets, was also designed by Jenney. But the Second Leiter Building is an early example of steel-frame construction at its best. In the late 1880s and early 1890s, architects such as Jenney were experimenting with building structure, attempting to develop a system whereby exterior masonry could be stretched over a steel frame like skin over bones, and aiming to provide commercial buildings with maximum height, space, light, and ventilation. Structural developments were paralleled by innovations in the design of exteriors, so as to reflect the internal metal structural frame. In the Second Leiter Building the structural system and a finely proportioned, beautifully detailed terra-cotta façade (fig. 2) are united in one building.

The Second Leiter Building is also notable for its size, each floor measuring 50,000 square feet and having sixteen-foot-high ceilings. Although Jenney designed the Leiter so that a floor could be subdivided to accommodate more than one tenant, upon completion the entire building was leased by Siegel, Cooper and Co. for its retail business. As Neil Harris noted in "Shopping—Chicago Style," in *Chicago Architecture, 1872–1922* (1987): "By the time of the World's Columbian Exposition in 1893, the structure that housed Siegel, Cooper and Co. claimed to occupy the largest retail floor area in the world. Extending 400 feet along State Street and 143 feet deep, it comprised 514,000 square feet of selling space, ten times the amount occupied by the firm five years earlier." Contemporary guidebooks praised the building as "an example of good taste, munificence, and wisdom." The Second Leiter Building was only surpassed in size by another

store that Jenney designed, The Fair Store (1890–91, now demolished), which was eleven stories high, each with 55,000 square feet of retail space.

Siegel, Cooper and Co. leased the Second Leiter Building for close to seven years. Several other companies would then occupy the building until 1931, when it was rented by Sears, Roebuck and Co. After fifty years on the site, Sears closed the store in the early 1980s, becoming one of the first big retail establishments to leave State Street. At the end of the decade, however, the building's fortunes reversed as the Leiter was renovated for offices and in 1991 the Harold Washington Library Center, designed by Hammond, Beeby, and Babka, was completed directly across the street. In 1997 the Leiter Building was named a landmark by the City of Chicago. —P.A.S.

Fig. 1. Burnham and Root.
Monadnock Building, southwest
corner of Dearborn Street and
Jackson Boulevard, 1890–91.
View from the northeast. The
Holabird and Roche southern
addition of 1893 is visible to the
left

8. Monadnock Building, 1884–91

53 West Jackson Boulevard
Burnham and Root
Addition to the south: Holabird and Roche, 1892–93
Restoration: John Vinci, begun 1979

Fig. 2. Burnham and Root. Preliminary elevation study for the Jackson Boulevard façade of the Monadnock Building, c. 1889 Canadian Centre for Architecture/Centre Canadien d'Architecture, Montreal

The Monadnock Building was one of John Root's last designs. Hailed by the *Architectural Review* in 1893 as "an achievement unsurpassed in the architectural history of our country," the sixteen-story building (fig. 1) is today the tallest wall-bearing structure in Chicago. Its harmony of structure and form is Root's greatest achievement.

The building was in every way a challenge to the architect. In 1881 the Chicago entrepreneur Owen Aldis bought for Peter Brooks, his Boston client, a 100-by-100-foot plot of land "on the ragged edge of town," south of the Board of Trade. When Dearborn Street was extended southward the following year, the site was narrowed to 68 feet on the north-south axis. To be profitable on such a narrow lot, the building had to be tall. Aldis and Brooks first approached the firm of Burnham and Root concerning the project in 1884, and according to William Donnell, president of the Montauk Corporation, current owner of the building, "generations of drawings ensued, many overtly Egyptian." Some five years later, on June 3, 1889, Chicago's first permit for a sixteen-story building was issued for the Monadnock Block.

For stability and "lasting strength," Brooks preferred masonry bearing walls to a steel frame, and so Root devised corner piers ranging in width from eight feet at the basement level to six feet above grade. To support the enormous weight of the building, Root reinforced the concrete raft footings with layers of steel beams. Certain formal qualities of the Monadnock are Egyptian in origin. The gentle swelling at base and cornice, as Donald Hoffmann demonstrated in *The Architecture of John Wellborn Root* (1973), "came very close to the bell-shaped column the Egyptians had derived from the papyrus." The papyrus motif appears in the tenth-story spandrels of an 1884 elevation drawing of the Monadnock (fig. 2); the plant was so universally used by the Egyptians in antiquity as to be a hieroglyphic symbol of Lower Egypt, as Root surely knew. Indeed Hoffmann further speculates that with the marshy composition of the soil below the Monadnock, "it must have occurred to [Root] that Chicago was a place astonishingly like Lower Egypt."

Root's quest for light, so evident in the Rookery (1885–88, see no. 2), continued in the Monadnock; but his solution to the problem was radically different. Four-window bays beginning at the third floor stretch up to the cornice of the later building and ripple across its length. Single windows are set in deep reveals between the bays. Instead of placing a light well in the building's center, as in the Rookery, Root positioned the open stairwells there (fig. 3), topping them with narrow skylights. Long corridors on either side of the staircases provide interior circulation (fig. 4). Corridor walls contain windows of bubble glass, which admit natural light from the exterior windows into the long hallways.

By 1885, Peter Brooks's brother Shepherd, also a

*Fig. 3. Monadnock Building,
detail of a staircase by
the Winslow Brothers Co.,
c. 1890–91*

*Fig. 4. Typical floor plan of the
Monadnock Building, c. 1989*

Bostonian, had bought the land to the south, and plans were made to build an extension to the Monadnock. The combined Brooks properties were divided into quadrants named for New England mountain peaks: Monadnock, Kearsarge, Wachusett, and Katahdin. The first two sections had been designed by Root. Following his death in January 1891, before the Monadnock and Kearsarge quadrants were completed, the firm of Holabird and Roche was commissioned to design the remaining two sections. These were finished according to somewhat different designs from Root's, in 1893. Although it is commonly believed the southern addition employs a skeleton construction, recent work on the Monadnock indicates that only the last quadrant is supported by a steel frame.

Since 1979, the building has been undergoing a meticulous restoration. The massive granite lintels above the major entrances on Jackson and Van Buren streets are once more visible, and the shop entrances on Dearborn Street have been reopened and their granite lintels and surrounds cleared of layers of black paint or replaced. The molded bricks that form the curved corners have been repaired or replaced, so that once more the vaulting line flows without interruption from base to cornice. Although office ceilings paralleling the corridors have been lowered to provide space for air-conditioning ducts and the wiring necessary for the electronic age, elsewhere original ceilings have been restored. Fragments of mosaic flooring discovered behind partitions have been painstakingly duplicated by Italian craftsmen. An aluminum staircase found on the first floor behind a temporary wall— perhaps the earliest use of the metal for architectural decoration—served as the model for recasting balusters, newel posts, and other elements for all the staircases in the lobby.

Root's biographer Donald Hoffmann has justly summed up the building with these words: "In its refinement and nobility, the Monadnock Block remains without peer in the history of the high office building." —J.H.C.

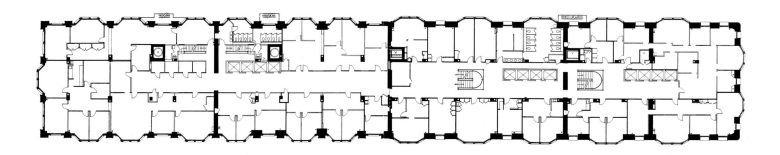

9. Marshall Field and Company Store,
1892, 1902, 1906, 1907, and 1914

*Block bounded by Wabash Avenue and State Street and
by Randolph and Washington streets
D. H. Burnham and Co. and Graham, Burnham and Company
Renovations: 1953–54, 1976, 1978, and 1988*

*Fig. 1. D. H. Burnham and Co.
Marshall Field and Company
Annex, northwest corner of
Washington Street and Wabash
Avenue, 1892*

In the early years of this century, the firm of D. H. Burnham
and Co. achieved world renown as a designer of department
stores. Its reputation spread as far afield as London, but it
began with the Marshall Field and Company Store in Chicago.
Occupying an entire city block, the store was designed by the
Burnham firm in five stages over a two-decade period. The
earliest surviving section, the Marshall Field and Company
Annex (fig. 1), was built in 1892 at the northwest corner of
Wabash Avenue and Washington Street. It was an annex to
the original Field store, then housed in the Singer Building on
the northeast corner of State and Washington. The building
of the annex was prompted by the forthcoming World's
Columbian Exposition of 1893, which was expected to bring
thousands of tourists to downtown Chicago and to Field's, the
city's most stylish department store. Designed for the firm by
Charles B. Atwood, the nine-story building was modeled after
a Renaissance palazzo and featured a heavily rusticated
exterior of granite, terra-cotta, and brick. The first four floors
were devoted to retail space and the upper five were reserved
for prestigious rental offices. According to Ann Van Zanten in
Chicago History (Fall–Winter 1982), the annex was an
advertisement for Field and for the Burnham firm itself,
reflecting the new urban image Daniel Burnham envisioned for
Chicago and realized at the Fair.

In 1902, Marshall Field commissioned Burnham to begin
the first section of the main State Street store, a project
described by Neil Harris in *Chicago Architecture, 1892–1922*
(1987), as a "five-year march along State Street from north to
south, on a journey around its square block that would take
more than a decade to complete." In contrast to the annex,
the twelve-story State Street store was devoted entirely to the
sale of dry goods, with no space for rental offices. Its severe,
classical exterior was repeated in the sections built later,
namely the southern half of the State Street façade (1907), the
middle building on Wabash Avenue (1906), and the final one
at the southwest corner of Wabash and Randolph (1914). A
similar style was used for the twenty-story annex building at
the southwest corner of Wabash Avenue and Washington
Street, built by Burnham's successor firm, Graham, Burnham
and Company (1914). The identical white-granite façades of
the State Street building consist of a three-story base, a seven-
story central section featuring uniform, flat Chicago windows,
and a two-story top with classical columns separating the
window bays (fig. 2). Originally the building was topped off
by a classical, overhanging cornice. The store's main entrance
on State Street was marked by four heroic-scale Ionic columns
topped by an entablature and a carved marble balustrade. By
the time the entire store opened in 1907, Marshall Field and
Company occupied 1,339,000 square feet of space and
employed 7,000 people. Its advertising boasted that it had
become the largest store in the world.

Fig. 2. D. H. Burnham and Co.
Marshall Field and Company
Store, northeast corner of State
and Washington streets, 1902–14

Other stores fronting on State Street, such as the Second Leiter Building, the Fair Store, and the Schlesinger and Mayer Store, were simple loft buildings with ornamented exteriors. William Le Baron Jenney's Second Leiter Building (1891, see no. 7), is renowned for its exterior expression of its interior steel frame, while Louis H. Sullivan's Schlesinger and Mayer Store (1899, 1903–04, see no. 14) has exquisite foliate ornament that wraps around the first two floors of the exterior. In contrast, Burnham focused attention on the interior of the Field Store by carving out two soaring atriums within the massive building. In the southern section, it is a six-story atrium whose dome is faced with a magnificent Louis Comfort Tiffany mosaic in an intricate, abstract design, shimmering in a palette of sapphire, emerald, and white. The atrium on the north side is unornamented except for its classical detailing (fig. 3), but both act as caesuras, as visual breaks, in a building whose massive size might otherwise seem overwhelming. The classical motifs of the store's exterior are repeated in the two-story Corinthian pilasters in the atriums and the massive fluted Corinthian columns on the store's main floor.

Burnham is thought to have been influenced in his use of the atrium by Parisian department stores such as the Bon Marché (1869–76), as well as by courts in the firm's own Chicago office blocks, such as the Rookery (1885–88, see no. 2) and the Railway Exchange Building (1903–04, see no. 17). Architects used open vertical courts in buildings of the time to add light, ventilation, and a sense of drama to otherwise solid structures. Marshall Field and Company, with its atrium spaces, classical detailing, and monumental scale, was a prototype for stores created by Burnham for numerous cities in the United States and Europe: the McCreery Store in Pittsburgh (1903), Wanamaker's in New York (1903), Selfridge's in London (1906), Gimbel's in New York (1909), Wanamaker's in Philadelphia (1909), the May Company in Cleveland (1912), and Filene's in Boston (1912).

The Marshall Field Store, as it is now known, undertook a $110 million renovation in the late 1980s. Although the changes affected every floor, the focus of the renovation was the conversion of the former loading dock on Holden Court, an alleyway separating the State Street and Wabash Avenue buildings, into a dramatic, eleven-story atrium. The renovation incorporated glass elevators and centralized escalators, reminiscent of those in Water Tower Place (1976, see no. 81), the city's first vertical shopping mall. Topped off by a barrel-vaulted skylight, the new Field's atrium also features walls faced in faux limestone and green marble, the company's corporate color. The centerpiece of the atrium is a fountain, based on a 1901 drawing, presumed to be by Burnham, found in the Field archive. —P.A.S.

10. Old Colony Building, 1893–94

407 South Dearborn Street
Holabird and Roche

Fig. 1. Holabird and Roche. Old Colony Building, 407 South Dearborn Street, 1893–94. View of the Van Buren Street façade, c. 1894

The Old Colony Building was constructed at a time when the southern end of Dearborn Street was beginning to develop as the center of the printing industry, serving not only Chicago but the entire Midwest. Like the Monadnock and Marquette buildings (see nos. 8 and 11), which were financed by Bostonians, the brothers Peter and Shepherd Brooks, the Old Colony was developed by another shrewd Boston investor, the lawyer Francis Bartlett, who also saw the potential for great financial gain by speculating in real estate in the growing city of Chicago. Given the expanding need for office space at the end of the nineteenth century, Bartlett's investment proved to be a wise one. The seventeen-story Old Colony Building provided 600 offices for lumber interests, publishing companies, and railroad corporations, including the Chicago, Milwaukee and St. Paul Railroad Company.

During the early years of the Holabird and Roche partnership, the firm developed a formula for producing tall commercial buildings that used steel-frame construction and had unified exteriors articulating the underlying structural system. Early experiments in that direction included the Tacoma (1887–89, demolished) and Pontiac buildings (1889–91, see no. 4), and many historians believe that Holabird and Roche's first fully integrated those functional and aesthetic concerns in the Marquette Building (1893–95, see no. 11). As Carl W. Condit wrote in *The Chicago School of Architecture* (1964): "The subsequent work of Holabird and Roche in the last decade of the nineteenth century reveals, with one exception, a systematic refinement and clarification of the fundamental form of the Marquette Building." That exception was the Old Colony Building.

What distinguishes the Old Colony from the Holabird and Roche buildings preceding and following it are the rounded, projecting window bays at the four corners. Running from the third floor to the roof, the distinctive corner bays may have been inspired by their use by Burnham and Root in contemporary buildings such as the Great Northern Hotel (1890–92), and the Ashland Block (1891–92), both demolished. The Old Colony is the only surviving example of a Chicago School building with this treatment of the corners.

The seventeen-story Old Colony has a three-story limestone base, an eleven-story shaft faced in cream-colored Roman brick and terra-cotta, and a three-story limestone top with a decorative, overhanging cornice. The long Dearborn Street and Plymouth Court façades of the building are composed of five bays, each containing pairs of double-hung windows. On the narrow, Van Buren Street façade, each floor has a single bay of Chicago windows, flanked by a double-hung window on either side. Continuous vertical brick piers on the long façades balance their breadth. The narrow north façade has no piers and instead emphasizes the horizontal through the projecting sills and lintels of the Chicago windows. These subtle design variations unify the wide and narrow façades of this tall building. A colonnade runs the length and width of its fifteenth and sixteenth floors. In the central portion, the gridlike arrangement of windows and masonry expresses the underlying steel frame, which is used throughout. There are no masonry bearing walls in this structure, making it innovative in its day. As in Jenney's Manhattan Building, the wind-bracing system was adapted from that developed earlier for railway truss bridges. The Old Colony system consists of four sets of portal arches running from the foundation to the roof to brace the horizontal and vertical structural elements.

The Dearborn Street entryway bears the Old Colony Building's name, which refers to the first English colony in America at Plymouth. The seal of this early Crown Colony is located beside the doorways of the building, whose east façade, appropriately enough, is located on Plymouth Court. It is a gesture similar to the incorporation of fish motifs on the Fisher Building (see no. 5), named for its owner and located directly to the north of the Old Colony. The building's original entrances were extensively altered over the years, and the one on Van Buren Street was closed and remodeled as commercial space. At the same time, the original two-story vestibule was divided into two floors to accommodate more rental space. Despite the changes, the Old Colony Building was declared a Chicago landmark in the early 1970s. —P.A.S.

11. Marquette Building, 1893–95

140 South Dearborn Street
Holabird and Roche
Addition: Holabird and Roche (bay on Adams Street),
1905–06
Renovation: Holabird and Root, 1979–81

William Holabird and Martin Roche's Marquette Building
(fig. 1) is their firm's quintessential Chicago School office
building, embodying all the functional, structural, and design
features for which their work of the late nineteenth and early
twentieth centuries is renowned. The building was
commissioned by Boston developer Peter Brooks, with Owen
Aldis acting as his representative. It was the same team that
had collaborated on the design and construction of several
other distinguished Chicago buildings, including the Montauk
(1881–82, demolished), the Rookery (1885–88, see no. 2) and
the Monadnock (1884–91, see no. 8). In the Marquette, Aldis
developed several fundamental principles for the design and
profitable management of a first-rate office structure:
providing the offices with as much light and air as possible;
incorporating only first-class spaces; creating the best in
public amenities, such as a lobby and elevators; and building
in flexibility to suit tenants' needs. The prescription proved
highly successful and was applied to countless subsequent
buildings, thereby making the Marquette a pioneer in
modern office design and planning.

The façade of the sixteen-story building, which is eight bays
wide and five bays deep, is particularly imposing. It is
decorated with Renaissance motifs of acanthus leaves and
meander patterns, and its brown brick, simple terra-cotta
ornament, and large repetitive window openings underscore in
a most striking and direct way its underlying steel structure.
Unlike many earlier buildings by Holabird and Roche, the
Marquette does not have projecting bays, and instead uses flat
windows that simply articulate the building's interior steel
frame, prompting Chicago School authority Carl W. Condit to
write in *The Chicago School of Architecture* (1964):

The street elevations of the Marquette set it off from all its
predecessors.... The general impression is that of a pattern of large
transparent areas set in narrow frames of piers and spandrels. The
wall is a nearly uniform array of rectangular cells vigorously
expressing the steel cage they cover. The deep reveals and unusually
fine proportions give the Marquette an incisive and dynamic quality
that raise it to the level of superior architecture in any style.

The sixteen-story structure has an E-shaped plan, fronting
to the east on Dearborn Street and to the south on Adams; a
large, open interior court lined with white enameled brick
provides the maximum reflection of natural light into the
interior offices. The long arms of the E contain offices, while
the short center arm contains a bank of elevators, an
uncharacteristically large space for this service. The building
has a two-story base, a twelve-story shaft of repetitive floors,
and two top floors originally capped by a decorative cornice,
which was removed in 1950 and replaced by a seventeenth
floor. The two-story base features large, Chicago windows. An
addition was built in 1905–06 when a single bay was added
on the Adams Street façade. Although the addition disrupts

Fig. 3. Marquette Building, view
of the lobby, with six Tiffany
mosaics illustrating the life of
Jacques Marquette

the symmetry of the façade, it utilizes the same materials and design as the original building, thus integrating it into the whole with some finesse.

A unique aspect of the Marquette is the abundance of sculpture and mosaics decorating the entrance and interior (figs. 2, 3). Generally Chicago School buildings of this period pared ornament down to a minimum, but the entrance and lobby of the Marquette feature elaborate panels that illustrate events in the life of Jacques Marquette, the French missionary who traversed the upper Mississippi area in the seventeenth century and explored the shores of Lake Michigan as far as Chicago. The main entrance doors have kick plates with tomahawks and bronze push plates with panther heads designed by Edward Kemeys (1843–1907), the renowned animal sculptor. Above the doors on the exterior are four bronze panels designed by Hermon A. MacNeil (1866–1947) illustrating Marquette's journeys. Above the lobby elevators are bronze portraits of the Indian chiefs Black Hawk and Keokuk and of Marquette's countrymen Sieur La Salle, and the Comte de Frontenac, who also led explorations to the New World in the seventeenth century.

The lobby is a two-story, white Carrara marble rotunda with stairs on either side of the entrance and a balcony separating the floors. The lobby's original grillework elevator cages (fig. 3) have been replaced by enclosed cabs, but a section of the original grilles can be seen in The Art Institute of Chicago's gallery of architectural fragments. On the face of the lobby balcony there are elaborate glass and mother-of-pearl mosaics, further illustrating the adventures of Marquette in six large panels. Designed by J. A. Holzer and the Tiffany Glass and Decorating Company, the mosaics were applauded by the contemporary journal *Architectural Review* (June 1897): "It is not the great size of these panels, but the bold treatment · · · that stamp[s] them beyond all question the most interesting example of glass mosaic in this country." Apparently the impetus for naming the building and depicting the exploits of Marquette stemmed from Owen Aldis himself, for he had translated Marquette's journal and was well-versed in the explorer's journeys.

The Marquette Building was designated a landmark in 1975, despite opposition from some developers and architects. Following its designation, the exterior (fig. 4) and first two floors of the interior were renovated by architects Holabird and Root, with backing from a subsidiary of Banker's Life and Casualty Company. The Marquette has been recognized as the building in which Holabird and Roche first resolved the design and engineering problems of the tall office building, and it was the prototype for many of their subsequent commercial buildings. Historian Nikolaus Pevsner said it all when he described the Marquette Building as "Holabird and Roche's classic moment." —P.A.S.

12. Montgomery Ward and Company Building, 1897–99

Now 6 North Michigan Building
6 North Michigan Avenue
Richard E. Schmidt
Addition: Holabird and Roche, c. 1923
Tower removed: 1947

Fig. 1. Richard E. Schmidt. Montgomery Ward and Company Building, 6 North Michigan Avenue, 1897–99 (since altered)

Fig 2. Richard E. Schmidt. Detail of drawing for terra-cotta tilework, twelfth-story cornice, Montgomery Ward and Company Building. Ink on linen. The Art Institute of Chicago

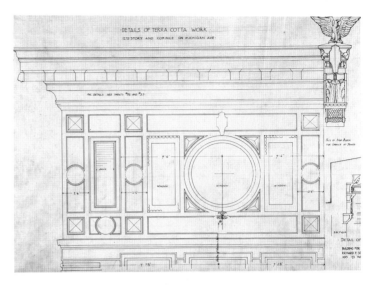

The Montgomery Ward and Company Building (fig. 1) has undergone numerous alterations since the turn of the century, with the result that what remains today at 6 North Michigan Avenue is a sad reminder of the original structure. When completed in 1899 as a combined office building and warehouse for Montgomery Ward and Company, one of the largest mail-order houses in the world, the main building was twelve stories high, with a tower rising from the center of the Michigan Avenue elevation to almost an equal height. Given the dual purpose of the building, constructed to house an array of merchandise and the office staff of the catalog empire, it was dubbed the "Busy Bee Hive" and was illustrated as such in an early advertisement for the building (fig. 3).

The Montgomery Ward Building, combining a functional Chicago School structure with Italian Renaissance ornamental motifs, was the first big commission for architect Richard E. Schmidt (1865–1959). In a 1966 *Prairie School Review* article titled "Hugh M. G. Garden," B. C. Greengard attributed the design of the Ward Building to Hugh Garden (1873–1961), who later became Schmidt's partner. The building's original three-story marble base featured an entrance portico with four pairs of Ionic columns topped by a marble pediment, dominated by a sculpture of two lions and two youths on either side of a large shield. Its rusticated corners and two-story, round-arched windows continued the Renaissance motif. The main nine-story block of the building was a straightforward Chicago School tower covered in mottled, buff-colored brick with light terra-cotta ornament depicting indigenous plants, birds, and fish (fig. 2). Bronze panels in the lobby floor represented various cereal grasses and a larger floor panel represented the company's corporate symbol, Commerce. Because the building housed the company's entire store of valuable merchandise, every precaution was taken to make it as fireproof as possible, and even the window casings were metal.

The most striking feature of the original building was its imposing square tower. Reminiscent of a Venetian campanile, it gave the Ward the distinction of being the tallest building in Chicago at the time of completion. The first five floors of the tower were offices; extending above them were a one-story arcade, an attic story, and a three-story pyramidal roof topped by a tempietto and a heroic-scaled weather vane. The pyramidal roof, tiled in gold terra-cotta panels, was dazzling, but it was the gilded weather vane, *Progress Lighting the Way for Commerce*, that generated the most interest among Chicagoans. The eighteen-foot-tall statue depicted Progress as a nude female figure poised on one foot, holding a torch in one hand and a caduceus, the ancient symbol of commerce, in the other. A long, curvilinear flame from the torch was designed to catch the wind, causing the figure to turn.

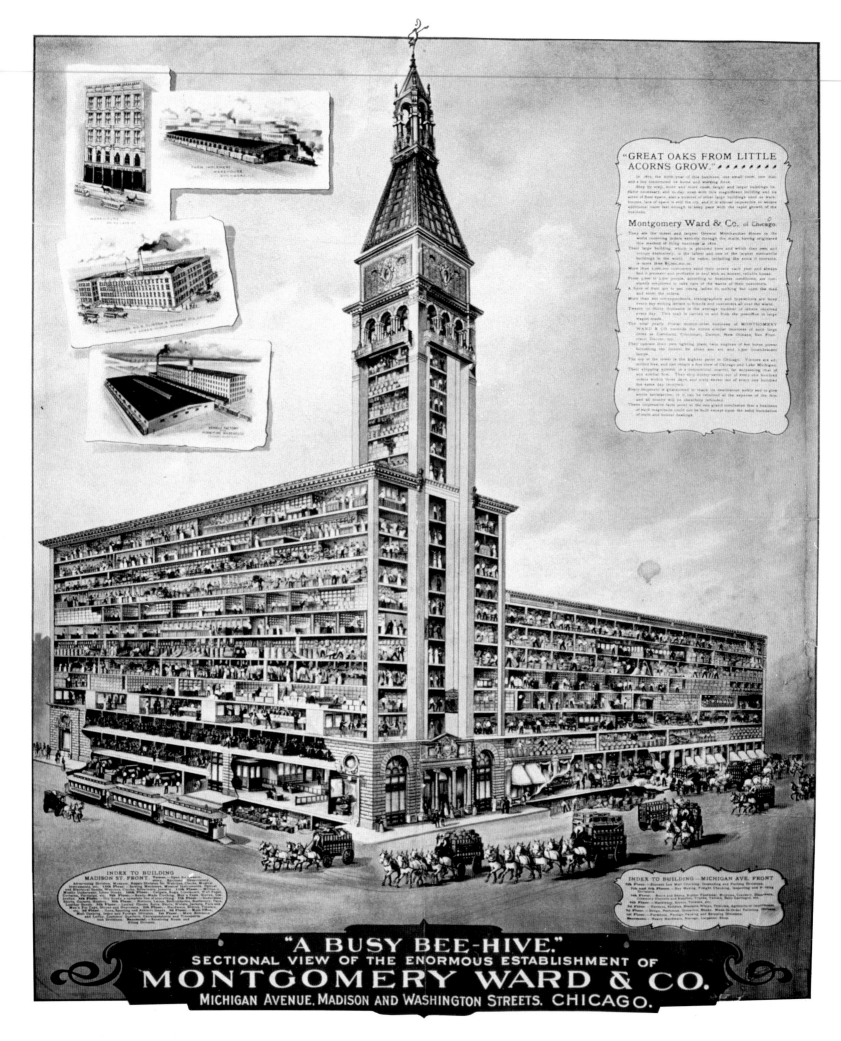

"A BUSY BEE-HIVE."
SECTIONAL VIEW OF THE ENORMOUS ESTABLISHMENT OF
MONTGOMERY WARD & CO.
MICHIGAN AVENUE, MADISON AND WASHINGTON STREETS, CHICAGO.

According to Margot Gayle, in a *Chicago History* article, "Montgomery Ward and Company and Three Statues on Chicago's Skyline" (Summer 1982), the figure of Progress is either the work of Scottish-American artist John Massey Rhind (1860–1936) or is a casting of *Diana, Goddess of the Hunt*, a sculpture designed by Augustus Saint-Gaudens (1848–1907) to top McKim, Mead and White's 1891 Madison Square Garden in New York and later installed atop the Agriculture Building at the 1893 World's Columbian Exposition in Chicago. However, Gayle noted: "Whether she was *Diana* reincarnated or a newly created *Progress*, the golden figure placed on top of the Montgomery Ward and Co. Tower Building in 1900 delighted Chicagoans."

The gleaming statue of Progress, standing at the highest point in the city, was lit by four electric beacons, each with the luminosity of a thousand candlepower. As Gayle also noted in *Chicago History*: "Progress actually did serve as a beacon in at least one instance. On September 5, 1918, Captain Ben Lipsner used these lights to guide his plane into Grant Park after making the first airmail flight between New York City and Chicago in nine hours and thirteen minutes of stormy weather."

In 1908, only nine years after completing the building, Montgomery Ward and Company sold it and moved to more spacious quarters at 618 West Chicago Avenue. That reinforced-concrete warehouse complex, designed by Richard Schmidt's successor firm of Schmidt, Garden, and Martin, stretches out along the Chicago River, providing easy access to transportation. In 1928 an Art Deco-style Administration Building was constructed for the company on Chicago Avenue and was topped by a new sculpture, *The Spirit of Progress*, most probably designed by Swiss-American artist Joseph Conrad (1867–1936). In 1974 Montgomery Ward completed another corporate headquarters, a twenty-six-story, travertine and glass tower designed by Japanese architect Minoru Yamasaki and located within the same warehouse complex. Although the new tower is the most visible structure in the complex, the silhouette of *The Spirit of Progress* still dominates the sky on West Chicago Avenue.

Once Montgomery Ward vacated the building at 6 North Michigan, it was renamed "The Tower Building," and numerous alterations were made over the years. Around 1923 the Holabird and Roche firm was hired to add five floors to the top of the building, thereby encasing the tower on three sides and visually diminishing it by five stories. Because the building was designed from the outset to accommodate very heavy loads, it was possible to add stories without reinforcing the columns on the lower floors. In 1947 what remained of the tower was judged to be structurally unsound, and it was demolished. At this point *Progress Lighting the Way for Commerce* was also dismantled. A *Chicago Tribune* article in July 1947 (which mistakenly referred to the work as *Diana*) reported: "The statue was cut into about 30 pieces before it was lowered. Diana's arm with outstretched spear [sic] came off at the shoulder, the head came off in one piece, and one leg below the knee. Most of the statue is at the company's office, but some parts have been claimed by Chicagoans to make metal ashtrays or keep as souvenirs." —P.A.S.

Fig. 1. Holabird and Roche. Gage Group: from right to left, the Gage, Edson Keith, and Ascher buildings, 18, 24–28, and 30 South Michigan Avenue, 1898–99. The façade of the Gage Building was designed by Louis H. Sullivan

13. Gage Group, 1898–99
Gage, Edson Keith, and Ascher Buildings

18, 24–28, and 30 South Michigan Avenue
Holabird and Roche
Louis H. Sullivan, façade of 18 South Michigan Avenue
Addition to 18 South Michigan Avenue: Holabird and Roche,
1902; remodeled: 1952; renovated: 1986
Addition to 30 South Michigan Avenue: Altman-Saichek
Associates, 1971

The buildings known as the Gage Group (fig. 1), also called the McCormick Buildings, were commissioned by various members of the McCormick family, descendants of Cyrus Hall McCormick, inventor of the reaper. The three adjoining buildings housed three of the city's leading wholesale millinery companies, previously located on Wabash Avenue. Although modest in scale, the buildings are superb examples of the late Chicago School style, having façades composed largely of glass and underlying steel structures that are clearly and poetically expressed.

The Gage Group consists of three steel-frame loft buildings clad in brick and terra-cotta. Originally, the southernmost building, at 30 South Michigan Avenue, designed for Theodore Ascher and Co., was two bays wide and six stories high. In 1971 a seventh story was added by Altman-Saichek Associates. The adjoining building, at 24–28 South Michigan, constructed for Edson Keith and Company, was larger from the outset, being three bays wide and seven stories high. Both buildings, designed by Holabird and Roche, featured extremely open façades composed of large Chicago windows. Consistent with the Chicago School aesthetic, the buildings were unornamented and were clad in simple red brick and terra-cotta.

The northernmost building, at 18 South Michigan Avenue, designed by Holabird and Roche for the Gage Brothers, was three bays wide and eight stories high when built. However its façade, unlike those of the other two, was designed by Louis H. Sullivan and featured buff-colored, terra-cotta sheathing with groups of four narrow windows in the outer bays and five in the center (fig. 2). The first floor was faced in cast-iron ornament that featured Sullivan's characteristic foliate designs, and the façade itself incorporated continuous vertical piers that terminated at the roofline in bursts of lush ornament. Sullivan's treatment is a classic expression of his philosophy that a skyscraper's design should elegantly and directly reflect the building's height. According to an article in *Brickbuilder* (December 1899), the Gage Brothers specifically requested that Sullivan design the façade of their building and offered to pay additional rent if he did so; the writer said further: "They thought it would benefit their business in an equal degree. They put an exact commercial value on Mr. Sullivan's art, otherwise he would not have been called in."

But according to an article quoted in Robert Bruegmann's *Holabird and Roche and Holabird and Root: A Catalogue of Works, 1880–1940*, Sullivan's design for the Gage Building façade did not receive unanimous approval. Holabird architect Edward A. Renwick, in his *Recollections* (1932), criticized Sullivan for having put four feet of ornament at the top of the windows, and suggested that the windows themselves should have been taller. When the building was constructed, artificial light was poor, and it was important to admit as much

daylight as possible. When the client questioned the design, Sullivan reportedly said: "If I came to you for a hat I'd use your judgment." Said Renwick: "The owner let him go ahead and the store was ruined for a good many years—until artificial light approximating daylight had been developed."

What Renwick did not know was that Sullivan was using for the first time "Luxfer prisms," a new prismatic glass that actually directed the light farther back into the deep recesses of the loft building. What Renwick thought were "four feet of ornament" at the top of the windows was actually the light-refracting prismatic glass. Despite this design issue, the firm occupying the building prospered, and in 1902 it announced in its magazine *The Gage* that it had become the largest millinery importer in the United States.

After the turn of the century, the Gage Brothers purchased the building, and in 1902 they commissioned the construction of a four-story addition. Designed by Holabird and Roche, the addition reflected the ornamentation of the lower floors; the bursts of ornament were continued to the roofline and the original cornice was reinstalled. In 1952, however, the building was remodeled, which included stripping the cast-iron ornament from the first-floor façade. Enraged by this act of destruction, architect Arthur Dubin managed to save several sections of the green-red ornament. He later donated several fragments of it to The Art Institute of Chicago, where a cast-iron panel is now on display in an installation of Chicago building fragments. The Gage Building was remodeled again in 1986, but the changes were sympathetic to the historic structure's original design. The Bovine Group, for Aubrey Greenberg Associates, cleaned the façade and removed an unsightly fire escape that had marred the exterior for many years. In addition, the lobby was remodeled, and the walls and floor incorporated designs based on Sullivan's stencils for the Chicago Stock Exchange Trading Room. —P.A.S.

14. Schlesinger and Mayer Store, 1899, 1903–04

Now Carson Pirie Scott and Company Store
1 South State Street
Louis H. Sullivan
Additions: D. H. Burnham and Co. (five bays on State Street), 1906; Holabird and Root (three bays on State Street), 1960–61
Restoration: John Vinci (rotunda and exterior ornament), 1979

Fig. 1. Louis H. Sullivan. Schlesinger and Mayer Store, now Carson Pirie Scott and Company Store, 1 South State Street, 1899, 1903–04

Fig. 2. Second-story pedestrians' walkway (now dismantled) connecting the store with the Wabash Avenue Elevated station, c. 1904

The Schlesinger and Mayer Store (fig. 1), since 1904 the home of Carson Pirie Scott and Company, was Louis Sullivan's last large commercial commission and the culmination of his career as the creator of skyscrapers. Because it is considered the climax of efforts to develop an architectural expression for the steel frame and the tall building, it stands as one of the most important structures in early modern architecture. In *The Chicago School of Architecture* (1964), Carl W. Condit succinctly summed up its virtues as one of the very best Chicago School buildings: "[It reveals] the thoroughness of Sullivan's exploitation of the aesthetic possibilities of the big steel frame, his superior sense of scale, proportion, rhythm, and organization, and his unparalleled imagination as an ornamentalist. . . . Formal, structural, and utilitarian elements are fully integrated into a new synthesis, the power and validity of which we have not yet been able to match."

As it stands today, the store is the result of several separate building efforts. The first section, which was designed by Louis Sullivan, is a nine-story structure, three bays wide, fronting on Madison Street. Sullivan and his former partner, Dankmar Adler, had a long-standing relationship with the merchants, having executed a series of remodelings between 1885 and 1897 of an earlier Schlesinger and Mayer Store, designed in 1873 by W. W. Boyington. Like the brothers who leased the Gage Building (see Gage Group, no. 13), Schlesinger and Mayer gave the commission to Sullivan with the hope that his design would enhance their public image.

Originally, Sullivan planned to clad the base of the building in bronze and the upper stories in white marble. However, the base was executed in cast iron painted to look like patinated bronze, and the upper stories were sheathed in white terra-cotta. According to Joseph Siry in his monograph *Carson Pirie Scott: Louis Sullivan and the Chicago Department Store* (1988), the decision to use terra-cotta was the result of a stonecutters' strike in Chicago in the summer of 1898. Although small in size, the first section designed by Sullivan was highly acclaimed. It elicited praise from *The Inland Architect and News Record* (January 1900):

The ornamentation of the soffits and jambs of the windows give the building a character of rich simplicity, and the ornamental iron door on the façade and canopy is highly ornate and possibly extreme, but the design is carried out in such rich ornamentation, the cartouches so delicate and well balanced, the lines of demarcation so carefully worked out, that it apparently expresses the climax of the capabilities of cast-iron and becomes a study for the student.

In 1903–04 a twelve-story addition was constructed, also designed by Sullivan. The focal point of the addition, which consists of three bays along Madison Street and seven along State Street, is a curved pavilion at the corner of State and Madison stretching from the ground floor to roof level. From the outset in 1898, the signature curved corner had been part

of the store's conception, repeating an element from the earlier Schlesinger and Mayer Store designed by Boyington. In a surprising revelation, Siry wrote in his monograph that the store's now-famous curved corner can be attributed to George Grant Elmslie, Sullivan's long-time assistant, and not to Sullivan himself.

The long, horizontal elevations of the store are sheathed in white-glazed terra-cotta and feature extremely large Chicago windows so as to admit as much light as possible. In contrast, the windows of the slender rotunda are vertically oriented to emphasize the height of the corner pavilion. The organization of the façades is remarkable for the way in which they clearly express the underlying steel structure. The interior of the building is organized like a warehouse, with large open spaces for the display of merchandise that are interrupted only by supporting columns with elaborate foliate capitals. The use of large windows and the uninterrupted flow of interior space are clear examples of Sullivan's often-quoted philosophy, "form follows function." Although the store is essentially a horizontal structure, its exterior exemplifies another of Sullivan's philosophies: that a tall building should be organized like a classical column with clearly defined areas for a base, shaft, and capital.

The cast-iron base on the first two floors is one of the store's most remarkable features (fig. 3). It is covered with decoration described by Condit as "profuse, delicate, and original foliate and floral ornament in low relief." The elaborate details frame ground-floor display windows larger than any previously used in commercial architecture. Above those windows on the first and second floors the architect incorporated bands of Luxfer prisms, small squares of prismatic glass that both cut down on glare and admitted light to the display windows and store interiors.

Details for the cast-iron base were sketched out by Sullivan in a general way, then were drawn up more precisely by Elmslie. Norwegian sculptor Kristian Schneider modeled the ornament in plaster molds, which were then used to cast the pieces in iron. The two-story base was painted with a red undercoat overlaid with green, in an attempt to imitate the color of oxidized bronze. The ornament, similar to that originally installed on the Gage Building, consists of leaves, berries, vines, and geometric forms, intertwined in lavish patterns. Within the ornament above the main entrance the architect cleverly incorporates his initials, "LHS." The panels sheathing the exterior of the entry rotunda, pierced by glazed porthole openings, have been described by Siry in his

Fig. 3. View of Sullivan cast-iron ornament on the corner pavilion, c. 1979

Fig. 4. Detail of cast-iron interior stairway

Fig. 5. Interior view of corner pavilion, c. 1979

monograph on the store as "a celebration of the lightness and delicacy of cast iron rendered in ornament."

Like the Fair Store (1890–91, demolished) and Marshall Field and Company (see no. 9), the Schlesinger and Mayer Store was built in stages so the merchants could do business while construction was in progress. However, the resulting loss of sales as well as the high construction costs led Schlesinger and Mayer to sell out to H. G. Selfridg and Company, which in turn sold out to Carson Pirie Scott and Company two months later. The economic decline was so rapid that by the time the store's interior was completed in 1904, it was Carson's and not Schlesinger and Mayer that christened the building. Carson Pirie Scott had purchased the business and store in 1904 because it was due to lose its lease in the Reliance Building (see no. 5) in two years. In 1906 Carson's commissioned D. H. Burnham and Co. to design five additional bays on the southernmost side of State Street, the last addition to the store for more than fifty years. No adequate explanation has been found to explain why Burnham, and not Sullivan, was hired to do the job, but Carson Pirie Scott was familiar with the firm from having been housed in Burnham's Reliance Building. Fortunately, Burnham's addition to the store adheres to Sullivan's original scheme in every detail, except the treatment of the top story, thereby maintaining a well-integrated façade along State Street.

Over the years, the building has been altered in various ways. In 1948 the original cornice was removed and replaced by a simple parapet. Other now-demolished features include a second-story enclosed bridge (fig. 2), which led to the Elevated trains on Wabash Avenue, and large festoons of ornament that were originally located between the first and second floors. In 1960 Holabird and Root were commissioned to construct three last bays on State Street, thereby extending the store south to the Mentor Building (see no. 19) on the corner of State and Monroe streets. Finally, in 1979, after having been designated a national landmark in 1975, the store's rotunda and first two floors were restored by the architect John Vinci (figs. 3, 5). Among the accomplishments of the award-winning restoration were the return of the mahogany paneling in the ground-floor rotunda to its original splendor and the repainting of the cast iron sheathing the first two floors in its original green color with a red undercoat. —P.A.S.

15. McClurg Building, 1898–99

Originally the Ayer, later the Crown Building
Now the Pakula Building
218 South Wabash Avenue
Holabird and Roche

Fig. 1. Holabird and Roche. McClurg Building. 218 South Wabash Avenue, 1898–99. View from the east, c. 1975

The McClurg Building, originally known as the Ayer Building, was commissioned by Boston investor Frederick Ayer. From its inception, it had been planned as a simple loft building with a minimum of external ornamental detailing. The eastern façade of the nine-story building, almost all glass, is composed of three huge bays of Chicago windows, with large glass storefronts on the ground level. Virtually all the light that would penetrate the building's deep loft spaces entered through those east windows. The knife-edged piers that separate the bays and run continuously from the second to the ninth floors give the building a tall, elegantly proportioned façade, originally topped off by a simple, overhanging cornice, which has since been removed. According to historian Robert Bruegmann, the reputation of Holabird and Roche was made on small, cost-efficient buildings such as the McClurg.

Considering the small size of the commission, the building received a great deal of attention when it was completed. As Bruegmann states in *Holabird and Roche and Holabird and Root: A Catalogue of Works, 1880–1940,* a rendering of it was included in the Chicago Architects' Club exhibition of 1899, and critic Peter Bonnett Wight listed the building in an influential 1899 *Brickbuilder* article titled "Recent Improvements in Fire-proof Construction in Chicago." Modern historians attribute the importance of the building to the fact that its simple exterior with enormous windows was a clear, direct expression of its interior steel frame. The McClurg has long been considered a predecessor of twentieth-century steel-and-glass skyscrapers, and was described by Stanley Tigerman in *Chicago Architecture* as "the frame 'become architecture.' "

More recently, however, historians have tended to view the building outside the context of twentieth-century Modernism. As Bruegmann noted, in "Holabird and Roche and Holabird and Root: The First Two Generations," *Chicago History* (Fall 1980), the façade of the McClurg Building is terra-cotta, and had the architects intended to do so, they would have been free to design it as simply and as flat as possible. Instead, they chose to create deep, fluted mullions, which add depth and shadow, enriching an otherwise simple elevation. Bruegmann also noted: "No matter how much it was abstracted, . . . the façade was still clearly derived from established architectural vocabularies and remained a wall with modeled depth."

At the time of completion, the McClurg Building accommodated a diverse group of tenants, including the Schaefer Piano Company, McMillan Publishing Company, Mr. Cox's Photography Gallery, and, on the ground floor, the A. C. McClurg Bookstore. The McClurg Company, which had one of the largest bookstores in the country in the 1870s, originally occupied a building bearing its name on the northwest corner of State and Madison, and moved to the site on South Wabash in 1899. Owned by General Alexander Caldwell McClurg, the bookstore was a popular meeting place for Chicago's literary community, including journalist Eugene Field, who visited the store almost daily. —P.A.S.

16. Chicago Savings Bank Building, 1903–04

Now the Chicago Building
7 West Madison Street
Holabird and Roche

The Chicago Savings Bank Building occupies a prominent site on the southwest corner of Madison and State streets, where State shifts thirty feet to the east, projecting the building beyond the line of properties to the north. As a result, the Chicago Building, as it is now known, comes directly into view when looking southward from North State Street, and its interiors enjoy an abundance of natural light. Located across the street from Louis Sullivan's renowned Schlesinger and Mayer Store (now Carson Pirie Scott and Company Store, see no. 14), the Chicago Building is one of Holabird and Roche's most characteristic Chicago School buildings, and it fully exemplifies the design and planning principles for a successful office building codified earlier by Owen Aldis and Holabird and Roche in the Marquette Building (1893–95, see no. 11). As Robert Bruegmann notes in *Holabird and Roche and Holabird and Root: A Catalogue of Works, 1880–1940*, the building was constructed for the Chicago Savings Bank, which was established in 1902 during the economic recovery following the depression of 1893. State Street was then experiencing phenomenal growth as the city's most important retail shopping district, and the directors of the bank elected to locate their new building in the center of activity at the corner of State and Madison streets.

The building's two main façades are composed of Chicago windows, in which a large, fixed, central pane of glass is flanked by double-hung windows on either side. Chicago windows may be either flat or bayed, and both variations are present in this building. Perhaps the earliest use of this type of large, commercial window occurred in Solon Spencer Beman's Studebaker Building (1885, see no. 1). Although the architects originally planned to clad the building in white-glazed terra-cotta, in the end they chose reddish-brown terra-cotta and brick with rusticated corners.

The narrow State Street façade of the Chicago Building features three bays of flat Chicago windows separated by continuous piers, making the building appear even taller than its fifteen stories. The longer Madison Street façade, where the main entrance is located, features three projecting bays of Chicago windows, which run from the second floor to the cornice and are separated by alternating bays of flat windows similar to those on the State Street façade. Like the State Street piers, the projecting bays give the building a strong vertical thrust. Holabird and Roche introduced projecting bays in the elevation of the Tacoma Building (1887–89; see introduction, fig. 9) and used them repeatedly in subsequent buildings both as a design convention and as a way to provide more light and ventilation to the offices within. Remarkably, the Chicago Building's decorative galvanized-steel cornice survives intact, an unusual occurrence when one considers that the terra-cotta cornices of most downtown commercial

buildings were simply removed when in need of repair or when the buildings were "modernized."

The architecture journals of the day praised the Chicago Savings Bank Building on several levels. *The Inland Architect and News Record* (July 1905) described the building as "prominent and impressive" and "unique in its simplicity of line." The real-estate journal the *Economist* (February 25, 1905) reported that several remarkable records were established during construction of the building: "The contractors, Wells Brothers Company, attained a high record for speed. They began to set steel on August 8 and by August 29 the entire steel frame work was finished. The setting of brick began September 1 and on October 1 it was all up."

Unlike the lavish treatment of the lobby in other buildings of the period, the Chicago Building has a small, but elegant, single-story vestibule clad in white Carrara marble with solid-bronze railings and grilles. A small stairway to the left of the entrance leads to the second story, where the Chicago Savings Bank was located. When the building opened, the floors above were leased to commercial and professional tenants (physicians and surgeons occupied floors nine through thirteen). The first floor was originally leased to small drug, jewelry, and tobacco stores.

Although the building's interiors and exterior are intact, its future is uncertain. In 1988 its owner, the Chicago Board of Education, considered razing the structure until it was discovered that demolition would cost more than $1 million, while the same amount of money applied to renovation could perhaps make the eighty-five-year-old structure profitable. The Board of Education then requested proposals from developers to renovate it. Late in 1989, the financial institution known as Citicorp submitted a bid to purchase the building; although preservationists hoped that the company would restore it, Citicorp instead threatened to demolish it to build a new corporate headquarters on Madison Street between State and Dearborn. Early in 1990, the bid was withdrawn. In the late 1990s, however, the building's future was finally secured. In 1997 the School of the Art Institute of Chicago purchased the building and completed its conversion into a residence hall for students. A year earlier, the building was designated a landmark by the City of Chicago.

The Chicago Building remains an example of the design and engineering developments that made the Chicago School of architecture an achievement without equal. —P.A.S.

17. Railway Exchange Building, 1903–04

Now Santa Fe Center
80 East Jackson Boulevard
D. H. Burnham and Co.
Restoration: Frye Gillan and Molinaro, 1982–85

Peoples Gas Company Building, 1910–11

Now 122 South Michigan Avenue
D. H. Burnham and Co.
Renovation: Eckenhoff Saunders Architects, 1985–87

Although most visitors enter the former Railway Exchange Building (fig. 1) from Michigan Avenue, the formal entrance is on Jackson Boulevard. When D. H. Burnham and Co. designed this center for the thriving railroad industry in the early part of the century, South Michigan Avenue, now a great boulevard, was narrow and brick-paved. Despite the presence of The Art Institute of Chicago (1892–93) across the street, such amenities as Grant Park did not yet exist. Therefore, an impressive entrance to an impressive building, a feature Burnham must have required, was better made from Jackson than Michigan. Burnham's firm not only designed the seventeen-story office block, Burnham himself was the building's major stockholder, and he moved the firm's offices onto the fourteenth floor. His descendants maintained an interest in the office block until 1952.

The building's organization is the classicization of the design of the Rookery (1885–88, see no. 2) and thus reflects the influence of John Wellborn Root, the firm's chief designer from 1873 to 1891, and of his successor, Charles B. Atwood, who filled that role from 1891 to 1895. As in Root's designs for the Rookery, a two-story enclosed court was built at the street level of the Railway Exchange, and above it an open light well was surrounded by a ring of offices. Although the Rookery's court recalled an airy birdcage, its Railway Exchange counterpart was square and followed a symmetrical, Beaux-Arts plan, echoing Atwood's design for the massive Ellicott Square Building in Buffalo (1893–94). On a direct axis across the court from the Railway Exchange's high, arched entrance, centered on the Jackson Boulevard façade, an imperial staircase led to the second-floor balcony and shops.

D. H. Burnham and Co.'s designer for the Railway Exchange was Frederick P. Dinkelberg (c. 1869–1935), who had joined the firm as an assistant to Atwood. Designer for Burnham of the famed Flatiron Building in New York (1902) and later of the Conway Building in Chicago (1912–13, see no. 27), Dinkelberg would in later years be associated with the firm of Thielbar and Fugard on the Jewelers Building (1924–26, see no. 33). As in 1895 Atwood had used white-glazed terra-cotta as exterior sheathing of the Reliance Building (see no. 5), so it was used by Dinkelberg on the Exchange's exterior façade and interior court. The designs for the ornamental dentils, balusters, column capitals, and other details were classical in origin. To brighten the inner offices, the light well was lined with white-glazed brick, as Root had done in the Rookery. And like the Reliance Building, the Railway Exchange is completely steel-framed, but its classical detailing makes no effort to exploit the appearance of skeletal construction.

The contemporary owner of the building is the Santa Fe Southern Pacific Corporation. The Santa Fe Railroad (originally the Atchison, Topeka and Santa Fe) had been a

Fig. 1. D. H. Burnham and Co. Railway Exchange Building, 80 East Jackson Boulevard, 1903–04. At far right is the Montgomery Ward and Company Building (see no. 12)

Fig. 2. D. H. Burnham and Co. Peoples Gas Company Building, 122 South Michigan Avenue, 1910–11

Fig. 3. Railway Exchange
Building, view of the renovated
light well, c. 1985

Fig. 4. Railway Exchange
Building, view of the restored
two-story entry court, c. 1985

removing the glass from the lower skylight, as Murphy/Jahn
had proposed, Frye restored it, adding a stenciled Pompeian
decoration from an early D. H. Burnham and Co. design
(never executed). The original marquee of lights was
reinstalled around the court (fig. 4). An early design for a
marble floor with a five-color border (also previously
unexecuted) was followed in the lobby. "A restoration better
than the original" was the proud assessment of the project by
both architects and clients.

As in both the Rookery and the Ellicott Square Building,
retail stores originally surrounded the court on both levels of
the Railway Exchange, with the mezzanine considered the
more desirable location. An early tenant was the Northwestern
Terra Cotta Company (supplier of the white-glazed terra-cotta
on the exterior), which displayed examples of its molds for
architectural details on the mezzanine balcony. During the
restoration of the building in the 1980s, actual terra-cotta was
used on the exterior where replacements were necessary, but a
synthetic tile, microcotta, was chosen for the interior.
Furthermore, the original mahogany on the storefronts was
refinished, and bronze framing was uniformly installed.
Although the building is air-conditioned, the windows on the
office floors actually open and shut.

The Railway Exchange is significant not only as an
architectural landmark but also as a historic site: it was here
that Daniel Burnham and a staff of assistants drew up the
Plan of Chicago, published in 1909. A small penthouse on the
northeast corner of the rooftop was the Plan office, and it was
retained by the restoration architects. From its windows,
Burnham could survey the bleak landscape surrounding The
Art Institute of Chicago and dream of a future lakefront park,
one of the keystones of the Plan. He could also observe the
progress of his own efforts to improve Michigan Avenue: the
construction of the adjacent Orchestra Hall (1905), at 218
South Michigan, and the Peoples Gas Company Building
(1910–11), another classically inspired skyscraper, three stories
taller than the Exchange, at 122 South Michigan Avenue
(fig. 2).

A renovation and restoration of the Peoples Gas Company
Building took place between 1985 and 1987 under the
direction of Eckenhoff Saunders Architects. The central
lobby, from which two retail arcades radiate axially at ninety-
degree angles, is considerably altered from the original, but it
follows the spirit of the building. On the exterior, the window
frames were repainted the original green, and the lighting
fixtures were restored. The building's mechanical facilities, as
in the Railway Exchange, have been completely modernized.
The two buildings, which were instrumental in the
development of South Michigan Avenue in the early years of
the century, were toward its close in the forefront in bringing
renewed vitality to the great boulevard. —J.H.C.

tenant of the building from its opening, so when the
diversified transportation company made Chicago its
headquarters in 1982, it elected to restore the Railway
Exchange Building rather than build or lease in another
location. The building was listed in the National Register of
Historic Places in June 1982, and a painstaking restoration
took place under the terms of the National Historic
Preservation Act. The most dramatic result was the newly
revealed interior court: the tarred-over skylight was replaced,
and the light well above it was capped with translucent,
insulating glass to create a fifteen-story atrium (figs. 3, 4).
Open corridors were constructed around the atrium to
provide interior circulation on every floor.

Although the original proposal to turn the light well into an
atrium was made by the firm of Murphy/Jahn, the commission
to supervise its restoration and renovation was given to Metz,
Train and Youngren. Lonn Frye, of the firm of Frye Gillan
and Molinaro, was the designer in charge. Instead of

18. Majestic Building, 1905

16–22 West Monroe Street
Edmund R. Krause

Fig. 1. Edmund R. Krause. Majestic Building, 16–22 West Monroe Street, 1905

Fig. 2. Edmund R. Krause. Study for terra-cotta ornament, Majestic Building (detail), c. 1905. The Art Institute of Chicago

Fig. 3. Edmund R. Krause. Front elevation of Majestic Building, (detail), c. 1905. The Art Institute of Chicago

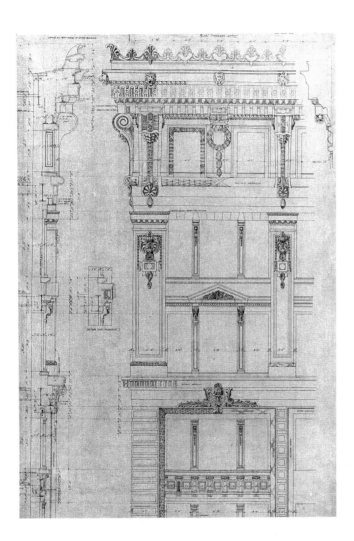

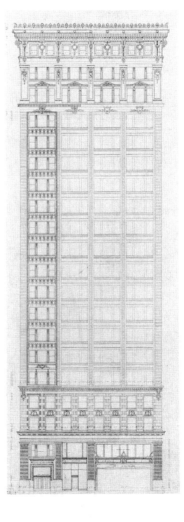

Edmund R. Krause was a German-born and trained architect who moved to Chicago in 1885 and established what became a thriving practice, perhaps because of the city's substantial German population. He received a number of important commissions, but many of the buildings were demolished, including the Alexandria Hotel (1891, additions 1914), at the southwest corner of Rush and Ohio streets; the Andrew Leicht House (1891), at the northwest corner of Fullerton and Lakeside avenues; the Kedzie Building (1892), at 87–91 West Randolph Street; and the Clock Building (1906), at 211–19 West Randolph Street. Although these are gone from the cityscape, his well-known Lessing Apartments and Annex (1897–1900) survive at 560–68 West Surf Street and were renovated in the 1980s. Those apartments and the Majestic Building (fig. 1) are among his few surviving works in the city.

The Majestic is a twenty-story multiuse theater and office building, whose basic functions were inspired by such Adler and Sullivan multiuse complexes as the Schiller Building (1891–92; see introduction, fig. 12) and the Auditorium Building (1887–89, see no. 3). The Majestic's street façade and top are elaborately detailed in white-glazed terra-cotta (fig. 2), perhaps reflecting the influence of D. H. Burnham and Co.'s Railway Exchange (see no. 17), completed the year before. When the Majestic was reviewed by the *Architectural Record* (June 1906), however, it was criticized for the "matter-of-fact," pedestrian nature of the ornament on the façade, yet praised for the use of white-glazed terra-cotta there and on the other sides of the building, particularly the corners. The choice of Chicago windows for the Monroe Street façade is related to the popularity of that form in commercial buildings of this time. This building, originally developed as a theater and office building for Mrs. Augustus Lehmann (fig. 3), functions today for the same purposes, with some alterations at the street level. —J.Z.

19. Mentor Building, 1906

39 South State Street
Howard Van Doren Shaw

Fig. 1. Howard Van Doren Shaw. Mentor Building, northeast corner of State and Monroe streets, 1906

Fig. 2. View of the ground-floor lobby, c. 1906

The Mentor Building is the only skyscraper by Howard Van Doren Shaw (1869–1926), an architect renowned for the many elegant estates he designed for Chicago's northern suburbs. Shaw, who studied architecture at Yale and the Massachusetts Institute of Technology, worked for two years in Chicago's most important atelier, the office of William Le Baron Jenney, before opening his own practice in 1897. Shaw's reputation was based in large part on his ability to design well in a great variety of historical styles, as in his Romanesque Lakeside Press Building (1897) in downtown Chicago, his Jacobean Market Square (1913) in Lake Forest, and the many Arts and Crafts and classical mansions that he designed on Lake Michigan's North Shore. Perhaps Shaw's best-known work is the Gothic Fourth Presbyterian Church (1912), at Michigan Avenue and Chestnut Street, which he designed with Ralph Adams Cram (1863–1942). Shaw, a Trustee of The Art Institute of Chicago, also left an architectural legacy there in his design of the Burnham Library of Architecture (1919) and the Goodman Theater (1925). In 1927 the American Institute of Architects posthumously awarded Shaw its highest honor, the Gold Medal, for his distinguished architectural career.

The seventeen-story Mentor Building (figs. 1, 2), at the northeast corner of State and Monroe streets, shares the block with Louis Sullivan's Schlesinger and Mayer Store (now Carson Pirie Scott and Company Store, see no. 14). It replaced an earlier Mentor Building on the same site, a seven-story structure that stood from 1873 until it was demolished to make way for the present building in 1905. Like the Marshall Field and Company Annex (see no. 9), the second Mentor Building was designed to combine two distinct functions in one structure, retail sales and commercial business. Later buildings, such as Benjamin Marshall's Lytton Building (1911), located to the south on State Street, followed that precedent and successfully combined a store and office building in one structure.

When the architect and historian Thomas Tallmadge wrote an article titled "The Chicago School" for the *Architectural Review* (April 1908), he identified the Mentor Building as a "Prairie School" skyscraper, noting that it could hold its own with the best of Sullivan's contemporary skyscrapers such as the Gage Building (1898–99, see no. 13). Even though the Mentor is a skyscraper, Tallmadge theorized that Shaw's preference for the use of horizontal elements over the vertical was "an absolute result of the inspiration of the prairie." The brown-brick and terra-cotta Mentor Building also combines the Chicago School concern for the frank expression of structure with classical detailing. The narrow State Street façade features flat bays of five double-hung windows separated by narrow brick piers. The longer Monroe Street façade is composed of three groups of the same double-hung windows that are separated by continuous brick piers running from the

second floor to the classical colonnade at the roofline. As in the Chicago Savings Bank Building (1903–04, see no. 16), a block to the north, the large, overhanging cornice of the Mentor Building survives intact. Despite the building's superior design and its importance as the only skyscraper by one of Chicago's most distinguished architects, the building is today nearly unoccupied. Although there is a store on the ground floor, the upper floors are either vacant or used for storage. —P.A.S.

20. Blackstone Hotel, 1908

630 South Michigan Avenue
Marshall and Fox

Fig. 2. Marshall and Fox. Blackstone Theater, 60 East Balbo Street, 1910, which adjoins the hotel to the west

Fig. 3. Marshall and Fox. Perspective study of the Blackstone Hotel (1908) and Theater (1910) with proposed tower annex, c. 1911–15 (unexecuted). Delineated by J. N. Tilton. University of Texas at Austin, Architectural Drawings Collection

The Blackstone was one of the first in a series of luxury hotels built in Chicago during the first two decades of the twentieth century (fig. 1). Designed in the opulent Second Empire style by Benjamin H. Marshall (1874–1944) and Charles E. Fox (1870–1926), it was built by John and Tracy Drake (sons of a Gilded Age developer famous for his Grand Pacific Hotel of 1872), on the site of their boyhood home. Its gilded-plaster interior detail and elaborate terra-cotta and brick exterior gave it such a stately presence that Chicago's social leaders soon chose it for their most exclusive events in preference to their homes. This was the Drake Brothers's intent, for according to Tracy: "The nearer a hotel can approach to the house itself, the more it appeals to the better class of discriminating American travelers."

The elegantly detailed Blackstone survives today with few alterations. Although some interiors have been renovated, on the whole they have been treated in the same spirit in which they were first created. The hotel is joined to the west by the Blackstone Theater (fig. 2), at 60 East Balbo Street, built by Marshall and Fox in 1910. Between 1911 and 1915 the same architects planned a tower annex (fig. 3) comparable in style to the hotel and intended to be sited to the west of the theater. Never executed, this planned expansion would have included an art gallery above the theater, and was doubtless intended to rival similar hotel and theater complexes nearby, such as Adler and Sullivan's Auditorium Building of 1889 (see no. 3). —J.Z.

Fig. 1. Holabird and Roche.
Monroe Building, southwest
corner of Michigan Avenue and
East Monroe Street, 1910–12

Fig. 2. Holabird and Roche.
University Club, northwest corner
of East Monroe Street and
Michigan Avenue, 1908–09

21. University Club, 1908–09

26 East Monroe Street
Holabird and Roche

Monroe Building, 1910–12

104 South Michigan Avenue
Holabird and Roche

Beginning in 1907 or 1908, Holabird and Roche designed a number of buildings that combined the direct expression of structure with a convincingly executed historical style, among them the Tudor Gothic University Club (1908–09), at the northwest corner of Michigan Avenue and East Monroe Street, and the Gothic Monroe Building (1910–12), on the southwest corner across the street. Grafting historical ornament onto Chicago School skyscrapers, the two buildings, along with the firm's Neoclassic City Hall–County Building (1905–11), were soon among the most beloved structures on the city's skyline.

The University Club, originally a private men's club established in 1887, was for its first two decades housed in two successive Loop buildings; then, in 1908, its members voted to construct new quarters solely for their own use. Selected as architects for the building were William Holabird and Martin Roche, both club members. And Holabird himself was a major stockholder in the Association of the University Club, whose members invested in the building and then leased it to the club.

The twelve-story building, a splendid mix of a steel-frame Chicago School skyscraper and a Tudor Gothic manor house, is linked by the Gothic style to some of the great universities of the world. The club has a two-story gabled roof ornamented by Gothic spires and gargoyles and windows that are framed in Gothic tracery. The most spectacular Gothic features of the building, however, are the second-floor Michigan Room and the ninth-floor Cathedral Hall.

The Michigan Room, paneled in carved wood, is dominated by a monumental limestone hearth and a striking coved ceiling, which is covered with fifty-six painted panels by Chicago artist and art collector Frederick Clay Bartlett (1873–1953); he did not depict, as one might expect, events in local history but rather scenes of the medieval hunt. Bartlett also designed many other features of the club, including its seal and the stained-glass windows in both the eighth-floor library and the Cathedral Hall on the floor above. Modeled after the fifteenth-century Crosby Hall at Bishopsgate (and moved to London in 1910), the great Cathedral Hall resembles the nave of a Gothic cathedral. The spectacular three-story space is replete with engaged limestone piers and pointed arches, a carved-wood vaulted ceiling, and twelve groupings of stained-glass windows set in stone tracery. Each of the twelve is composed of fifteen individual stained-glass windows set into a pointed-arch opening. Seven of the twelve depict Literature, Law, Science, Religion, the Fine Arts, Music, and Commerce, while the other five represent individual American colleges and universities. Other features of the club include squash courts and an open-air balcony on the twelfth floor, various restaurants and meeting rooms on the seventh floor, and guest rooms on floors three through six. The lobby and second floor,

as well as the stained-glass windows throughout, were restored for the club's centennial in 1987, and the exterior of the building was cleaned in 1988 and 1989.

Like the University Club, the fourteen-story Monroe Building is essentially a twelve-story Chicago School skyscraper, but it is topped off with a two-story gabled attic, which immediately after completion housed the offices of Holabird and Roche. Although the Gothic style of the gable and lobby is repeated in the varicolored façade, the sculptured, continuous, vertical piers, and the ornamented spandrels, the building nevertheless follows the structural tradition of the Chicago School. The base, which features large storefronts on the first floor and Chicago windows on the second, originally accommodated such tenants as Capper and Capper, a distinguished clothier, and French, Schriner and Urner, a boot and shoe store. The building's continuous piers reveal the steel structure beneath, and separate pairs of double-hung windows form five bays on the narrow Michigan Avenue façade and nine bays on Monroe Street. The building's gable end on Michigan Avenue features three round arches filled with pairs of small windows separated by pilasters with elaborately carved capitals, while the roofline on the Monroe Street side is opened up by three dormers.

The lobby of the Monroe Building, which is accessible from doorways on both Michigan Avenue and Monroe Street, is a long, narrow arcade running through the center of the first floor. The lobby is a fantasy of glazed Rookwood tile and contains elaborate Gothic detail such as a ribbed, vaulted ceiling enhanced by checkered borders, twisted columns, and a patterned floor. The building's elaborately appointed interiors included woodwork of dark English oak and Gothic window sashes.

The Monroe Building was designed in the Gothic style at the request of its developer, Shepherd Brooks, who wanted its silhouette to harmonize with the University Club across the street. As a result, he also requested that the Monroe not exceed it in height and thus not be built to the full limit allowed by city ordinance. In a speech to the Building Managers' Association in 1921, Holabird applauded Brooks's action as "an illustration of how an owner sacrificed his own interests for the benefit of the community." —P.A.S.

22. McCormick Building, 1908–10, 1911–12

332 South Michigan Avenue
Holabird and Roche
Original ten bays: 1908–10
Additional eight bays: 1911–12

The McCormick Building is part of an impressive wall of masonry structures built during the late-nineteenth and early-twentieth centuries along South Michigan Avenue, fronting on Grant Park. This wall of structures—which includes Adler and Sullivan's Auditorium Building of 1887–89 (see no. 3), D. H. Burnham and Co.'s Railway Exchange of 1903–04 and Peoples Gas Company Building of 1910–11 (see no. 17), and Graham, Anderson, Probst and White's Straus Building of 1924 (see no. 35)—forms one of the most enduring and cosmopolitan images on the Chicago skyline.

The McCormick Building was commissioned by Robert Hall McCormick, the son of Leander McCormick, who with his brother Cyrus had run the enormous McCormick Harvesting Machine Company. After retiring from the business in 1881, Leander began to invest in real estate, a practice that his son Robert pursued after his father's death in 1900. The twenty-story McCormick Building was constructed in two stages, the southern ten bays being completed in 1910 and the northern eight in 1912. The two parts have identical elevations: a two-story granite base; a seventeen-story shaft of starkly unornamented, gray Roman brick; and a decorative overhanging cornice. The building's original tenants included many lumber and construction firms, as well as Spaulding and Co., gold- and silversmith, and Allegretti Chocolate Cream Company.

The building follows a U-shaped plan, surrounding an enclosed interior light court facing the alley. Offices in the building were exceptionally bright, owing to their exposure to the light court and the building's frontage on the open expanse of Michigan Avenue. Because of the good light, the offices were also unusually deep. However, the windows in the McCormick were considerably smaller than those of its contemporary, the Brooks Estate Building (see no. 23), perhaps to forestall problems of heat loss.

Although functional, the straightforward, simple design of the McCormick Building inspired little enthusiasm among contemporary critics. Peter Bonnett Wight, in an article titled "Additions to Chicago's Skyline," in the *Architectural Record* (July 1910), said: "Its architecture is not calculated to attract remark. If there is beauty in simplicity, here it is. But certainly there is very little design." In 1996–97 the top six floors of the McCormick Building were converted into luxury residential units. The 78 condominium units are the first office-to-residence conversion on South Michigan Avenue, following the successful lead of other buildings, such as the Manhattan (1889–91, see no. 6) on South Dearborn Street. —P.A.S.

Fig. 1. Holabird and Roche. McCormick Building, 332 South Michigan Avenue, 1908–10 (the first ten bays), 1911–12 (the last eight bays)

23. Brooks Estate Building, 1909–10

223 West Jackson Boulevard
Holabird and Roche

A hallmark of the Chicago School, the Brooks Estate Building demonstrates that the design and engineering innovations of the 1880s and 1890s continued to be used successfully after the turn of the century. By this time, Holabird and Roche had worked them into a formula, which the firm readily applied to commercial commissions such as the Brooks Estate Building. Characteristic of the formula, the building's underlying steel structure is clearly expressed on its exterior, and its terra-cotta-clad façades, largely devoid of ornament, are composed primarily of large windows. The Brooks Building, as it is also known, was commissioned by and named for Boston real-estate developer Peter Brooks, who, with his brother Shepherd, invested heavily in late-nineteenth-century Chicago architecture, evidently without ever setting foot in the city.

The double-hung sash windows of the Brooks Building are arranged in groups of three, separated by piers with round moldings. As historian Carl W. Condit wrote in *The Chicago School of Architecture* (1964): "It is one of the most open and vigorously articulated of the Holabird and Roche designs by virtue of the round moldings on the piers, which elongate and narrow their appearance and enliven the whole elevation." The piers terminate at the cornice line in a burst of foliate ornament similar to that by Louis Sullivan at the top of the Gage Building (see no. 13), which he designed in collaboration with Holabird and Roche in 1898–99. The first floor of the Brooks Building featured large, open storefronts. Because it originally was a mercantile building, housing silk, ribbon, knitting, glove, and lace concerns, the floors above had open plans. Later, in the 1920s, the building became prime office space, its central location and proximity to public transportation answering the growing need for business offices in the West Loop.

Like other Holabird and Roche buildings of the period, such as the Oliver at 159–69 North Dearborn (1907–08) and the Crane at 836 South Michigan Avenue (1912–13), the twelve-story Brooks Building is significant because it follows the Holabird and Roche formula for late Chicago School design, described by Condit as "the familiar cellular pattern of the articulated wall." But as architectural historian Robert Bruegmann has noted, the Brooks is unusual in that its top is set off in green terra-cotta rather than white. And to place the ornament against the green surface is a Sullivanesque decorative scheme, but one that is highly simplified.

In 1976 the Brooks Building was nominated for Chicago landmark status and in 1983 that nomination was submitted to the City Council of Chicago. In 1997 the Brooks Building was designated a Chicago landmark. —P.A.S.

Fig. 1. Holabird and Roche. Brooks Estate Building, 223 West Jackson Boulevard, 1909–10

24. Lumber Exchange Building, 1913–15

Later the Roanoke, now the Eleven South LaSalle Building
11 South LaSalle Street
Holabird and Roche
Additions: Holabird and Roche (five stories), 1922; Holabird
and Roche with Rebori, Wentworth, Dewey and McCormick
(thirty-seven-story tower), 1925
Renovation: Hammond Beeby and Babka, 1981–83

Otis Building, 1911–12

Now Manufacturers Hanover Plaza
10 South LaSalle Street
Holabird and Roche
Reconstruction: Moriyama and Teshima Planners and Holabird
and Root, 1987–89

Two Holabird and Roche skyscrapers that stood across the street from one another virtually intact for over seventy years were altered in the 1980s to meet the needs of new tenants. The Lumber Exchange Building (1913–15), including the exterior and the ground-floor lobby (figs. 1, 2), was completely renovated between 1981 and 1983 with the goal of making changes sympathetic to its original Chicago School structure. In contrast to this contextual approach to renovation, the top twelve stories of the Otis Building (1911–12) were removed a few years later, leaving only the façade of its four-story-high granite and terra-cotta base intact, and a new thirty-seven-story tower of blue glass and aluminum was constructed above it. The preservation of the building's lower stories, a technique more common in Europe than in the United States, was labeled "façadism" by the *Chicago Tribune* critic Paul Gapp, who defined it as "saving a secton of an historic building, usually a front wall, as a sop to preservationists when the rest of the building is torn down. We haven't seen much of that in Chicago, mostly because the practice here is to tear down famous buildings completely, without leaving a trace" ("LaSalle Languishes," *Chicago Tribune*, August 14, 1988).

As Dennis E. Rupert, architect in charge of the 1983 Lumber Exchange renovation, observed in *Threshold* (Autumn 1984), the building had undergone three periods of construction, one of which paralleled a change in Chicago's zoning laws permitting increases in the allowable height for buildings. Constructed between 1913 and 1915, the Lumber Exchange was a sixteen-story commercial block typical of Holabird and Roche's late Chicago School work (fig. 3). Although the architects used a steel-skeleton structure sheathed in a brick, terra-cotta, and glass skin, they also applied a variety of Gothic, Renaissance, and Greek ornament to the building's base. In 1922 a five-story Holabird and Roche addition was constructed on top, and in 1925 a thirty-seven-story tower building was added to the east on Madison Street (fig. 4).

The 1925 addition, designed by Holabird and Roche in association with Rebori, Wentworth, Dewey and McCormick, was primarily the work of Chicago architect Andrew Rebori (1886–1966). His first office tower, it incorporated setbacks, predating Holabird and Roche's highly acclaimed setback skyscraper 333 North Michigan Avenue (see no. 41) by two years, and may well have been the firm's first use of that design device. In the interim between 1922, when the five stories were added, and 1925, when the thirty-seven-story

Fig. 1. Holabird and Roche. Lumber Exchange Building, now Eleven South LaSalle Building, 1913–15. View of entryway as renovated by Hammond Beeby and Babka, 1981–83

Fig. 2. Lobby of Eleven South LaSalle Building as renovated by Hammond Beeby and Babka, 1981–83

tower was constructed, the name of the building was changed
to the Roanoke. In 1928, as commercial aviation was
becoming more common, a forty-five-foot beacon tower was
constructed at the top; featuring twenty-four neon tubes and
two rotating beacons, the light was visible for a hundred
miles.

Over the years the building's original ornament was
removed piecemeal in numerous alterations, and a 1950s
"modernization" stripped the entrance and lobby of all the
rest. In 1981, the building's owners, LaSalle Partners Ltd.,
commissioned the firm of Hammond Beeby and Babka to
design a major renovation, which aimed to reestablish the
building's identity by basing the alterations on its original
features. The ground-floor storefronts were sheathed in green
marble,(fig. 1), and the lobby was redesigned using classical
forms, including an entryway in the shape of a Palladian
window (fig. 2). According to Rupert, in his *Threshold* article,

Fig. 5. Holabird and Roche. Otis Building, 10 South LaSalle Street, 1911–12. View from the northeast soon after completion

Fig. 6. Otis Building, now Manufacturers Hanover Plaza (center), after reconstruction by Holabird and Root, 1987–89, adding a thirty-seven-story glass-and-aluminum tower above the original four-story base

the renovated white marble and polychrome lobby evokes "through reference and abstraction the elegant character that the original lobby had achieved with intimate scale, rich materials, and profuse figural ornament."

The Otis Building, located directly across the street from the Lumber Exchange, was a sixteen-story, granite-and-brick office building (fig. 5), with a light court on the west elevation, which acccording to the 1911 *Chicago Central Business and Office Building Directory* allowed for "exceptional and permanent light on all four sides." In 1984 the developer Fidinam [USA] Inc. announced plans to build a thirty-seven-story tower on the site, using the exterior walls of the first four floors as its base, The new tower (fig. 6), completed in 1988, bears the name of its major tenant, Manufacturers Hanover Trust, which leased five floors in the building. Acccording to the developer, the decision to retain the base of the Otis Building was made in an attempt to

maintain the street-level ambience and scale of La Salle Street. However, the structure's combination of the historic and the contemporary has been criticized on the grounds that the forms, colors, and materials of the two confront rather than complement one another. Among the major design features of the new tower are its painted blue frame, with glass tinted to match; a vertical strip of bay windows that runs from the nineteenth floor to the roof; a semicircular indentation in the same wall that runs from the sidewalk to the top of the seventh floor; and a painted, bright-green piping that outlines corner moldings and window reveals.

By experimenting with a combination of historic and contemporary designs, the Toronto-based architects of Manufacturers Hanover Plaza have provided a solution that is new and not necessarily welcome to Chicago. Thus far, this is the first such treatment of a Chicago historic building. —P.A.S.

25. Franklin Building, 1912

720–36 South Dearborn Street
George C. Nimmons

*Fig. 1. George C. Nimmons.
Franklin Building, 720–36 South
Dearborn Street, 1912. View from
the southeast, 1989*

*Fig. 2. Franklin Building, view of
terra-cotta façade ornament
depicting the history of printing,
1989*

The Franklin (fig. 1) was one of many buildings constructed along South Dearborn Street to serve the printing industry in the early years of this century. Then called Printing House Row, the area was bounded by Polk Street on the south and Van Buren on the north, and housed printing companies as well as an array of related businesses devoted to typesetting, photoengraving, etching, mapmaking, binding, publishing, and photography. The industry, which served the entire country, established itself in the South Loop where there was access to four nearby railroad stations, namely the Illinois Central at Eleventh and Michigan, the Grand Central at Harrison and Wells, the LaSalle Street at LaSalle and Van Buren, and the Dearborn at the foot of Printing House Row, on Polk and Dearborn streets.

The printing industry flourished in the area until after the Second World War, when the need for large presses and other advances in technology forced many companies to set up large suburban plants; transport by rail gave way to truck transport, and new, expansive expressways were built. By the early 1970s, as most of the buildings became deserted, Printing House Row took on the character of skid row. At that point, however, developers and architects began to rehabilitate the derelict loft buildings, such as the Donohue (built in 1883 for the Donohue and Henneberry Company, at 711 South Dearborn), turning them into apartments and offices. Because Printing House Row played such an important role in the industrial history of Chicago (and because its numerous red-brick buildings were so consistently well-designed), the area has been placed on the National Register of Historic Places.

As a result of the massive rehabilitation of Printing House Row (renamed Printers Row in the 1970s), Dearborn Park, a residential community housing 10,000 people, was constructed to the south on abandoned railroad land in 1977. The master plan for the community was drawn up by the architectural firm of Skidmore, Owings and Merrill, while clusters of white-brick townhouses and red-brick mid-rise and high-rise apartment buildings were designed by five Chicago firms. Additional developments resulting from the success of the area's rejuvenation include a second phase of Dearborn Park, which in the late 1980s was being constructed to the south, and the first phase of River City, a self-contained riverfront apartment and commercial complex, designed by Bertrand Goldberg and completed in 1986 (see no. 64).

Industrial loft buildings such as the Franklin, the Lakeside Press (1890, at 731 South Plymouth Court), and the Mergenthaler Linotype (1917, at 501 South Plymouth Court), were constructed with heavy timber and reinforced-concrete floors that could sustain the weight of the printing presses and other machinery housed within. The Franklin Building at 720 South Dearborn (fig. 1) was actually the second of the same

Fig. 3. Franklin Building, view of
glass-covered top story, 1981

name designed by George C. Nimmons (1865–1947) for the
printing industry. The earlier Franklin, at 525 South Dearborn,
was a seven-story brick building constructed in 1888. The
Franklin completed in 1912 is a thirteen-story brown-brick loft
building noted for the beautiful multicolored terra-cotta
ornament skillfully incorporated into its Dearborn Street
façade (fig. 2). A variety of vertical piers and pilasters further
define its features. The two-story base has nine tapering
pilasters that separate individual ground-floor storefronts and
multicolored terra-cotta panels that sketch the history of
printing from Gutenberg onward. The main part of the
building features five vertical piers running uninterrupted
from the second to the ninth floors and terminating in a
flourish of colored terra-cotta ornament. The groups of three
double-hung sash windows are separated by brick spandrels
with terra-cotta insets. The windows of the top two floors are
separated by tapering ornamented piers and spandrels, with a
central crest at the highest point of the peaked roof. The top
floor of the Franklin Building was originally a spectacular
three-story space bathed in natural light from the sloping
skylight that filled the entire ceiling (fig. 3). As part of the
growth of Printers Row, the Franklin Building has been
converted into loft condominium units. —P.A.S.

26. Fort Dearborn Hotel, 1912

Now the Traders Building
401 South LaSalle Street
Holabird and Roche
Renovation: Booth Hansen and Associates, 1983–84

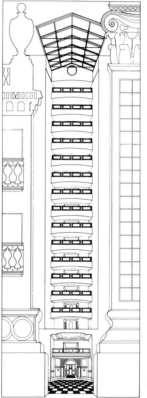

Fig. 1. Holabird and Roche. Fort Dearborn Hotel, now the Traders Building, 401 South LaSalle Street, 1912

Fig. 2. Perspective elevation of light court, enclosed and renovated by Booth Hansen and Associates, c. 1983

The Fort Dearborn was a relatively modest hotel designed in 1912 by the firm of Holabird and Roche (fig. 1), which a few years before had designed the opulent LaSalle (1908–09, demolished) and a decade later would design even larger, more luxurious hostelries such as the Sherman House, the Stevens (now the Chicago Hilton and Towers; see no. 39) and the Palmer House (see no. 40). Although the later hotels would have ornate interiors patterned after elaborate New York predecessors, the Fort Dearborn reflected the simplicity of the frontier outpost for which it was named.

Commissioned by Edward A. Renwick (1860–1941), a partner in the Holabird and Roche firm, the Fort Dearborn was a rather simply detailed, 500-room, seventeen-story establishment. Its red-brick and terra-cotta exterior features classical ornament at the street level that is Georgian in ancestry. Although the plan of the first two floors is a square, with a two-story lobby in the center, that of the upper fifteen is U-shaped because arranged around a light court. The two-story lobby, which was modest in size, was luxuriously sheathed in Circassian walnut panels and Rookwood tile, and had a black-and-white marble floor. The mezzanine level, which still features two large oil murals depicting Chicago's early history as a frontier trading post, was originally intended to be used as a promenade and writing room. The lobby's

decorative plaster ceiling, capitals, and bronze railings repeat
the classical motifs of the building's exterior.

By the time the hotel was almost seventy years old, it had
fallen into a state of serious disrepair. At that point, the
developer Richard G'Sell commissioned the renovation of the
building and converted it into a 140,000-square-foot office
building, designed to house traders from the nearby Board of
Trade, Chicago Board Options Exchange, and Midwest Stock
Exchange. The new program called for the building to be
completely gutted inside. The exterior was restored, new
mechanical systems were added, and the light court was
enclosed and converted into a soaring atrium topped by a
skylight (fig. 2). Although the interior has not been given a
historically accurate restoration, it has been beautifully
renovated, with the lobby in particular being treated with a
sensitivity to both historical and contemporary design features
(figs. 3, 4). The new color palette of muted green and brown
is sympathetic to the original features, which include some of
the decorative bronze railings and the two large murals. As an
example of what developers and preservationists of the 1980s
termed "adaptive reuse," the Traders Building is a successful
illustration of how to bestow new life on an aging structure.
—P.A.S.

27. Conway Building, 1912–13

111 West Washington Street
Now Burnham Center
D. H. Burnham and Co. and Graham, Burnham and Company
Renovation: Jack Train Associates, 1986

*Fig. 1. D. H. Burnham and Co.
and Graham, Burnham and
Company. Conway Building,
111 West Washington Street,
1912–13*

The twenty-one story Conway Building was the last office building designed by the architectural firm of D. H. Burnham and Co. before Daniel Burnham's death in 1912. Built for the Marshall Field Estate, the Conway was named for Field's birthplace, the city of that name in Massachusetts. Directly following the formula for office blocks perfected by the Burnham firm in the early years of this century, the Conway is an atrium building sheathed in light-colored terra-cotta decorated with classical ornament.

Following a scheme used in the Rookery (1885–88, see no. 2) and the Railway Exchange (1903–04, see no. 17), the lobby of the Conway originally contained a two-story enclosed light court and above it a large, square open well, which was surrounded by the floors of offices. Just as in the earlier buildings, the Conway's open well provided much-needed light and ventilation to the offices surrounding it. Following the office-building formula further, the Conway was covered inside and out with white-glazed terra-cotta featuring an array of classical details—egg-and-dart moldings, meander-pattern friezes, and urns and acroteria. In addition, the organization of the Conway's façades is very similar to that of other classically inspired Burnham buildings, particularly the 1892 annex to the Marshall Field and Company Store (see no. 9). The Conway features a three-story base with large storefront windows and monumental classical pilasters. The tall shaft of the building is faced in white terra-cotta blocks and is topped by a three-story colonnade and an elaborate rooftop balustrade. The building's curved corner on Clark and Washington streets is reminiscent of Burnham's most famous classically inspired skyscraper, the Flatiron Building (1902; see introduction, fig. 16), in New York. Both were the work of Frederick P. Dinkelberg (c. 1859–1935), who in 1926, would also design the domed Jewelers Building (see no. 33).

The use of classical forms and a white palette for office buildings reflected the tremendous importance to Burnham of the Beaux-Arts buildings in the White City of the World's Columbian Exposition in 1893. Using successful aspects of the Fair as models, Burnham had developed a far-reaching blueprint for the future of Chicago. His world-renowned 1909 Plan of Chicago called for a variety of inspired improvements to the city, including the construction of Grant Park, the Michigan Avenue Bridge, and Lake Shore Drive. In addition, in order to instill a "new civility" into Chicago's business district, he called for an end to the dark ring of soot-encrusted buildings surrounding the Loop, encouraging instead the construction of white and light-colored buildings, such as the Conway.

In 1944 Chicago Title and Trust Co. purchased the Conway Building and filled in the interior court to the height of six stories, thus providing more floor space for offices. In 1986, the company commissioned Jack Train Associates to renovate the ground floor and to recreate a two-story lobby in the spirit of the original building. When that renovation took place, sections of white-glazed terra-cotta from the lobby were donated to The Art Institute of Chicago for display in its gallery of Chicago building fragments. The classically detailed blocks, even when seen out of context, provide a clear idea of the design conventions that dictated the detailing of the Conway and so many other buildings during the period between the World's Columbian Exposition of 1893 and the onset of the Great Depression in 1929. —P.A.S.

II. MID-AMERICAN METROPOLIS

Chicago in the 1920s and '30s

28. Drake Hotel, 1919

140 East Walton Street
Marshall and Fox

In the early years of the twentieth century Benjamin H. Marshall (1874–1944) and Charles S. Fox (1870–1926), designers of the Drake Hotel (fig. 1), were Chicago's leading high-society architects. They set new standards for the creation of luxury hotels and apartment buildings for Chicago's elite, increasing numbers of whom were deserting their single-family mansions on Prairie Avenue and the South Side for apartment life along the lakefront of the Near North Side. That turn-of-the-century exodus increased after the Michigan Avenue Bridge opened in 1920, and "The Avenue" became a major transportation artery between the North Side and the Loop. In all, Marshall designed ten fine hotels in Chicago and two dozen sumptuous apartment buildings— including 1550 North State Parkway (fig. 2)—before the Stock Market Crash of 1929 and the subsequent economic depression robbed him of his clientele.

Among Marshall's best-known apartment and hotel designs are those located in Streeterville, on East Lake Shore Drive, the city's most prominent residential lakefront address. Ironically, the area is named for George Wellington Streeter, a boat captain and gunrunner, who in 1886 took up residence on a small boat that had run aground on the shore of Lake Michigan just south of Chicago Avenue. By dumping garbage in the lake, Streeter created a landfill that eventually grew to a gargantuan 150 acres. Streeter laid claim to the newly created land, arguing that it was not part of the original 1818 Federal land grant establishing the State of Illinois. His fight for possession of the land was unsuccessful, but it continued until his death in 1921. Meanwhile, the area became dotted with luxury apartment buildings, including four designed by Benjamin H. Marshall: 999 North Lake Shore Drive (1911), the Breakers at 199 East Lake Shore Drive (1911), 209 East Lake Shore Drive (1924), and the Drake Towers Apartment Hotel at 179 East Lake Shore Drive (1928). It is at the corner where Lake Shore Drive and Michigan meet that an earlier Marshall and Fox monument stands: the Drake Hotel of 1919.

The thirteen-story Drake was commissioned by the same brothers, John and Tracy Drake, who in 1908 had hired Marshall and Fox to design the Blackstone Hotel (see no. 20), on South Michigan Avenue. According to C. William Westfall in *The Chicago Architectural Journal* (1982), heirs of Potter Palmer, the nineteenth-century hotel man, had been working with Holabird and Roche since 1911 on plans for a major hotel at the junction of Michigan and Lake Shore Drive. However, the honor of constructing that jewel in the crown of Michigan Avenue went not to the Potter Palmer heirs but to their long-time competitors, the Drakes.

The 800-room Drake Hotel is organized in an H-plan that may well be a response to its beachfront site: every room is provided with an outside exposure. The hotel's rather plain limestone exterior incorporates Italian Renaissance motifs, its façades resembling a Renaissance palazzo. A colonnade stretches between the two end wings, enclosing a dining room that faces the lake. The interior of the Drake Hotel, designed by Marshall and Fox with the decorator William Jennings Sinclair, incorporated the newest and most luxurious appointments available at the time; in the opinion of Westfall, the Drake's "massing and refinement in detail made it a paragon among Marshall's and the city's buildings."

In addition to hundreds of guest rooms, the Drake provided, according to Henry W. Frohne in the May 1921 *Good Furniture*, "charming surroundings of lakeshore and park." The Drake also allotted space for permanent residents: an entire floor was reserved for bachelors who would live for extended periods in the hotel. And every floor had apartments for families wishing to live there permanently. Furthermore, the two- to six-room apartments could easily accommodate servants if the tenants so desired. This combination of temporary guest rooms and apartments gave the Drake a homelike quality lacking in other hotels of the period. Frohne commented on the ambience with the following praise: "Here is a hotel which is as like a home as a hotel can be. With the air of genuineness evident in its spacious public apartments, a yet more lasting texture has been woven into the very fibre of the structure, which warmly says 'welcome' to the guest."
—P.A.S.

29. Wrigley Building, 1919–22

410 North Michigan Avenue
Graham, Anderson, Probst and White
Additions: Graham, Anderson, Probst and White (north building and connecting bridge), 1924–25; Louis R. Solomon, John D. Cordwell Associates (Wrigley Building Plaza), 1957; Powell-Kleinschmidt (lobby renovation), 1984

Fig. 1. Graham, Anderson, Probst and White. Wrigley Building, 410 North Michigan Avenue, 1919–22, prior to the addition of the north building, 1924–25

Fig. 2. Wrigley Building, c. 1921–22, illuminated front façade

The centerpiece of the Plan of Chicago (1909) initiated and organized by Daniel H. Burnham was a domed civic center and broad plaza located at the junction of Halsted and Congress streets on Chicago's steadily expanding West Side. It was Burnham's dream to give coherence to the Plan and expand the business center by providing this great edifice on the far side of the river. Burnham's dream was never realized, however, because two other recommendations of the Plan were implemented within ten years of its publication, directing growth to the north and overshadowing development of the West Side. These improvements were the widening of Michigan Avenue from Twelfth Street north to the Chicago River and the building of the double-level Michigan Avenue Bridge connecting the newly broadened boulevard with Pine Street on the north bank. Completion of the bridge by Burnham's colleague, Edward H. Bennett, in 1920, linked the two halves of the widened boulevard. The Plan also called for raising the level of Michigan Avenue from Randolph Street north to the bridge, providing for access to its lower level, with similar construction on the north side.

One of the first to recognize the possibilities of the north side of the river was William Wrigley, Jr., head of the Wrigley Company, a singularly profitable enterprise based on the five-cent package of chewing gum. His company purchased the corner immediately to the northwest of the bridge in 1918 and commissioned Burnham's successor firm, Graham, Anderson, Probst and White, to design a new corporate headquarters. The site commanded sweeping views up and down the river, and it merited and received a commanding edifice from the firm's designer, Charles Beersman (1888–1946). The seventeen-story, trapezoidal office block (fig. 1), with its impressive entrance facing the river, angles to the southwest and northeast, and is capped by a tall, slender, eleven-story tower based on the Giralda Tower in Seville. Creative alignment with the irregular site broke up the massing of the Wrigley and gave it high visibility on the skyline, further emphasized by its profusion of Renaissance-style ornament. And as its loading docks were consigned to the new lower level of Michigan Avenue, the Wrigley presented clear façades on all sides. As architectural historian Sally Chappell observed in *Chicago Architecture, 1872–1922* (1987): "The Wrigley Building meets the rest of the city with urbanistic grace at every level."

The form of construction followed was by then standard: a steel frame resting on caissons. But the glittering terra-cotta sheathing was anything but standard. An echo of the famous White City of the 1893 World's Columbian Exposition and a direct descendant of Charles Atwood's terra-cotta clad Reliance Building (1894–95, see no. 5), it also recalled McKim, Mead and White's Municipal Building (1914) in New York. The Wrigley exterior is described by Chappell: "Six different shades of a special enamel finish were baked on the terra-cotta, varying from gray to pale cream and getting progressively lighter toward the top." Atwood had achieved a similar variation on a smaller scale in the cladding of the 1892 Marshall Field and Company Annex (see no. 9). Since the 1920s, ranks of spotlights have illuminated the Wrigley's white expanse after dark (fig. 2), turning it into a beacon for nighttime sailors and a landmark for evening strollers on Michigan Avenue.

Another recommendation of the 1909 Plan was that the city capitalize on the river's edge, and this was accomplished in the Wrigley Building landing stage, where tour boats now dock. The semicircular plaza at the upper level, owned by the city but maintained by the Wrigley Company, also follows the spirit of the Plan. In 1924–25, an addition skillfully extended the Wrigley complex northward, adding a building and joining the two with a third-floor bridge (fig. 3). The landscaped public courtyard between them, built over East North Water Street, was completed by the company in 1957.

Wrigley's pioneering move to the north in territory newly opened by the Michigan Avenue Bridge established his company on a site of great significance in the city's history. Indians and early French explorers had camped on land where the Wrigley Building now stands; the first permanent settler, the Haitian trader Jean-Baptiste Point du Sable, built his cabin nearby, and Fort Dearborn (1803–12) was located just across the river. To celebrate the city's history, Wrigley was joined by the Ferguson Fund, established by Benjamin F. Ferguson, a nineteenth-century lumberman, in endowing sculptures for the Michigan Avenue Bridge. Installed in 1928, the two reliefs by James Fraser on the north pylons honor early pioneers and explorers, and those by Henry Hering on the south end memorialize the Battle of Fort Dearborn and the "I Will" spirit that rebuilt Chicago following the Great Fire of 1871. The Wrigley Building, cleaned and restored in recent years, is itself a memorial to the great skyscraper age of the 1920s and stands now as it did in 1922 as a gateway to the city's greatest avenue. —J.H.C.

Fig. 3. Wrigley Building, view from the south, c. 1925, with Michigan Avenue and the Chicago Tribune Tower (1925, see no. 32) at right

Fig. 1. Holabird and Roche.
Chicago Temple Building (First
Methodist-Episcopal Church),
77 West Washington Street,
1922–23

30. Chicago Temple Building, 1922–23

First Methodist-Episcopal Church
Now the First United Methodist Church
77 West Washington Street
Holabird and Roche

The Chicago Temple Building, constructed in 1922–23 by the First Methodist-Episcopal Church, is the unlikely combination of a church and office tower located on a downtown Chicago site (fig. 1). According to historian Robert Bruegmann, in *Chicago History* (Fall 1980), the Methodist-Episcopal congregation, which had owned the land since 1845, had repeatedly considered selling it at an enormous profit and leaving the downtown area, but the trustees of the church had at least twice before decided not only to remain in that location but to build ever larger structures combining church and commercial space.

When in 1922 architects Holabird and Roche were offered the opportunity to design the latest building on the site, they met the challenge by planning a twenty-one-story office tower topped by an eight-story Gothic spire. A fifteen-hundred-seat chapel was made easily accessible at street level by means of an entrance on Clark Street, and a separate entrance to the office block was located around the corner on Washington Street. By separating the two entrances to the building, the architects accommodated two very different functions in one structure. Their choice of Gothic ornament was consistent with imagery for both ecclesiastical architecture and commercial buildings of the time. A precedent for the latter was the Woolworth Building in New York (1913)—dubbed the Cathedral of Commerce by a contemporary critic—which freely borrowed elements from Gothic architecture in order to give visual expression to the unprecedented height of this extraordinary skyscraper. And in 1922 the winning design for the Chicago Tribune Tower (see no. 32) featured buttresses and gargoyles in the Gothic style. In fact, an article on the Chicago Temple in *Architecture* magazine (November 1924) suggested that using any other was inconceivable. "The great height of the building and its relation to the lot area suggested, if not demanded, the use of the Gothic style."

The eight-story-high spire presented a particularly thorny problem, however. According to city zoning laws in effect in 1922, the tallest a building could be was no more than 260 feet high. Instead, Holabird and Roche designed the Chicago Temple tower to top off at 556 feet above street level. Disregarding the ordinance, the firm began construction of the building long before the permit for the tower was applied for. As Bruegmann noted in *Chicago History*, however, the tower on the architectural model was detachable, suggesting that the architects had an alternate plan in mind should the City Council have turned down their request for a zoning variance.

But the City Council did grant the Chicago Temple an exception to the zoning law, thereby stirring up a controversy and paving the way for the eventual relaxation of the city's strict zoning ordinance regarding the maximum height of skyscrapers. Critics of the day expressed concern that the action set an unfortunate precedent for other developers, who would try to coerce the City Council into granting them exceptions to the law:

Certain it is that, with the aid of the architects and those who have studied this subject thoroughly, no revision of the building code making "the sky the limit" should be permitted. The City Council opened an old and vexing question when it granted the permit to the Methodist Church for its new tower. It is difficult to determine how it can refuse to grant similar permits to others. In short, there is now no limit on the height of buildings in Chicago; or, shall we say, the establishment of height limits depends upon the force of appeal to the City Council (*Western Architect*, January 1923).

The same article indicated that these fears were well founded:

The *Chicago Tribune* already has consulted the architects of its new building as to the possibility of exceeding the height permitted by ordinance and which governed the competition just closed. The *Tribune* editorially congratulated the City Council on its action, and published revisions of the competition sketches for its new building, rising not only to the height permitted the Methodists, but to 650 feet.

At the time of its completion in 1923, the Chicago Temple was the tallest building in Chicago, the tallest church in the world, and the second tallest building in the world. Although surpassed in height during the next decade with the construction of the Chicago Board of Trade (1929–30, see no. 53) and the One North LaSalle Building (1930, see no. 42), the Chicago Temple is still the tallest church in the world, in a city that boasts the world's tallest building.

The Chicago Temple was cleaned and restored in 1989.
—P.A.S.

31. London Guarantee and Accident Building, 1922–23

360 North Michigan Avenue
Alfred S. Alschuler

Fig. 1. Alfred S. Alschuler. London Guarantee and Accident Building, 360 North Michigan Avenue, 1922–23

Fig. 2. Alfred S. Alschuler. Site plan of London Guarantee and Accident Building, c. 1922. Ink on linen. The Art Institute of Chicago

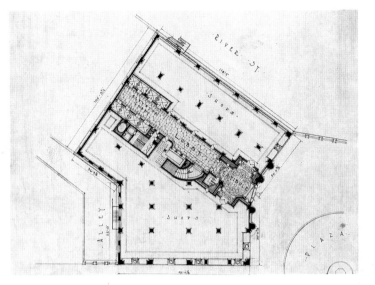

Alfred S. Alschuler (1876–1940) was a native of Chicago who, after graduating from the Armour Institute of Technology, entered the office of the renowned engineer and architect Dankmar Adler shortly before the latter's death in 1900; Alschuler worked first with Adler and then with Samuel Atwater Treat until 1907. It was then that he started an independent practice specializing in industrial architecture; his three most famous buildings were the Thompson (1912) at 350 North Clark Street, the John Sexton and Company (1916, addition 1919) at 500 North Orleans Street, and the Ilg Electric Ventilating Company (1919) at 2850 North Pulaski Road. Since he rarely designed office buildings (the now-demolished 140 North Dearborn Street of 1916 and the nearby 180 North Michigan Avenue of 1926 are exceptions), it is not known how or why he obtained the commission to design the headquarters (fig. 1) for the prestigious London Guarantee and Accident Company, a British-owned insurance company. The answer may well be through his acquaintance with John S. Miller, the developer of the site, whose son was a friend of Alschuler's. Or perhaps the connection was made by Frank O. Tupper-White, an English-trained architect in Alschuler's office, who worked as the chief designer for the London Guarantee building.

This structure was to face the prestigious Wrigley Building (1922, see no. 29) from a location on the south side of the Chicago River adjacent to the newly completed Michigan Avenue Bridge. It was a position of great prominence: the handsome London Guarantee building was being constructed in an up-and-coming area of the city that was intended to rival Paris in its limestone classicism yet serve the needs of 1920s Chicago in its connections with upper and lower Wacker Drive and the newly widened Michigan Boulevard. The London Guarantee's irregular plan (fig. 2) was dictated in part by the odd shape of the site at the intersection of Michigan Avenue, the Chicago River, and the newly built Wacker Drive. Moreover, this building occupied the historic site of Fort Dearborn, where Chicago was founded in 1803, and in addition to an overall prevalence of classical imagery (figs. 3, 4), would contain sculptural references to that early history. Finally, imagery related to the London parent company—the coat of arms of the City of London and the rampant griffin—would be found throughout the lobby and exterior, some of it to be carved in situ.

The working drawings for the building were developed in early 1922, with the sculptural details designed late that year and early in 1923. The cornerstone-laying ceremony of December 3, 1922, was attended by representatives of the London Guarantee and Accident Company, the Chicago Historical Society, and the State, City, and Army, with an escort of fifty-five men from Fort Sheridan representing the soldiers from Fort Dearborn who had been massacred at

Eighteenth Street and Calumet Avenue in 1812. Speeches at
the ceremony stressed the civic contributions that this new
building would make, drawing comparisons with the
monuments of ancient Greece and Rome.

Although the distinctive Roman tempietto (fig. 3) later set
atop the building served on occasion as a backdrop for
performances staged by members of the prestigious Tavern
Club, whose quarters were across the street in 333 North
Michigan Avenue (1927–28, see no. 41), this was perhaps not
what the speakers had in mind. Alschuler himself drew a
parallel with civic architecture when in a 1934 speech he
spoke of his admiration for the tempietto form, particularly as
used in the Stockholm Town Hall (1909–23); according to
some who practiced with the architect, however, the London
Guarantee lantern actually derives from the Choragic
Monument of Lysicrates (334 B.C.) in Athens.

Construction of the London Guarantee and Accident
Building was completed in 1923 at a cost of $5 million, and
the building won the Lake Shore Trust and Savings Bank
Gold Medal that year. The prominence of this structure

doubtless led to other large commissions for Alschuler, such
as the 180 North Michigan Avenue Building in 1926 and
the Chicago Mercantile Exchange in 1927 (see no. 91). The
London Guarantee building remained essentially unchanged
until after the Second World War, when it was sold. In 1956,
the new owners hired Cone and Dornbusch to modernize
the structure. Although the architects incorporated new
elevators and an air-conditioning system, they unfortunately
removed the elaborate iron detailing of the grand entrance,
and the original dome and lobby vault (fig. 5) was covered
with accoustical tiles. It is hoped that one day the importance
of this building, which was declared a landmark in 1996,
will be recognized and that the entrance and lobby will be
fully restored. —J.Z.

32. Chicago Tribune Tower, 1922–25

435 North Michigan Avenue
Hood and Howells
Addition: Hood and Howells (WGN Building), 1935
Renovations: Wiss-Janney Elstner Associates (exterior), 1980–92; John Vinci (lobby and offices), 1986–90

Fig. 1. Hood and Howells. Chicago Tribune Tower, 435 North Michigan Avenue, 1922–25

Fig. 2. Walter Gropius and Adolf Meyer. Chicago Tribune Tower Competition, study for south elevation, 1922. Ink on paper. Busch-Reisinger Museum, Harvard University, Cambridge, Massachusetts, gift of Walter Gropius

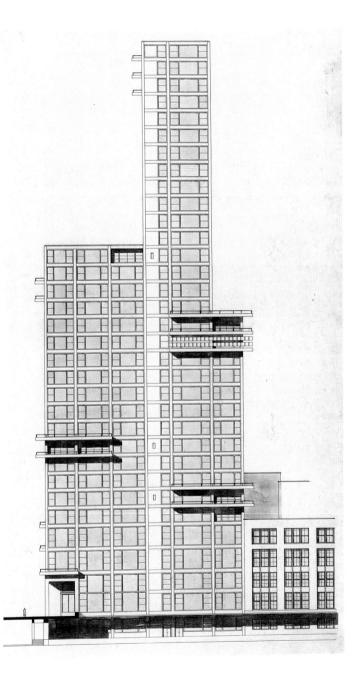

Although William Wrigley, Jr., made the first land purchase at the new urban crossroads created by widening Michigan Avenue and bridging the Chicago River, the newspaper publisher Colonel Robert R. McCormick, president of the Chicago Tribune Company, was not slow to follow. In 1919, the company purchased the property to the northeast of the unfinished bridge. On June 9, 1922, at the annual meeting of the American Institute of Architects, held that year in Chicago, the *Tribune* announced an architectural competition for the design of its new corporate headquarters. The next day, which was the seventy-fifth anniversary of the newspaper's founding, the story appeared on the front page of the paper. The competition's stated aim was "to provide for the world's greatest newspaper . . . the world's most beautiful office building." Entries were due November 1, with a one-month grace period for deliveries from distant countries. Some 263 architects responded—eventually to be 264 when Finnish architect Eliel Saarinen's late entry arrived from Helsingfors (now Helsinki); the entrants represented twenty-three countries in what some would consider the most important such competition ever held.

The significance of the competition lay not only in the choice of the winning design, a Gothic skyscraper by John Mead Howells (1868–1959) and Raymond M. Hood (1888–1934), of New York (fig. 1), but also in the diversity and power of some of the other entries. Publication of 260 of them by the *Chicago Tribune* and the newspaper's organization of a traveling exhibition featuring many of the original drawings, in 1923, gave wide circulation to the ideas represented by the designs, some of which were clearly prophetic and others idiosyncratic to an astonishing degree. The submission by Walter Gropius (fig. 2) of the Weimar Bauhaus was widely praised for its modernity, although fellow European Adolf Loos's 400-foot-tall, Doric-columned tower (fig. 3) may have been perceived as eccentric. But Saarinen's second-prize-winning entry (fig. 4) was to have an enormous influence on the development in Chicago of the Art Moderne style in the late 1920s (see 333 North Michigan Avenue Building, no. 41) and even on Hood's own design for the RCA Building (1931–34) in New York. Indeed in 1986 architect Cesar Pelli would allude to this design in his Chicago skyscraper the PaineWebber Tower (see no. 108).

The Chicago Tribune Tower, framed in steel, is sheathed in Indiana limestone and follows the standard form of base, shaft, and crown, with Gothic details embroidering the base and top. The design, with its great arched entrance, richly carved ornament, and trophy wall (inset with fragments from the Great Wall of China and historic buildings all over the world), carried gothicizing of the skyscraper to an extreme. Although frequently derided, particularly in the 1960s when the International Style reigned supreme, the Tribune Tower's

vertical thrust and open tracery give this building an unsurpassed visual presence on the skyline. In the catalog of the 1923 exhibition, the architects Hood and Howells described their design as unified: "It is not [just] a tower or top, placed on a building—it is all one building."

The Tribune Tower's most distinctive feature, the ring of flying buttresses at the crown ("stage scenery to the last degree," in the words of one critic), was purely decorative but tied the top to the straightforward shaft of the office block. Skilled stone carvers worked on site creating the gargoyles, grotesques, and other ornament that encrust the base and the uppermost 100 feet. (The addition of a tower not exceeding 400 feet above grade level had been "left to the judgment of each competitor," according to the 1922 instructions for the Chicago Tribune Tower Competition, although the city's zoning law in 1922 prohibited a building's being occupied above 260 feet; the Tribune anticipated a 1923 amendment of the ordinance permitting not only the raising of a tower to that level but also the occupying of it.) The ornament, as Gothic carving has always been, was also practical. It shed water, thus to a degree protecting the stonework from the elements.

Hood and Howells, who had both attended the Ecole des Beaux-Arts in Paris, as well as the Massachusetts Institute of Technology in Boston, based their design on the famed Butter Tower of the Rouen Cathedral. It is not surprising that the judges chose a building in the Gothic style; a well-known precedent was Cass Gilbert's Woolworth Building (1913) in New York—called by critics the Cathedral of Commerce—for the architects had received hints. The competition announcement stated: "The Tribune sees naught incompatible between ancient beauty and modern uses." And in the summer of 1922, according to Cynthia Field (unpublished master's thesis, Columbia University, 1979), the Tribune's Sunday rotogravure section ran a series of articles under such headings as "Will the Tribune Building look like this?" illustrated with Gothic cathedrals and Gothic-style New York office towers, including the Woolworth and the Bush Terminal Building on West Forty-second Street (Hemle and Corbett, 1918).

The complex engineering that made the thirty-four-story, 450-foot Chicago Tribune Tower possible began with caissons on bedrock at the base and a steel-column-and-girder frame up to the twenty-fifth floor, where, as Carl W. Condit explains in Chicago, 1910–29 (1973), "a dense grillage of girders and beams carries the frame of the octagonal tower and the ring of flying buttresses that rise around it; at the thirty-third floor, where the area again contracts, a similar grillage supports the topmost discontinuities."

The Plan of Chicago (1909) had envisioned the northern extension of Michigan Avenue to be elegantly European and lined with low-scale, classical buildings. Although the Wrigley and the Tribune Tower, just north of the bridge, do not fit that description, their position across the wide boulevard from one another, each with an adjacent plaza, allows the two to work exceptionally well as a symbolic gateway to what the Tribune Competition's program called "the potential wonder mile of North Michigan Avenue."

Beginning in 1980, the Tribune headquarters underwent a thorough renovation. The lobby was restored, the office floors were modernized, and the exterior was stabilized. Where steel pins holding the stonework had rusted, they were removed, sanded, and coated with a rust-resistant sealer. The carvings, including a dragon at the twenty-fifth-floor level, were repaired or replaced by a master stone carver, Walter Arnold.

The 1989 construction of NBC Tower (see no. 102) to the south and east of Tribune Tower led to the redesign of Pioneer Court as part of the ongoing renovation of the Tribune complex by Vinci/Hamp Architects, Inc.; collaboration on the Court was with Douglas Hoerr, Landscape Architect. Realigned to provide an entrance to NBC, and with extensive new plantings, the court harks back to the ideals of the City Beautiful Movement. Throughout 1997, the newspaper proudly celebrated its 150th anniversary. One of the commemorative events took place on September 23 when the first of an eventual 100 Chicago Tribute Markers of Distinction to be installed throughout the city was dedicated in the new Pioneer Court. The marker honors the first permanent Chicago settlers, Jean Baptiste Pointe du Sable and his wife Catherine, whose eighteenth-century log cabin was built at the river level approximately where the Tribune Tower now stands. Another tribute marker, to be placed on Wabash Avenue at the site of the first Tribune Building, will honor the newspaper's founder, Joseph Medill.

Highly visible on its spacious site, the Tower is an instantly recognizable symbol of the city. However, its splendid isolation has been threatened by the Tribune Company itself. According to the terms of an agreement reached early in 1989 by the newspaper and the City of Chicago regarding landmark designation for the Tower, the company may erect a skyscraper immediately to the east. Thus the Tower's fate would be like that of the Wrigley, Michigan Avenue's other "gatepost," whose western façade, one of its most striking features, has been lost to view by the building of a new skyscraper. —J.H.C.

33. Jewelers Building, 1924–26

*Later the Pure Oil, then the North American Life Building
Now known as 35 East Wacker Drive
Thielbar and Fugard
Associate architects: Giaver and Dinkelberg*

The Jewelers Building (fig. 1), as its name suggests, was originally intended to house jewelry designers, wholesalers, and retailers and their related businesses. However, by 1926, when the Pure Oil Company became the major tenant of the building, its name was changed to reflect that fact. One of the designers of the distinctive building was Frederick P. Dinkelberg, who had worked with Daniel Burnham on several classically inspired skyscrapers including the Railway Exchange (1904) and the Conway (1913) buildings in Chicago (see nos. 17 and 27), as well as Burnham's most famous skyscraper, the Flatiron Building (1902) in New York. Dinkelberg died penniless in 1935, despite his earlier successes.

The forty-story Jewelers Building is composed of two sections. The main block, twenty-four-stories high, has small domed temples (concealing water tanks) at each of its four corners. Rising from the center is the narrower, seventeen-story tower, topped by a large, domed pavilion (fig. 2), which conceals mechanical equipment. Except for the ground floor, the building is sheathed in lavishly patterned, cream-colored terra-cotta that incorporates the letters "JB," signifying the building's original name. Indeed Carl W. Condit, in *Chicago, 1910–29* (1973), wryly observes that "terra-cotta has never been used more lavishly for strictly ornamental ends." According to a rental brochure produced at the building's completion, the design of the structure is based on the fifteenth-century chapel for the Certosa of Pavia, an Italian monastery noted for its extensive detail. The brochure also boasted that at the time of completion, the Jewelers was the tallest building west of New York.

From the outset, the Jewelers Building was designed as a first-class office building with countless amenities, the most dramatic being a thirty-eighth-floor lounge, a restaurant on the floor above it, and an observation deck and dining room with a thirty-foot-high vaulted ceiling on the floor above that. The breathtaking fortieth-floor room was called the Belvedere and provided an unprecedented 360-degree view of the Chicago skyline. The building also featured an open-air terrace on the twenty-sixth floor, at the base of the Belvedere tower, and a roof promenade at the twenty-fourth floor, both designed to enrich the lives of tenants and their visitors.

A then-unique feature of the Jewelers was an internal parking garage in the central core of the building, where a light court would have been located (because the building fronted on public thoroughfares on all four sides, it received abundant natural light). The garage extended from the lower level of the newly completed Wacker Drive to the twenty-second floor. According to Condit, this was the first garage in Chicago to be constructed as an integral part of the structure and was possibly the first in the United States to be completely mechanized. He described the complex parking system in *Chicago, 1910–29:*

Cars were moved to their locations on a particular floor by three elevators electrically driven and controlled by a key-operated switchboard. These elevators possessed the novel feature of movable floors: when the elevator car reached the designated level the floor tipped forward, allowing the automobile to roll onto a horizontal carrier which conveyed it to its parking berth. The process was reversed when the driver called for his car.

Despite the building owner's best intentions, the complex parking system was subject to frequent mechanical failures. In 1940, after the parking system had been in operation for fourteen years, it was shut down when the size and proportions of American automobiles changed and the elevators were no longer large enough to hold them. At that point, the area occupied by the elevator shafts and parking stalls was converted to office space.

Like other skyscrapers of the 1920s, such as the Wrigley, Chicago Tribune Tower, Palmolive, LaSalle-Wacker, and Chicago Board of Trade buildings (see nos. 29, 32, 45, 51, and 53), the Jewelers Building was originally designed to be illuminated at night. The seventeen-story tower was brightly lit, a dramatic foil for the main building on which it rested, and the domed top of the fortieth-floor Belvedere was ribbed with bands of lights. During the blackouts of the Second World War and the energy crisis of the 1970s, the building's dramatic lights were extinguished. However, when the Jewelers was renovated in the early 1980s, it was relit (fig. 2), thereby restoring the building to a prominent position in Chicago's evening skyline. This sentiment was expressed in the forementioned original rental brochure: "With its lofty ornamental dome-crowned tower, its stands as a seal to Chicago's sense of the beautiful and an inspiration to all future builders for the Queen of the Lakes." —P.A.S.

34. Federal Reserve Bank, 1920–22

230 South LaSalle Street
Graham, Anderson, Probst and White
Additions: Naess and Murphy (southwestern), 1957; Holabird and Root (northwestern), 1984–89

Illinois Merchants Bank, 1923–24

Now Bank of America
231 South LaSalle Street
Graham, Anderson, Probst and White
Renovation: Skidmore, Owings and Merrill, 1989–90

LaSalle Street, even in Chicago's early days its chief financial center, was terminated with a flourish in 1885 with the construction of W. W. Boyington's Board of Trade Building (demolished 1930). This nerve center of the Midwestern economy was impressively framed in the early 1920s by a pair of sober classical buildings that face each other across LaSalle Street: to the east, the imposing Illinois Merchants Bank (figs. 1, 3), and to the west, the prestigious Federal Reserve Bank (fig. 2). The six massive columns of the Federal Reserve building, which houses the Chicago branch of the United States central banking system, are capped by Corinthian capitals; their counterparts, which stand before the Illinois Merchants, a regional bank, are topped by capitals of the lesser, Ionic order. Above the third-floor cornice of both banks, the limestone shafts rise virtually unadorned.

Few of the great banking rooms that such institutions once boasted exist today in Chicago. For example, the great room in the D. H. Burnham and Co. First National Bank of 1903 was demolished with the building in 1965, and the hall in the Straus Building of 1924 (see no. 35) has been divided into smaller spaces. However, neither situation is the case in the two banks on LaSalle Street. Traditionally, banking halls were sited above street level. In a 1980s renovation by Holabird and Root, the original three-story hall in the Federal Reserve Bank was combined with the street-level room directly below to create a grand, four-story court. This magnificent space functions as the Federal Reserve's entrance lobby, serving its many visitors, including tourists and school groups.

The basilican banking hall of the 1924 regional bank building rises four stories from the second floor, and it has retained its fifty-three-foot height through the years. However, a 1993 renovation shortly before the merger of the Continental Illinois National Bank with the Bank of America in 1994 altered the hall's use and vast open space. The central area and the side aisles have been discreetly converted to offices for private banking, and the west end now is the Burnham Club, an executive meeting center. The elegant columns, elaborate lighting standards supported by rampant griffins, and iron chandeliers are the only survivors of the original luxurious furnishings.

Jules Guerin (1866–1946), delineator of many of the most beautiful drawings in the 1909 Plan of Chicago, painted the murals that ring the banking hall above its twenty-eight Ionic columns. A testimonial to world trade, the mural panels include some of the principal buildings of the World's Columbian Exposition of 1893. The bank's street level is a retail concourse, designed by Skidmore, Owings and Merrill in 1990. —J.H.C.

Fig. 2. Graham, Anderson, Probst and White. Federal Reserve Bank, 230 South LaSalle Street, 1920–22. View of façade, 1989

Fig. 3. Graham, Anderson, Probst and White. Illinois Merchants Bank, now Continental Illinois National Bank, 231 South LaSalle Street, 1923–24. View of façade, 1989

35. Straus Building, 1923–24

Later Continental National Insurance Co. Building
Now Britannica Center
310 South Michigan Avenue
Graham, Anderson, Probst and White

Fig. 1. Graham, Anderson, Probst and White. Straus Building, 310 South Michigan Avenue, 1923–24

In 1923 the City of Chicago passed a new zoning law that for the first time allowed occupancy in buildings exceeding 260 feet in height, providing that requirements for setbacks were met (see introduction). The first building designed to take advantage of the 1923 zoning ordinance was commissioned by the investment banking firm of S. W. Straus and Co. The required setbacks begin at the twenty-first floor of the Straus skyscraper, and a nine-story tower tops this shaft, with a further setback before the last two stories. The building's crown is a stepped pyramid, recalling both the tenth-century campanile of St. Mark, in Venice (which had collapsed in 1902 and was reconstructed in 1911), and its echo in New York, the tower of the Metropolitan Life Insurance Company Headquarters (Napoleon LeBrun and Sons, 1909). At the top of the Straus pyramid is a glass beehive representing thrift, supported by the heads of four bison, symbols of strength, thrift, industry, and the City of Chicago. Far more visible than the bison were beacons that sent shafts of light in the four directions of the compass, symbolizing the Straus Company's extensive financial activities. In 1954, however, the beacons were replaced by a glowing blue light in the beehive, and the stepped pyramid is separately illuminated.

Like the Wrigley Building and Chicago Tribune Tower a few blocks to the north on Michigan Avenue (see nos. 29 and 32), the Straus Building was a corporate headquarters, so that considerable effort was lavished on its plan by the premier designers of princely skyscrapers, Graham, Anderson, Probst and White, the successor firm to D. H. Burnham and Co. The architects' attention to detail was so great that their sidewalk barricade to protect passersby during construction, superior to the normal makeshift wall of old doors, drew the attention of the *American Architect* (January 1924), which illustrated it with both a photograph and elevation drawings.

The Straus Building exterior, clad in Indiana limestone, exemplifies the classicism that was the architectural firm's hallmark. In deference to the Railway Exchange (see no. 17), the building's neighbor to the north, the Straus Building architects placed the cornices decorating its base at approximately the same height as those of the Exchange, a harmonious contribution to the streetscape. The towering shaft of the Straus is in the unadorned style of the Federal Reserve Bank (see no. 34), the firm's immediate predecessor building, on LaSalle Street.

So as to recoup its investment as quickly as possible, the Straus Company requested and received a sixteen-month contract from the architects and building contractors. The completed interior, wrote Andrew N. Rebori (1886–1966), a contemporary architect, resulted in "massive impressiveness, surpassing in grandeur and costliness any work of like character in Chicago." Cleaned in the 1980s, the dignified skyscraper adds distinction to South Michigan Avenue, even though its former magnificence is much diminished: elaborate bronze elevator doors, decorated with classical relief sculptures representing the arts, are virtually the only remnant of the once opulent lobby. The grand staircase leading to the two-story banking hall on the second floor has been demolished and the great room divided, replaced with two floors of undistinguished offices.

The base of the building has also been considerably altered over the years, beginning in the 1930s when the Straus interests moved to LaSalle Street (see no. 55). Following the building's sale to the Continental Companies (later CNA Financial Company) in 1943, the entrance with its coffered bronze doors by the sculptor Leo Lentelli (1879–1961) was destroyed, and the two-story arched windows on the level above were reduced to smaller rectangles. Although no longer part of CNA, in 1961–62 the Straus Building was directly connected to CNA's new corporate headquarters, Continental Center, designed by the firm of C. F. Murphy Associates. This twenty-two-story, unadorned steel and glass skyscraper at the corner of Wabash Avenue and Jackson Street was originally painted black. Later painted red, this far-from-anonymous modern building with its clearly defined walls makes an elegant backdrop for the richly classical Straus Building.
—J.H.C.

Fig. 1. Henry Raeder Associates, with Nimmons and Dunning. American Furniture Mart, now 680 North Lake Shore Place, 1922–24 (east end) and 1925–26 (west end). View from the northwest

36. American Furniture Mart, 1922–24, 1925–26

Now 680 North Lake Shore Place
Henry Raeder Associates with George C. Nimmons and N. Max Dunning (east end), 1922–24; Nimmons and Dunning (west end), 1925–26
Renovation: Lohan Associates (conversion to apartments), 1982–84

Fig. 2. American Furniture Mart, view of tower, c. 1989

Fig. 3. American Furniture Mart, view of Whiting Hall, grand entryway extending from Lake Shore Drive on the east side to McClurg Court on the west

When the massive American Furniture Mart (fig. 1) opened, Chicago was the central marketplace for home furnishings in the country, and by 1932, the building was described in a local publication as "the largest in the world devoted to a single industry." The writer, V. L. Alward, went on to say that the furnishings on view came from 235 cities, and "it would take a furniture buyer eight months to visit the factories represented."

Conceived in 1922, the year of the Chicago Tribune Tower Competition, the building was finished in brick and terracotta and combined two typical Chicago architectural forms: the loft building and the tall office block. It was built in two sections, each of which had, according to Carl W. Condit in *Chicago, 1910–29* (1973), not only different architects but also a different form of construction. The complex took over four years to complete. The sixteen-story east end, facing Lake Michigan, wrote Condit, "is a column-and-girder frame of reinforced concrete carried on wood piles, but the higher [twenty-story] west portion, with its skyscraper tower, is steel-framed and caisson-supported."

The distinctive 474-foot Gothic Revival tower centered on the west end (fig. 2) resembles that of the British Houses of Parliament (1840–68) by Sir Charles Barry and A. W. N. Pugin, and is a fine foil for the Wrigley and Tribune towers to the south. The Mart's blue-glazed, terra-cotta crown was a beacon to the thousands of buyers who attended the semiannual June and January furniture shows in the American Exposition Palace, occupying almost the entire first floor. A forerunner to McCormick Place, the facility opened in 1924, and the building was entered from either Lake Shore Drive or McClurg Court through Whiting Hall (fig. 3), a baronial

lobby named for the Mart's original owners General Lawrence Whiting and his brother Frank. Display rooms on the floors above, rented by companies on a long-term basis, were reached through a lobby on Erie Street and served by separate elevators.

The interior architecture, as befits a furniture mart, featured a number of period styles. The Furniture Club on the sixteenth floor, a mecca for leaders in the industry, providing them with unparalleled views of the lakeshore and skyline, was furnished, according to N. Max Dunning (1873–1945), one of the building's architects, in "Elizabethan, Jacobean, Adam, Georgian, Early American, and Spanish [styles] used with perfect propriety" (*Western Architect*, April 1925).

The furniture industry began moving to the South in the late 1950s, and the last big show was held in January 1979. The enormous building, set in a prime location, became a white elephant. It was sold that spring and soon imaginative plans were made by the developer for its conversion to a mixed-use building. The architects, Lohan Associates, capitalized on the separate entrances and banks of elevators in the complex to give individual identities to each area. The lakefront and the south side were made residential, as was the tower, which has a separate apartment on each floor. Whiting Hall is the entrance lobby on the lake. The north side was given over to offices and parking floors. In 1988 Golub + Co. purchased the entire building with the exception of the tower, sold the apartments as condominiums, and expanded the retail area. Although the Furniture Club no longer exists, the blue tower, once more lit from below as it was in the 1920s, is a dramatic image on the night skyline. —J.H.C.

37. Allerton House, 1924

Now Allerton Hotel
701 North Michigan Avenue
Murgatroyd and Ogden
Associate architects: Fugard and Knapp

The Allerton House chain of "club hotels" was established in New York to provide residences for single men and women. The intent was to give the single professional a home at a reasonable rate, with the service of a good hotel and the sociability of a private club. The designer of a number of Allerton houses in New York was Arthur Loomis Harmon (1878–1958), later a partner in the firm of Shreve, Lamb and Harmon, architects of the Empire State Building in New York (1931; see introduction, fig. 17). The Allerton houses were often built in the North Italian Renaissance style. Harmon collaborated with the architectural firm of Murgatroyd and Ogden on the Allerton Hotel for Women, located at Lexington Avenue and Fifty-seventh Street, New York. Completed in 1923 (published *Architecture and Building*, March 1923), it, too, followed the style of those previously designed by Harmon. Murgatroyd and Ogden's association with him on that project probably led to their being hired to design the twenty-five-story Chicago Allerton House, which was completed in 1924. When announced in *North Central Magazine* (December 1922), the building was described as having "eleven hundred well lighted and well ventilated rooms," said to be "ample in size without being unduly large," as well as "furnished comfortably and in excellent taste." The building's top originally contained a sun parlor and roof garden. Fugard and Knapp, well known in Chicago for such luxury apartment buildings as 60–70 East Scott Street (1917), 229 East Lake Shore Drive (1918), and 219 East Lake Shore Drive (1922), were the local associate architects who doubtless supervised the working drawings and construction.

The Allerton House (fig. 1) was the first such club hotel on the newly opened Michigan Boulevard. In 1928–29 it was joined by the Woman's Athletic Club, by Philip B. Maher, at 626 North Michigan Avenue. Nearby were two similar hotels designed by Oman and Lilienthal, the fifteen-story Eastgate (1926, now the Richmont), at 162 East Ontario Street, and the twenty-two story St. Clair (1928–29, now the Best Western Inn of Chicago), at 162 East Ohio Street. The Allerton's Italian brick style clearly influenced the design and materials of the two nearby hotels. —J.Z.

Fig. 1. Murgatroyd and Ogden, with Fugard and Knapp. Allerton House, now the Allerton Hotel, 701 North Michigan Avenue, 1924

Fig. 1. James Gamble Rogers.
Northwestern University, Chicago
Campus, aerial view after
completion of Montgomery Ward
Building (upper left), 1925–26

38. Northwestern University, Chicago Campus, begun 1924

Bounded by Lake Shore Drive and Fairbanks Street to the east and west and by Chicago Avenue and Huron Street to the north and south
James Gamble Rogers, with additional buildings by various architects

Architect James Gamble Rogers (1867–1947) achieved renown as a designer of colleges and universities in the Gothic style. He was born in Kentucky and educated at Yale University and at the Ecole des Beaux-Arts in Paris. After completing his studies abroad, he returned to the United States in 1897, establishing an independent practice in Chicago before moving east to New York.

Best remembered for the Harkness Memorial Quadrangle and Tower (1921) at Yale, he was invited soon after its completion to plan a number of buildings for Northwestern University's new Chicago Campus (fig. 1) on the Near North Side. The Montgomery Ward Building (1925–26, fig. 2) was one of six Gothic structures he designed in association with Chicago architects Frank A. Childs and William J. Smith, whose firm was otherwise well known for its industrial buildings. In 1932 Rogers would also design the Gothic-style Deering Library for Northwestern's Evanston campus.

The ground-breaking for the Montgomery Ward Building, at the southeast corner of Chicago Avenue and Fairbanks Street, was held May 8, 1925, and the eighteen-story structure was completed in the following year. Underwritten by Mrs. A. Montgomery Ward, widow of the mail-order-company founder (she donated $4.5 million for this purpose in 1923), it was heralded when opened as the first skyscraper university building in the United States. It preceded by ten years the University of Pittsburgh's famed Cathedral of Learning (the latter, designed by Charles Z. Klauder [1872–1938] in 1924, was begun in 1926 and completed only a decade later). In time, several buildings with some relationship to the collegiate Gothic style were added to the Northwestern University Law and Medical schools complex, among them the Passavant Hospital (1928), at 303 East Superior Street, by the Chicago architects Holabird and Root, and the Wesley Memorial Hospital (1940–41), at 250 East Superior Street, by Thielbar and Fugard, also from the local architectural community.

Between 1970 and the end of the 1980s, other notable buildings were constructed by the university. The Prentice Women's Hospital and Maternity Center and the Northwestern Institute of Psychiatry were housed in an expressionistic, quatrefoil concrete shell (1974–75), designed by Bertrand Goldberg (born 1913), at 333 East Superior Street. And Gerald Horn (born 1934) of Holabird and Root designed the metal-paneled, modernist Olson Pavilion (1979), at 250 East Huron Street, and the contextually responsive Arthur Rubloff Building (1984), constructed for the Law School at 750 Lake Shore Drive.

Finally, in 1989, Ralph Johnson (born 1948) of the architectural firm of Perkins and Will designed a Gothic-influenced addition to the 1926 Ward Building (fig. 3), matching it in height and achieving a comfortable fit with the earlier building. —J.Z.

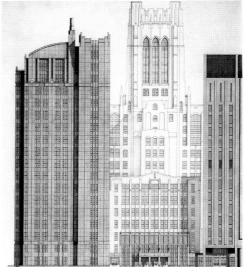

39. Stevens Hotel, 1925–27

Now Chicago Hilton and Towers
700–46 South Michigan Avenue
Holabird and Roche
Renovation: Solomon Cordwell Buenz and Associates
(architects) with Hirsch/Bedner and Associates (interior
designers), 1986

The Stevens Hotel (fig. 1) was founded by James W. Stevens (1853–1936), president of the Hotel LaSalle Company and owner of the Holabird and Roche-designed LaSalle Hotel (1909, demolished). According to Robert Bruegmann in *Holabird and Roche and Holabird and Root: A Catalogue of Works, 1880–1940*, the planning stages of the Stevens Hotel were shrouded in secrecy. Stevens and Edward A. Renwick (1860–1941), architect from the Holabird and Roche firm, met on the fourth floor of the LaSalle Hotel to discuss plans as they developed, each man coming and going separately to maintain secrecy. When after two years the commission was finally announced, there was great consternation because of the hotel's unprecedented size; a contemporary periodical, the *Economist* (March 4, 1922), billed it as "the largest and most sumptuous in the world." So complex were the arrangements that Holabird and Roche architect Frank Long (1864–1939), a

renowned hotel planner, had sixty draftsman working full time on the project.

The twenty-five-story brick and stone building was designed in a modified Louis XVI style and cost more than $17 million to build. It was the city's largest hotel, having three thousand guest rooms, and because of three deep light wells, each room had an outside view. From the outset, it was the city's premier convention hotel, with a four-thousand-seat hall and an exhibition area of thirty-five thousand square feet, nearly twice as much as its conventions competitor, the Chicago Coliseum. To house the large building's considerable support services, it had five basements, with separate areas designated for the ash tunnel and pits, incinerator, coal bunkers, and tin-can baling room. The first through the fourth floors housed hotel offices and public areas such as the grand banquet hall and main dining room, while floors five through twenty-five were guest

Fig. 1. Holabird and Roche.
Stevens Hotel, now Chicago
Hilton and Towers, 700–46
South Michigan Avenue, 1925–27

Fig. 2. View of renovated lobby,
1986

rooms. According to the *Western Society of Engineers* (December 1926), the Holabird and Roche structural engineer, Benjamin Shapiro, encountered difficulties in constructing the large public rooms on the lower floors. The most complicated, he wrote, were those that housed large trusses for the grand banquet hall and other large, open rooms.

George A. Fuller won the construction contract, reported by the *Economist* as the largest ever awarded for a single structure. The interior decorator was Norman Tolson, and Marshall Field and Company received the $500,000 commission to provide the furniture. When the Stevens Hotel was completed, it received rave reviews, including an extremely detailed, fifty-five-page article in a 1927 issue of *Hotel Monthly* in which the author apologized for not having sufficient space to describe fully the wonders of the hotel. The Grand Stair Hall was said to be "an architectural creation that compels admiration." The ballroom was found "magnificent" and the public rooms "luxurious." Centered on the stairways in the Grand Stair Hall, which led to the opulent formal dining room and ballroom, were bronze fountains, designed by sculptor Frederick C. Hibbard (1881–1950), with figures modeled after Stevens's three sons.

However, the success of the hotel was short-lived. The onset of the Depression in 1929 dealt the hotel a blow that was relieved only temporarily by the Century of Progress Exposition in 1933–34. The hotel had gone into receivership in 1932, and it was declared bankrupt in 1936. In 1942 the United States War Department purchased the building for $6 million with plans to use it as an Army Air Force technical school and barracks, housing as many as nine thousand soldiers. Responding to Congressional criticism, the Army sold the building at a loss six months later to Arnold Kirkaby, who then owned the Blackstone and Drake hotels (see nos. 20 and 28). After a renovation, the Stevens almost immediately was restored to its former position as the city's premier convention hotel. According to the *Saturday Evening Post* (June 17, 1944), the grand establishment simultaneously hosted both the Democratic and Republican national conventions in 1944.

In 1945 Conrad Hilton purchased the hotel and remodeled it once again, reducing the number of guest rooms from three thousand to twenty-seven hundred; and he closed off the great two-story lobby windows overlooking Grant Park. Six years later the hotel's name was changed from the Stevens to the Conrad Hilton. In the late 1970s the Hilton Corporation announced plans to shut down the huge hotel and build a major new establishment in the North Loop, following the exodus of department stores and office buildings from downtown. However, the corporation ultimately renovated the existing structure on South Michigan Avenue instead. In 1986, the $150 million renovation, accomplished in eleven months, consisted of remodeling public areas, restoring the lobby

windows, enlarging the guest rooms (once again reducing the number, from twenty-seven- to sixteen hundred), and constructing a health club and new parking garage with a porte cochère on the northwest corner of the block. The hotel was renamed the Chicago Hilton and Towers, and its magnificent public spaces, such as the lobby (fig. 2) and the twenty-thousand-square-foot grand ballroom, were restored to their Classical/Rococo elegance, while other public areas were reoriented to accommodate the new vehicular entrance. The most luxurious suite in the hotel's new reincarnation is a duplex on the twenty-ninth and thirtieth floors. With a magnificent view of Grant Park and Lake Michigan, the five-thousand-square-foot suite is carved out of two former hotel ballrooms. Its Louis XVI décor includes a Flemish tapestry, marble and mahogany fireplaces, and restored French doors that open onto original balconies. —P.A.S.

40. Palmer House, 1925–27

101–29 South State Street
Holabird and Roche

Fig. 1. Holabird and Roche.
Palmer House, 101–29 South
State Street, 1925–27

The Palmer House (fig. 1) was six years in the planning stages, from 1919 until 1925, but it was constructed in just two, between 1925 and 1927, at the same time as the Stevens Hotel (see no. 39). The twenty-five-story brick and limestone building was commissioned by the Palmer Estate, of which Honoré and Potter Palmer, sons of nineteenth-century real-estate baron Potter Palmer, were Trustees. The Palmer House was slightly smaller than the Stevens Hotel—at 2,268 rooms, 732 less than the Stevens. Nonetheless, at the time it was constructed, the Palmer House, known for its Second Empire exterior, was one of the largest structures in the world.

From Chicago's early days, the city's most famous hotel was a Palmer House. Four different establishments were built under that name, three of them occupying the same site at State and Monroe streets. The first opened only weeks before the Great Fire of 1871 and was lost in the conflagration. The next, which immediately preceded the Holabird and Roche building, was a renowned, seven-story structure built in 1875. Designed by John M. Van Osdel (1811–1891), also the architect of the 1871 Palmer House, it was the most modern hotel of its day, having, according to Carl W. Condit, in *The Chicago School of Architecture* (1964), electric lights, telephones, and elevators. But shortly after the First World War, the owners decided that the city could support a much larger hotel. The new Holabird and Roche structure was built in two phases: as business continued in the old Van Osdel building, construction of the new hotel's State Street and Wabash Avenue section began. Once it was completed late in 1925, the old building was demolished to make way for the second section, which was completed in 1927.

In a distinctive approach to designing a hotel, the lobby is located on the second floor, while the lower level and first floor have been entirely turned over to restaurants and shops. The elegant first-floor commercial arcade is T-shaped and runs without interruption from State Street to Wabash Avenue. Just off the second-floor lobby, which is dominated by a huge overhead mural, is one of the city's most famous restaurants, the Empire Room, renowned for a décor including dark-green walls, tapestry panels, ebony pilasters, and gold-leaf trim. In keeping with this use of French Empire-style design motifs, guest rooms in the hotel were furnished in a variety of historical styles. The department store Carson Pirie Scott was awarded the commission to supply the furniture for the large hotel, and turned over one floor of the store to holding the stock for the hotel's extensive furnishings.

Among the shops that Holabird and Roche designed for the arcade was the C. D. Peacock Jewelry Store (1926–27), one of the city's oldest and most venerable stores (its predecessor having been founded by Elijah Peacock in 1837). The most striking feature of the opulent establishment was the seventeen thousand square feet of *verde antico* (antique green) marble that covered its walls and columns. According to Robert Bruegmann in *Holabird and Roche and Holabird and Root: A Catalogue of Works, 1880–1940*, the entire American supply of this handsomely veined green marble was reserved for the Peacock commission. Indeed, because the material was so rare, there was some doubt whether enough of it could be quarried to complete the jewelry store.

Over the years, Holabird and Root (the successor firm to Holabird and Roche) continued to be associated with the hotel's renovations, such as the 1935 transformation of a French Empire-style café on the lower level into Le Petit Café, a chic, modern restaurant. The new room, which served as both a lunchtime café and an evening cocktail lounge, was notable for its unique glass Venetian blinds. Designed by the Holabird firm, the blinds were fabricated in a new unbreakable glass, called "Tuf-flex," made by the Libbey-Owens-Ford Glass Company. The translucent, sandblasted Tuf-flex blinds were hung in artificial windows, where colored lights on dimmers were adjusted throughout the day to simulate a range of effects from bright noonday sun to dim, colored light for the evening.

In 1945 the Palmer Estate sold the hotel to Conrad Hilton for $20 million. In the 1950s, a number of changes were made, including the installation of an escalator to connect the Monroe Street entrance to both the lower arcade and the second-floor lobby above. Another major remodeling took place in the 1960s, and in 1989 the Monroe Street entrance was refurbished. But the character of the venerable hotel remains intact, with the opulent Empire Room fully restored.
—P.A.S.

41. 333 North Michigan Avenue, 1927–28

Southeast corner of Michigan Avenue and Wacker Drive
Holabird and Root

Chicago Motor Club, 1927–28

Now Wacker Tower
68 East Wacker Place
Holabird and Root

Fig. 1. Holabird and Root.
333 North Michigan Avenue,
southeast corner of Michigan
Avenue and Wacker Drive,
1927–28

Fig. 2. Holabird and Root. Chicago
Motor Club Building, now Wacker
Tower, 68 East Wacker Place,
1927–28

When in 1922 the *Chicago Tribune* hosted an international competition to design its new headquarters, the most influential scheme was not the winning entry by New York architects Hood and Howells (see no. 32), but the one that took second place, by the Finnish architect Eliel Saarinen. John Holabird and John Wellborn Root, Jr., heirs to the firm of Holabird and Roche, were greatly influenced by the Saarinen design in their late 1920s skyscrapers, particularly in their handling of the individual setback blocks of 333 North Michigan Avenue (fig. 1). As Robert Bruegmann observed in *Chicago History* (Fall 1980):

Saarinen had solved the problem [of composing the skyscraper façade] by making a number of small setbacks and unifying them by the continuous deep channels of windows between the wall surfaces and by eliminating all horizontal stops. The eye tended to follow the vertical lines straight up to the top of the building, minimizing the breaks in massing and emphasizing the verticality. Holabird & Root used essentially this solution at 333 N. Michigan.

The architects further refined their treatment of the setback in subsequent buildings, including the Palmolive (see no. 45) and the Chicago Board of Trade (see no. 53). A not-so-well-known example is the slender Chicago Motor Club Building (1927–28, fig. 2), at 68 East Wacker Place. An elegant Art Moderne structure, it clearly reflects the design philosophy of the Ecole des Beaux-Arts in Paris, where both Holabird and Root studied architecture. Following the aesthetic of the Ecole, the Motor Club features an elegant, symmetrical façade that is based on stripped-down classicism. The lobby of the fifteen-story tower originally contained a large mural (fig. 4) designed by John Warner Norton (1876–1934), who also created works of art for other Holabird and Root buildings of the decade, including the Board of Trade, the Chicago Daily News (see no. 52), and 333 North Michigan Avenue.

The more imposing 333 North Michigan is composed of two sections: the main block, which is twenty-four stories high, and a sleek tower to the north that rises to a height of thirty-five stories. The tower is composed of graceful setbacks reminiscent of the Saarinen design. The building is in one of the most prominent locations in the city—at the corner of North Michigan Avenue and the Chicago River, where along with the Wrigley, London Guarantee and Accident, and Chicago Tribune buildings (see nos. 29, 31, and 32) it forms a gateway between the Loop and North Michigan Avenue. The architects sited the building so its narrow tower faced north, overlooking the open expanse created by the Chicago River and according to the author of a contemporary article in the *Economist* (April 28, 1928), the open site gave "a sentinel quality to the structure."

At the fifth floor of the building, a series of seven-foot-high carved limestone panels line the façade. Designed by Chicago

sculptor Fred M. Torrey, the panels depict events in early Chicago history including the meeting of *Père* Jacques Marquette with the Indians, the Fort Dearborn Massacre, and the eventual pacification of the Indians. The panels are enclosed by borders of geometric ornament at top and bottom. Torrey was associated with Lorado Taft's Midway Studios. According to Ira Bach and Mary Gray, in *Chicago's Public Sculpture* (1983), Torrey had become acquainted with John Root, Jr., through the architect's aunt, Harriet Monroe, who was perhaps better-known as the editor of *Poetry* magazine. Bach and Gray also commented on the way the Torrey sculpture enhances the sleek design of the modern skyscraper:

By keeping his sculptures in very low relief, Torrey made his work compatible with the fundamentally geometric expression of the building. In fact his work adds variety to the surface texture, provides a transition between the dark polished granite base accented with portholelike windows and the lighter treatment of the upper elevations, and enhances the strong, slim outline the whole building has when it is seen from north of the Michigan Avenue bridge.

Fig. 3. 333 North Michigan Avenue, interior of Tavern Club, c. 1927–28

Fig. 4. Chicago Motor Club, view of lobby with mural by John Warner Norton, c. 1928

Among the original tenants of the building were the architectural firms Granger and Bollenbacher, George C. Nimmons Co., and Charles L. Morgan, architect and artist. Holabird and Root also occupied two floors of the building, and in fact Root himself was a member of the corporation that owned the land on which 333 was built. When the building was being designed, the Women's Athletic Club originally expressed interest in leasing space—and even had the architects draw up special plans for them. But in 1928 the Club's leaders instead commissioned Philip Maher to design a building for them at the southwest corner of Michigan Avenue and Ontario Street. However, the exclusive Tavern Club (fig. 3) leased the twenty-fifth and twenty-sixth floors, where it is still housed today. The Club's interiors, originally designed by Winold Reiss of New York, have since been altered.

The striking presence of 333 North Michigan won it many admirers and at least one award—a gold medal granted in 1929 by the Lake Shore Trust and Savings Bank for being the year's most attractive building in the new North Michigan

Avenue area. In the year following the building's completion, an article in the *Chicago Tribune* (February 3, 1929) hinted at its popular acceptance, calling it "one of the finest examples of modernistic architecture in the city, if not in the country. . . . The lines of the building, when observed in perspective, do not present a series of right angles as is often the case in New York structures employing setbacks. The result is softer lines which many admirers of skyscraper architecture find more to their taste."

According to Robert Bruegmann in *Holabird and Roche and Holabird and Root: A Complete Catalogue of Works, 1880–1940*, even before the building was completed, there were plans to put up a large addition. To have been called the Chemicals or Publication Building, it would have been constructed to the east over Beaubien Street and above the Illinois Central freight house and tracks. Like so many other buildings that were on the drawing boards in 1929, the onset of the Depression put an end to the plans. —P.A.S.

42. One North LaSalle Building, 1930

Now American National Bank Building
Vitzhum and Burns

Fig. 1. Vitzhum and Burns. One North LaSalle Building, now American National Bank Building, northeast corner of LaSalle and Madison streets, 1930. View of tower (at left) from the northeast, with the Foreman State National Bank Building (see no. 55) to its right

Fig. 2. Vitzhum and Burns. Steuben Club Building, now Randolph Tower, 188 West Randolph Street, 1929. View from the west, c. 1989

Fig. 3. Vitzhum and Burns. Bell Building, now Old Republic Building, 307 North Michigan Avenue, 1925. View from the west, c. 1989

Steuben Club Building, 1929

Now Randolph Tower
188 West Randolph Street
Vitzhum and Burns

Bell Building, 1925

Now Old Republic Building
307 North Michigan Avenue
Vitzhum and Burns

Although the firm of Vitzhum and Burns is little known in the history of Chicago's architecture, its partners designed several of the city's most visible tall office buildings, among them the Bell (1925), Steuben Club (1929), and One North LaSalle (1930) buildings. Designers, as well, of the sixteen-story De Paul University Building (1928), at 64 East Lake Street, Karl Martin Vitzhum (1880–1967) and John J. Burns (1886–1956) reveal in these skyscrapers their progression between 1925 and 1930 into mainstream design, from the terra-cotta classicism of the Bell Building (fig. 3) through the limestone Modernism of the Steuben Club (fig. 2) and the elegant setbacks of One North LaSalle (fig. 1). The last is their tallest, at forty-nine stories and 530 feet high. According to Carl W. Condit, in *Chicago, 1910–29* (1973), this building "has the

most emphatic vertical pattern of all Chicago skyscrapers." The building's name marks its location in the heart of the city's financial district. The seventeen relief panels at the fifth-floor level commemorate the man for whom Chicago's version of Wall Street is named, the seventeenth-century French explorer René Robert de La Salle who, according to legend, camped on the very site of this building during his search for the mouth of the Mississippi River.

The Depression of the 1930s and the Second World War allowed the firm of Vitzhum and Burns few visible commissions, until they completed St. Peter's Church and Friary, at 110 West Madison Street, in 1953. But their three high rises of the 1920s have survived and are well maintained despite alterations and renovations over the years. —J.Z.

43. Builders Building, 1927

Now 222 North LaSalle Street Building
Graham, Anderson, Probst and White
Renovation and addition: Skidmore, Owings and Merrill,
1980–86

Fig. 1. View of the Builders Building, now 222 North LaSalle Building; at left is the original portion by Graham, Anderson, Probst and White of 1927, and at right is the addition by Skidmore, Owings and Merrill of 1980–86

Fig. 2. Builders Building, view of four-story-high rotunda renovated c. 1986 by Skidmore, Owings and Merrill

Constructed in eleven months in 1927, the twenty-three-story Builders Building was conceived as a center for disseminating the "ideas and new methods" of the American construction industry, according to *Real Estate News* at the building's opening. The central feature of this skyscraper designed by Graham, Anderson, Probst and White, successor firm to D. H. Burnham and Co., was a great four-story rotunda, similar to one in the Pittsfield Building (see no. 44), designed by the same firm and completed in the same year. However, the Builders' interior court was not to be a center for retail shops, as in the Pittsfield, but of showrooms for the display of materials and equipment vital to the construction industry. It had supplied the initial money to raise this building at the corner of LaSalle Street and Wacker Drive, with the expectation that the offices and exhibition spaces would be occupied by merchandisers serving a thriving industry. And for a few brief years, that was the case.

Although the resemblance between the interiors of the two is evident, the Builders bears little external relationship to the towering structure of the Pittsfield. The Builders is a continuation of the classically inspired design basic to the work of Graham, Anderson, Probst and White. Their use of the blocklike form, clearly defined base, straightforward shaft, and screen of classical columns at the top recalls the design of the Peoples Gas Company Building (1910, see no. 17) by D. H. Burnham and Co. The contemporary journal *Through the Ages* (March 1932) reported approvingly that the Builders Building was "without any of the setback or extremist features that characterize many of our skyscrapers."

Within four years of the opening of the mart, the onset of the Depression left the construction industry in desperate straits, and it no longer needed a great display center. New tenants moved into the building on LaSalle and Wacker, chiefly the Chicago Board of Education. The rotunda was divided to create a meeting room for the school board, and the building became a bureaucratic headquarters.

In 1980, developers began to look at Wacker Drive and the river front with new eyes. The owners of the Builders Building bought the adjacent narrow lot and commissioned the architectural firm of Skidmore, Owings and Merrill to renovate the existing plant and propose a plan for an addition. The result (fig. 1), designed by partner in charge Adrian Smith, was an addition to the west that respected the older building and provided a glass-and-steel penthouse that linked the two buildings and added 120,000 square feet of new space. Finally, the rotunda of the Builders was fully restored (fig. 2). Inexplicably, the address was changed at the same time, from 228 to 222 North LaSalle Street.

For the new addition, the architects chose different exterior materials, primarily granite instead of the glazed brick and terra-cotta of the original building. Instead of recessing the windows, the designers incorporated oriel bays, an old Chicago School tradition, which enlivens the river façade.

Behind the dropped ceilings of the floored-over rotunda, the architects found intact the rounded arches and most of the original plaster ornament. Restored to view, these elements further enriched a splendid interior space. Since the light well over the original four-story rotunda has been enclosed (and turned into six atriums), the rotunda's glass ceiling is now illuminated from above by artificial light. For the owners, the result of this renovation and addition is a modern building enlarged sufficiently to be profitable. For Chicago, according to Cheryl Kent, in the *Inland Architect* (January 1988), "The renovation of 222 signifies a commitment to the fabric of the city, its scale, character, and history." —J.H.C.

44. Pittsfield Building, 1927

55 East Washington Street
Graham, Anderson, Probst and White

Michigan Boulevard Building, 1913–14, 1923

Now Michigan Avenue National Bank
30 North Michigan Avenue
Jarvis Hunt

Willoughby Tower, 1929

8 South Michigan Avenue
Samuel N. Crowen

Although Gothic ornament is relatively uncommon in the work dating from the 1920s of architects Graham, Anderson, Probst and White, it appears in profusion on their 1927 Pittsfield Building (fig. 1). This New York-style skyscraper, which derives from that city's famous Woolworth Building (1913), has a seventeen-story tower that rises from a twenty-one-story block; at the twenty-second, thirty-fifth, and thirty-eighth floors of this limestone building, turreted cornices mark the setbacks. At the pinnacle the tower is square, with arched windows and turrets, topped by a peaked roof of green oxidized copper. A striking addition to the skyline in 1927, the Pittsfield claimed the title of the city's tallest skyscraper at the time; it remains highly visible today.

The Pittsfield Building was commissioned by the trustees of the Marshall Field Estate and named for the town in Massachusetts where the young entrepreneur got his first job (another Field building commemorated his home town of Conway, Massachusetts; see the Conway Building, no. 27). The trust maintained ownership of the Pittsfield Building until 1944. Since then it has changed hands several times but has been carefully maintained. Remarkably, neither the exterior nor the interior has been altered.

The first-floor façade is clad in polished black granite, one of the earliest uses on a Chicago skyscraper of this material usually associated with the Art Moderne style. Gothic screens set at intervals in the cornice at the fifth-floor level define the building's base. A similar but more delicate screen repeated in bronze appears above the exterior and interior shop windows. A secondary entrance to the building faces Wabash Avenue, but the main entrance is on the long façade fronting on the more fashionable Washington Street and is centered on the base of the tower. Single-story-high passages, sumptuously decorated with coffered ceilings and bronze fittings, lead from both entrances into the dramatic five-story rotunda. Ornamental detail here includes grillework, decorative iron frames around the Chicago windows overlooking the court at the east and west ends, and a reversing tulip motif which appears both as brackets and in relief panels. According to *Through the Ages* (December 1930), a marble-trades magazine, the walls and floors in the public areas are predominantly of marble.

The Pittsfield was a mixed-use complex when it opened in 1927. Aimed at a specific clientele, members of the medical and dental professions, it continued to be occupied by doctors and dentists decades later. Retail shops filled the first five floors surrounding the rotunda. Open balconies on the north and south sides gave visibility to window displays and invited strollers to shop. In contemporary terminology the rotunda would be called a vertical mall, although it undoubtedly was inspired by the great atriums in the Marshall Field and Company Store (1902, see no. 9), a block away on State Street

Fig. 1. *Graham, Anderson, Probst and White. Pittsfield Building, 55 East Washington Street, 1927, as published in* The American Architect, *December 5, 1928*

Fig. 2. *Jarvis Hunt. Michigan Boulevard Building (foreground), now Michigan Avenue National Bank, 30 North Michigan Avenue, 1913–14/1923. Rising above it is the Pittsfield Building tower*

Fig. 3. View of Michigan
Boulevard Building prior to
addition of five stories in 1923

Fig. 4. Samuel N. Crowen.
Willoughby Tower, 8 South
Michigan Avenue, 1929

and built by the architects' predecessor firm of D. H. Burnham and Co. Although at present shops remain only on the lobby and first-balcony levels, the rotunda is structurally and decoratively intact. In the late 1980s, Wabash Avenue, despite the presence of the Elevated train rattling above it, was slowly metamorphosing into a lively street of shops, which the owners of the Pittsfield intended to capitalize on by returning the rotunda to its original purpose as a retail center.

In part, Graham, Anderson, Probst and White may have been inspired to design the Pittsfield along Gothic lines by Jarvis Hunt's Michigan Boulevard Building next door, at 30 North Michigan Avenue (fig. 2). And Hunt (1859–1951) in turn may have found inspiration in two nearby clubs, the Chicago Athletic Association (1891–93), a fanciful Venetian palazzo at 12 South Michigan, by Henry Ives Cobb (1859–1931), and Holabird and Roche's Gothic-style University Club (1909, see no. 21), at the corner of Michigan Avenue and Monroe Street—although New York's Woolworth Building doubtless played a part as well. Hunt's building, its main entrance originally located on Washington Street, is a typical office block of the early years of the century. When completed in 1914 it was fifteen stories high; five more floors were added in 1923, although not to the original design. As constructed, the building was U-shaped above the second story, providing a light well on the Washington Street side (fig. 3). The exterior is clad in glazed terra-cotta, and its ornament includes grotesques in the first-floor cornice and trefoil bands in the spandrels all the way to the top. Regrettably, the façade at street level has been stripped of ornament and faced with polished granite. Both the original entrance on Washington Street and the large interior lobby have disappeared, although a small vaulted passage and arched entrance remain at the south end of the Michigan Avenue façade.

One block south in this Gothic enclave is the gracefully proportioned Willoughby Tower (1929, fig. 4), by Samuel N. Crowen (1872–1935), an architect about whom little is known. Like the Pittsfield, the Willoughby was built from a base-plus-tower design and equals the former in height. Gargoyles, escutcheons, and leafy medallions enliven the Willoughby's limestone façade. A turreted cornice marks the tower setback. Additional setbacks are ornamented, and the final one provides for a small, octagonal, castellated tower that resembles a medieval keep. Carvings and a Gothic arch frame the Willoughby entrance, located at the south end of the Michigan Avenue façade. The small, richly appointed foyer and elevator lobby give the impression that one is entering a medieval bishop's palace rather than an office building. The Willoughby replaced an eight-story building of the same name and together with its neighbor, the Pittsfield, was the last of the Gothic skyscrapers rising on the lakefront following the completion of the Michigan Avenue Bridge. —J.H.C.

45. Palmolive Building, 1927–29

Later the Playboy Building
Now known by its address
919 North Michigan Avenue
Holabird and Root
Remodeling: Ronald L. Dirsmith, 1967
Renovation: Skidmore, Owings and Merrill, 1982

Fig. 1. Holabird and Root. Palmolive Building, now 919 North Michigan Avenue Building, 1927–29, in a night view, c. 1930

When the Palmolive Building (fig. 1) was constructed on North Michigan Avenue in the late 1920s, it was the tallest structure in the area, towering above its nearest neighbors, the Fourth Presbyterian Church (1912) and the Drake Hotel (1919, see no. 28). At the time, only a few widely spaced buildings lined the newly developed Michigan Boulevard. The Palmolive-Peet Company chose the location, so distant from the Loop business center, for the area's quiet atmosphere and the site's stunning views of Lake Michigan. Soon the office building developed a prestigious reputation and attracted a host of distinguished tenants, many in advertising and publishing.

The thirty-seven-story Palmolive Building is a limestone tower with six symmetrical setbacks and indentations that telescope upward to a flat roof. Described as "prismatic volumes" by historian Carl W. Condit, in *Chicago, 1910–29* (1973), the receding setbacks create an elongated effect that is heightened by continuous channels of windows and vertical piers, which minimize the effect of the horizontal breaks created by the setbacks. In the daytime, the elegant appearance of the building is attributed to the graceful way in which the setbacks fold into one another (fig. 2). At night, when the building is illuminated, however, the effect is reversed as the bright-colored floodlights dramatically contrast one vertical cliff against another.

The building was actually constructed in the winter of 1928–29, one of the most brutal in Chicago's history. The hardships encountered by the workmen were considerable, as detailed in the *Architectural Forum* (May 1930):

Located on the edge of Lake Michigan, the Palmolive Building presented a perfect target of the zero winds that came tearing down over the 360-mile open stretch of water to the north. Under these conditions working upon the scaffolds was impossible, and men working upon open floors were often lashed to beams to prevent them from being blown overboard. It was impossible to hoist steel or stone, and then on calm days men had to employ blow torches to melt away the snow and ice.

Despite these difficulties, the building was constructed on schedule and with few accidents.

At the time of completion, the building was topped by a 150-foot mast carrying a powerful beacon for aerial navigation. According to Robert Bruegmann in *Holabird and Roche and Holabird and Root: A Catalogue of Works, 1880–1940*, the lamp was originally named for Charles Lindbergh, who in 1927 was the first man to fly a solo mission across the Atlantic Ocean. Because Lindbergh never accepted the honor publicly, the powerful light was renamed the Palmolive Beacon in 1931. After serving as a navigation tool for over thirty years, the beacon was partially shielded in 1968 because it disturbed tenants in nearby high rises, particularly the 100-story John Hancock Center (1965–70, see no. 75), where

Fig. 2. View of Palmolive
Building. In the foreground is the
Fourth Presbyterian Church,
1912, by Ralph Adams Cram

Fig. 3. View of renovated façade
of the Palmolive Building, c. 1982

apartment-dwellers caught the beams dead in the eye. The beacon was extinguished in 1981, long after it had become obsolete as a navigation tool and had, instead, become a constant source of irritation to area residents. In 1990 the beacon was replaced with a stationary light that glows rather than flashes.

The storefronts and entryways of the building's two-story base were originally framed with elaborate decorative lintels and canopies in cast iron and nickel bronze. The richly appointed offices had terrazzo floors and wainscotting of walnut-trimmed marble. Unfortunately, many of the building's original features were removed after it was leased by the Playboy Company in 1965, and interiors from the first through the fifteenth floors were stripped.

The Palmolive was part of a design tradition that evolved after passage of the 1923 Chicago zoning law, which paved the way for setback skyscrapers, but it was also influenced by the training received by both Holabird and Root at the Ecole des Beaux-Arts in Paris, which stressed symmetrical axial plans and the marriage of simplified classical forms with the structural volumes underlying them. As a result, the architects produced an impressive and cohesive body of work in the late 1920s and early 1930s that included such elegant limestone setback towers as 333 North Michigan Avenue (1927–28, see no. 41) and the Chicago Board of Trade (1929–30, see no. 53). The Palmolive is undoubtedly one of their most

sophisticated designs; according to historian Robert Bruegmann, in *Chicago History* (Fall 1980), the building "can perhaps be considered the firm's most exemplary work of the late 1920s. Here, because there was an ample site and no tall neighbors to block the view, the architects created a nearly perfect expression of the high set-back skyscraper."

In 1979 the building was sold to a group of Chicago businessmen headed by Jerrold Wexler and Edward Ross. One year later, the architectural firm Skidmore, Owings and Merrill was hired to renovate the building. As the architects in charge of the renovation, Adrian Smith and William Drake, stated it, their design goal was "to complement the original architectural vocabulary within a budget that would not permit full restoration." They succeeded in creating a semblance of the building's original spirit. Their renovation concentrated primarily on the first two floors and lobby of the building. Rather than recreate the original storefronts, they designed rectangular bays on the Michigan Avenue and Walton Street façades. The storefronts are framed by ribbed lintels and fluted columns whose limestone color harmonizes with the façade (fig. 3). The lobby was renovated with back-painted glass, patterned terrazzo, and Tennessee pink marble. Elements that could be preserved, such as the elevator cabs and carved wooden elevator doors, were retained, thereby maintaining and restoring the original elegance of this important setback tower of the 1920s. —P.A.S.

46. Engineering Building, 1928

205 West Wacker Drive
D. H. Burnham and Co. (The Burnham Brothers)
Renovation: Himmel Bonner Architects, 1982

Fig. 1. D. H. Burnham and Co. (The Burnham Brothers). Engineering Building, 205 West Wacker Drive, 1928. View from northeast, across Wells Street Bridge, 1989

Fig. 2. Interior view of Engineering Building lobby, renovated by Himmel Bonner Architects, 1982

The Engineering Building is in a sense a legacy of the great Daniel H. Burnham, for it was designed by the sons of the renowned architect, the name of whose practice they had adopted in 1917. After their father's death in 1912, his business had continued briefly under the name D. H. Burnham and Co. and then, as Ernest R. Graham, in practice with Burnham since 1888, moved to the forefront, as Graham, Burnham and Company. When Graham left the firm in 1917 to form Graham, Anderson, Probst and White, subsequently designing such renowned Chicago skyscrapers as the Wrigley Building and Civic Opera Building (see nos. 29 and 50), the sons Hubert Burnham (1882–1968) and Daniel H. Burnham, Jr. (1886–1961), in an effort to attract commercial clients with large-scale commissions, reinstated the name of their father's highly successful firm. The most famous commission of the second D. H. Burnham and Co. was the green and gold Carbide and Carbon Building (1928–29, see no. 47) on North Michigan Avenue.

The Engineering Building (fig. 1) fronts on Wacker Drive, also a legacy of the elder Burnham and his renowned 1909 Plan of Chicago. The twenty-three-story building, simple in its detailing, features uniform window openings, except at the corners where the offices have larger windows. Stylized ornament is found at the third level and is continued at the top, from the twentieth to the twenty-third floors. The ornament projects above the roofline on the major piers, thereby enlivening the building's skyline silhouette, as is typical of Art Deco skyscrapers. The Engineering Building is located directly to the east of a Holabird and Root building also completed in 1928; originally known as the Chicago Evening Post Building, it later was called the Times Building when it housed the *Chicago Sun-Times*, the morning newspaper. The nineteen-story structure complements the Engineering Building in its window treatment and its stripped-down, austerely modern style.

In the early 1980s, the Engineering Building was completely renovated, both inside and out. The entrance to the building was shifted from Wells Street to Wacker Drive, and the lobby was revamped to accommodate the change; a black-and-white checkerboard floor was installed on a diagonal to establish a new traffic pattern leading to the existing elevators (fig. 2), which still have their original, highly ornamented brass doors. Near the banks of elevators, the new ceiling is pulled back to reveal the lobby's original ornate, gilded cove ceiling.

Another approach to the design of the 1920s-style skyscraper was followed in the stark, unornamented simplicity of the twenty-four-story Victor M. Lawson YMCA, at 30 West Chicago Avenue, completed in 1931. It was designed with several dramatic setbacks that are more typical of Art Deco skyscrapers in New York and elsewhere. The building was named for its donor, noted philanthropist Victor F.

Lawson (1850–1929), who founded the independent *Chicago Daily News* in 1876, when he was just twenty-six years old.

Two years after the YMCA was completed, its designers, Melville C. Chatten (1873–1957) and C. Herrick Hammond (1882–1969), merged with the Burnham Brothers, forming Burnham and Hammond. They produced small-scale buildings during the Depression and Second World War years; and after the war they specialized in factories, hospitals, and university buildings. The firm continued under that name until the early 1980s, when it went out of business. —P.A.S.

Fig. 1. D. H. Burnham and Co.
(The Burnham Brothers). Carbide
and Carbon Building, 230 North
Michigan Avenue, 1928–29

Fig. 2. View of Carbide and
Carbon Building tower, 1989

47. Carbide and Carbon Building, 1928–29

230 North Michigan Avenue
D. H. Burnham and Co. (The Burnham Brothers)

Until the Burnham Brothers joined C. Herrick Hammond in the partnership of Burnham and Hammond in 1933, the firm built a number of Chicago high rises, including the Bankers Building (1926), the City-State Building (1927), and the Engineering Building (1928, see no. 46), all classical, limestone and terra-cotta structures, historicist in their detailing. The Carbide and Carbon Building (figs. 1, 2) represents a departure from those designs in many respects.

At forty stories high, the most prominent of their buildings, the Carbide and Carbon is distinguished by a dramatic black, green, and gold color scheme, perhaps inspired by the black brick and gold terra-cotta of Raymond Hood's American Radiator Building (1924) in New York. The base of the Carbide and Carbon Building consists of black granite with black-marble and bronze trim. The shaft is clad in dark-green and gold terra-cotta, while the mottled-green top is trimmed in gold leaf. The richly decorative appearance of the green façade, heightened by its contrasting gold details, is no doubt related to its initial function as regional headquarters for the Union Carbide and Carbon Company.

When the New York-based company, inventor of the dry-cell battery and originator of the Eveready brand name, decided to build, it looked for a "distinctive and perpetual advertisement for its occupants," according to a 1932 promotional booklet. It further noted: "The effect of such beauty in a building upon the morale of the people employed in it is unquestionably beneficial and inspiring; and to clients, business associates, and visitors, it is constant assurance that the organization they are dealing with are [sic] of the highest calibre."

According to the *Western Architect* (April 1930), the building's local prominence enabled the Burnham Brothers to secure the commission for the Cuneo Building—another skyscraper of contrasting colors—which was planned in mid–1929 for the northeast corner of Michigan Avenue and Randolph Street and was intended to be 657 feet tall, or sixty stories high! However, the Stock Market Crash of October 1929 and the Great Depression that followed forced the cancellation of that project, as they did so many other high rises being planned. —J.Z.

48. Mather Tower, 1926–28

Now known by its address
75 East Wacker Drive
Herbert Hugh Riddle
Restoration and renovation: Harry Weese and Associates,
1982–83

Fig. 1. Herbert Hugh Riddle. Mather Tower, 75 East Wacker Drive, 1926–28. At left, the London Guarantee and Accident Building (see no. 31)

Fig. 2. View of the renovated lobby of Mather Tower, 1983

This unusually slender Gothic skyscraper, with its rectangular base topped by an octagonal tower (fig. 1) is only half of what Chicago was promised in 1926. In that year Alonzo C. Mather (died 1941), real estate developer and philanthropist and the inventor of the Palace Stock Car for the humane transport of horses and cattle, announced plans to build twin towers on Michigan Avenue and Wacker Drive; the towers were to have been connected by an arcade at the base and at the top by a radio aerial. No drawings of this project exist, but the arcade presumably would have run to the southwest of the asymmetrical London Guarantee and Accident Building, of 1923 (see no. 31), with the second tower rising just south of it on Michigan Avenue. The Mather Tower's unconsummated twin was only one of many projects abandoned after the 1929 Stock Market Crash, and the existing building, designed by Herbert H. Riddle (1875–1939), was apparently the architect's last major commission.

The twin towers would have made interesting brackets for the London Guarantee and Accident Building. However, the single completed tower stands as an urbane cousin of the Wrigley Building (see no. 29) directly across the river; both are glazed in creamy white terra-cotta, feature historicizing ornament, and are topped by decorative pinnacles. In 1928, the Mather Tower stretched above its neighbors on both sides of the river, reaching a height of 553 feet 6 inches at the top of its lantern.

Fronting on Wacker Drive, which departs from Chicago's grid by following the line of the river, the Mather site has an unusual configuration, inspiring an innovative design. Riddle dealt with his small, narrow, 65-by-100-foot site by extending the base building to the property line in the front and placing his first setbacks to the rear, at the ninth- and sixteenth-floor levels. Thus, facing the street and the river is a façade of unbroken verticality for the first twenty-four floors. Here the octagonal tower begins, at this point only forty-one feet ten inches in diameter. The tower narrows by means of other setbacks as it approaches the forty-second-floor lantern, which is just nine feet six inches in diameter. The result of this composition is maximum rental space, an abundance of windows with a river view, and a well-proportioned and distinctive skyscraper.

Between 1923 and 1928 Riddle had designed buildings for the Chicago Theological Seminary in Hyde Park as well as for a number of other churches and institutions, but apparently the Mather Tower was his first and only skyscraper. No interviews with the architect are known to exist, and so questions about the sources of the tower's distinctive design remain unanswered.

The unusual form presented complex framing problems, which were described in detail in an issue of *Engineering News-Record* (November 24, 1927): "Owing to the height and

comparatively small horizontal area of the building, a definite uplift may be developed by certain wind conditions. For this reason, there is introduced the unusual feature of anchoring the four corner columns deeply into the piers." Wind bracing was particularly important in the slender octagonal tower and was "applied at connections to both the interior and exterior columns." According to the article, the workmen "placing the terra-cotta curtain walls and other work commented upon the steadiness of the tower even during high winds."

The interior of the entrance level reflects the building's shape. From Wacker Drive a narrow entrance hall flanked by generous shop spaces opens into a rectangular lobby, which has a handsome marble staircase at the south end (fig. 2). The stairway originally continued to the sixth floor, perhaps as a link with the unexecuted arcade. The lobby ornament of marble, bronze, and terra-cotta is classical in style, contrasting with the Gothic arches and quatrefoils decorating the exterior. All are in pristine condition, following the 1982–83 renovation by Harry Weese and Associates. This renovation gives the owners a thoroughly up-to-date office building with splendid river views and provides the city with a graceful tower that once more gleams brightly in the sunlight and glows radiantly from its lantern at night. —J.H.C.

49. Medinah Athletic Club, 1927–29

Now Hotel Inter-Continental, Chicago
505 North Michigan Avenue
Walter W. Ahlschlager
Restoration and renovation: Harry Weese and Associates,
1988–89

Fig. 1. Walter W. Ahlschlager.
Medinah Athletic Club, now
Hotel Inter-Continental, Chicago,
505 North Michigan Avenue,
1927–29, as published in The
American Architect, *1929*

Fig. 2. Detail of Medinah Athletic
Club exterior

Perhaps no skyscraper in Chicago more completely exemplified the exuberant optimism of the 1920s real-estate boom than the Medinah Athletic Club, completed in 1929 (fig. 1). It reached for height at forty-five stories; it stressed the vertical in its soaring shaft and setback tower; it celebrated the skyscraper with an extravagantly ornamental pinnacle; and it provided lavish interior spaces and facilities for an anticipated membership of 3,500 men.

From its Saracenic portal on Michigan Avenue to its minaret and dome 513 feet above the street (figs. 2, 3), the building speaks of the exotic Orient. The club was commissioned by a group of Medinah Nobles; affiliates of the Shriners, a nationwide fraternal and philanthropic organization said to have ancient roots in the Middle East and whose members sometimes refer to themselves as "Sons of the Desert," the Medinah Nobles had been successful in building Arabic-motif structures in other parts of the country. In 1925 one group had established the Medinah Country Club (Richard G. Schmid), which still flourishes on 400 acres in Du Page County, Illinois. Another founded the in-town Medinah Athletic Club, on Michigan Avenue. The organizers of the two clubs were purely social affiliates of the Shriners, and were not linked officially or financially with the Medinah Temple (Huehl and Schmid, 1912) at the corner of Wabash Avenue and East Ohio Street.

Walter W. Ahlschlager (1887–1965), architect of a number

of hotels and movie theaters, including the Belmont and Grove (both 1926), in Chicago, was commissioned to design the club on Michigan Avenue. The organizers' purpose was to provide extensive athletic facilities, luxurious dining and entertainment spaces, and 440 hotel rooms and suites. The planners' desire, according to a descriptive brochure, was a "strictly twentieth century structure...which in general atmosphere and tone was to be that of 1300 A.D." Ahlschlager was ideally suited to this task, since the interiors of his two New York movie palaces of the same years, the Roxy (1927, demolished 1961) and the Beacon (1928, altered but still extant), were opulent fantasies out of the Arabian Nights.

Among the twentieth-century amenities offered by the Medinah were the largest swimming pool in any Chicago club, a rifle range, an eighteen-hole miniature golf course on the twenty-third floor, automatic floor stops on the elevators, and, like every other men's club in Chicago at the time, special areas reserved for women. It was the décor of the lower floors that recalled A.D. 1300: the lobby had a grand double staircase sweeping up to a five-story entrance hall of Assyrian inspiration (the Stair Hall of the Lions, fig. 4). There was also a Spanish tea court and numerous other large public spaces, elaborately finished in styles that ranged from Byzantine to Celtic. To decorate and furnish the interior, according to the promotional brochure, "the far corners of the earth were searched for those things most precious."

Fig. 3. View of Medinah Athletic
Club Moorish dome and minaret,
with a zeppelin in the background, c. 1930

The ancient Middle East was the source of the exterior ornament, including a Moorish dome and minaret at the top (fig. 3), monumental carved figures (seers, perhaps, or prophets) on both the south and west façades, and a frieze recalling Assyrian and Egyptian art above the ninth-floor windows. This relief was designed by George Unger (dates unknown) and carved by Leon Hermant (1866–1936). Its theme is the celebration of the building processes, which refers to the historic beginnings of the Freemasons (of which the Shriners are a part) in the stonemasons' guilds of England and Scotland. Paradoxically, this tower, which publicly celebrated building in the past, was also innovative in its time. The great limestone shaft with its terraced setbacks is "almost neutral in its simplicity," wrote Carl W. Condit in *Chicago, 1910–29* (1973); furthermore, he said, "the modern style came to the Chicago hotel with the construction of the Medinah Athletic Club."

The club opened to its charter members on April 15, 1929. Despite the building's many attractions, it could not survive the Great Depression and went bankrupt in 1934. It reopened first as the Chicago Towers and then as the Continental Hotel, the last new hotel in Chicago for thirty-five years, according to Condit. In 1958 the Sheraton Corporation took over its operation and in 1961 built an undistinguished addition to the north. The Medinah was purchased in 1978 by MAT Associates, which closed it for restoration in 1986. The skyscraper, which is included on the National Register of Historic Places, reopened in early 1990 as the Hotel Inter-Continental, Chicago. A few months earlier, in 1989, an addition at 525 North Michigan opened as the Forum Hotel Chicago.

Harry Weese and Associates, architects for the conversion, could not replace the spire that once graced the Medinah's minaret, but the owner's program specified careful cleaning of the exterior sculptures and the restoration of the reception halls, grand ballroom, Spanish tea court, swimming pool, and most of the other splendid public spaces. As in the Stevens Hotel (now the Chicago Hilton and Towers, see no. 39) to the south on Michigan Avenue, the rooms have been completely rebuilt. The Weese renovation was sensitive to the 1920s ambience of the surrounding historic district, which includes the Wrigley Building and Tribune Tower (see nos. 29 and 32), as well as to a new urban complex, the Cityfront Center, to the east (see NBC Tower, no. 102). As in its days as the Medinah Athletic Club, the restored skyscraper's symbol is the regilded, pear-shaped dome. After dark, lighting accents the tower's upper terraces, and the dome is illuminated from below, similar to the treatment of the Chrysler and Empire State buildings in New York. A glittering pinnacle from the Jazz Age was restored to Chicago's skyline. —J.H.C.

P-2455
CHICAGO ARCHITE

50. Civic Opera Building, 1927–29

20 North Wacker Drive
Graham, Anderson, Probst and White

Fig. 1. Graham, Anderson, Probst and White. Civic Opera Building, 20 North Wacker Drive, 1927–29

The Civic Opera House (fig. 1), which opened in Chicago on November 4, 1929, with a performance of *Aida*, thrilled its first-night audience, according to newspaper reports, with its colonnaded entrance on Wacker Drive, its opulent foyer, and its lavishly decorated auditorium. The building was found newsworthy in the business world, as well, because its forty-two-story central shaft was a potentially lucrative office building. Chief organizer of the dual-purpose building was Samuel Insull (1859–1938), in 1927 not only the owner of the Midland Utilities Company but also president of the Chicago Civic Opera Company and personal guarantor of the second mortgage for the 20 North Wacker Drive complex. He and the other investors, many of them also opera subscribers, were convinced that the building would pioneer redevelopment of the old warehouse district at the western edge of the Loop. Their enthusiasm was fueled by the construction of the Chicago Daily News Building (see no. 52) across the river, as well as by the proximity of the North Western and Union railway stations. As Anne Lee wrote in *Architectural Forum* (April 1930): "Sanguine, and believing in their idea, its backers look forward to a self-supporting opera by reason of the yield the building will eventually net." Bolstering this optimism was an anticipated street improvement growing out of the 1909 Plan of Chicago: the extension of lower Wacker Drive, which would provide an automobile entrance to the complex as well as adjacent parking.

Designed by Graham, Anderson, Probst and White, the building is typical of the firm's schemes from the 1920s. The main shaft is an unadorned cliff of masonry; but bands of ornament below the hipped roof, at the top of the two transverse wings, and surrounding the windows and doors at street level provide the requisite richness for the home of opera. Alfred P. Shaw (1895–1970), chief designer for the project, said the firm chose what it called the French Renaissance style, "modernized for adaptation to American skyscraper construction," because it would "offer [a] sympathetic background for the old, conservative traditions of opera." The building's western façade, which faces the river, is also carefully finished, and the limestone cladding and setbacks are an appropriate counterpoint to the similar but more severe lines of the Chicago Daily News Building, constructed almost simultaneously on the opposite bank. The splendid composition of the Opera House's river façade was somewhat marred after the Second World War by the installation of corrugated structures housing air-conditioning equipment on top of the transverse wings framing the opera stage, as well as on the setback roof of the stage itself.

The masks of comedy and tragedy and the motifs of lyre, trumpet, palm leaf, and laurel wreath appear in terra-cotta and bronze on the exterior of the building and reappear in the foyer and auditorium. Jules Guérin (1866–1946), noted for

his watercolor renderings for the Plan of Chicago and for his murals in other skyscrapers (see nos. 34, 56), supervised the interior design, choosing as the predominant colors for the auditorium vermilion and orange accented with gold leaf. The most dramatic decoration was his hand-painted fire curtain, lowered in place before every performance.

The coherence of the building's plan is clear from the entrances along the seventeen-bay colonnade facing Wacker Drive. Sculptured pediments mark the doors to the Opera House and the smaller Civic Theatre at the south and north ends. Separate doors serve the opera box office and the entrance to the office tower.

The engineering required to construct a building encompassing an office tower, an auditorium with fine acoustics, and a small separate theater was so formidable that *Architectural Forum* devoted a special section of its April 1930 issue to all aspects of the impressive achievement; according to Carl W. Condit in *Chicago, 1910–29* (1973), the caissons had to be carried to bedrock, and in some cases existing concrete piers from previous buildings, joined by steel plates to the new piers, were utilized to help carry the load. Even the river wall had to be reinforced to prevent damage from errant ships. According to the contemporary trade journal, *Through the Ages* (March 1930), the stage was "one of the marvels of modern science. Nowhere is the mechanical and lighting equipment equaled. A fourteen-story building could be placed between the stage floor and the gridiron floor."

The irony, however, is that the Chicago Opera Company lasted only three years in its new home. The Stock Market Crash had a dire effect on Samuel Insull; his utilities empire collapsed in 1932, forcing him into bankruptcy. The opera company, too, declared bankruptcy shortly thereafter. Yet, though three opera companies also failed in the next twenty years, the stages at 20 North Wacker Drive were seldom dark. In the 1940s, both theaters were regularly used for bond rallies and other wartime events. Then in 1954, the world-renowned Lyric Opera of Chicago was founded, and it has been the resident company in the Civic Opera House since that date.

The opera building remained a highly visible if somewhat solitary pioneer on the western edge of the Loop until the early 1980s, when developers took renewed interest in Wacker Drive. The office building was renovated by new owners in 1983, and the Opera House itself was completely modernized in 1995–96. To make way for an improved stage and other facilities, the jewel-like Civic Theatre was demolished, a loss mourned by theater-goers throughout the city. However, the Civic Opera building has survived real estate ups and downs and cultural wars and will celebrate its seventieth birthday in 1999. —J.H.C.

51. LaSalle-Wacker Building, 1929–30

221 North LaSalle Street
Holabird and Root in association with Rebori, Wentworth,
Dewey and McCormick

Fig. 1. Holabird and Root.
LaSalle-Wacker Building, 221
North LaSalle Street, 1929–30

Fig. 2. Night view of Chicago,
with the LaSalle-Wacker Building
at left, c. 1930

The LaSalle-Wacker Building, located at the top of LaSalle Street, Chicago's financial canyon, was dubbed "The Gateway to Finance" shortly after its completion in 1930. The building was a collaboration between two architectural firms, Holabird and Root and Rebori, Wentworth, Dewey and McCormick, which had first worked together on the tower for the Lumber Exchange Building (see no. 24), also located on LaSalle Street. For Andrew Rebori (1886–1966), the LaSalle-Wacker Building may well have marked the high point of his career. According to Wim De Wit, in the *Chicago Architectural Journal* (1984): "Rebori's contribution to this building embodied his conception of the architectural profession as he had worked to define it since his arrival in Chicago in 1911.... Speaking of the LaSalle-Wacker Building, Rebori declared that the success of any tall building was based on 'the three essentials of suitable location, proper planning, and adequate financing.'"

There is some confusion about the authorship of the building's design. Although its stripped-down classicism and elegant setbacks mark it as typical of Holabird and Root's structures of the late 1920s, similar to the Palmolive Building or the Chicago Board of Trade (see nos. 45 and 53), early drawings in the Rebori Archive at the Chicago Historical Society suggest that he may well have been the originator of the design, perhaps starting the project in 1928 and later calling upon Holabird and Root to assist as the proposed building grew in plan and height. What further suggests that Rebori and not Holabird received the original commission is

that the clients were Joseph Medill Patterson and Colonel Robert McCormick, the latter the cousin of Rebori's wealthy partner, Leander J. McCormick, Jr.

The LaSalle-Wacker Building, as built, was a forty-one-story, limestone-and-granite structure with a beacon on top that could be seen by aviators for 200 miles (figs. 1, 2). The structure's first three stories form a solid base. Above them the building rises to the twenty-fourth floor in an H-shaped plan with light courts on the north and south façades. In the center of the building, at the cross in the H-plan, is a tower that rises uninterrupted from the third to the forty-first floor. The vertical thrust of the building is heightened by the piers that run straight up through the center of each section of tower. Likewise, the symmetrical setbacks on the central tower both emphasize its height and give it slender and elegant proportions. Originally the building was dramatically lit at night to emphasize its soaring towers and deep setbacks. It was constructed on LaSalle Street to house banking offices, brokerage firms, and other financial concerns. There is a famous anecdote in Chicago lore asserting that it was on the windy rooftop of the LaSalle-Wacker Building that Andrew Rebori held an audition for fan dancer Sally Rand, who would take part in the Streets of Paris exhibition at the 1933 Century of Progress Exposition, which Rebori designed with John Root, Jr. It is well recognized today that much of the success of the 1933 Exposition can be attributed to the legendary Sally Rand. —P.A.S.

52. Chicago Daily News Building, 1929

Now Riverside Plaza Building
400 West Madison Street
Holabird and Root

Fig. 2. View of Daily News Building Grand Concourse leading to the Chicago and North Western Railway Station, with murals by John Warner Norton

The Daily News Building (fig. 1) was completed in 1929 at a time when the fifty-three-year-old newspaper was at its peak of influence and success, attracting a host of distinguished creative talent, including cartoonist Vaughan Shoemaker, humorist Robert J. Casey, and writer Carl Sandburg. The building designed by Holabird and Root to house the newspaper was equally distinguished. A critic for the *Western Architect* (August 1929) wrote: "In many ways the new home of the *Chicago Daily News* is a pioneer both in modern American architecture and in the utilization of land heretofore believed impractical for the erection of skyscrapers." The sleek, Art Deco building was the first in Chicago to be constructed using air rights over railroad tracks; in doing so, the *Daily News* broke the barrier to westward expansion beyond the Loop, crossing the Chicago River and building over the unsightly railroad tracks running next to it. To do so, however, required a major technical feat, which was ably achieved by Holabird and Root's engineering associate, Frank E. Brown: the thick smoke from the coal-fired steam engines of the trains running underneath the building had to be vented out the top.

The twenty-six-story Daily News Building occupies an entire city block, and its east and west façades are long, limestone cliffs pierced by floor after floor of uniform window openings, intended to make each office "a roomful of light." The mass of the building, however, is relieved by prominent setbacks at the base and roofline and by vertical piers that give an upward thrust to the long, horizontal structure. One of its most prominent features is the elegant outdoor plaza, which runs parallel to the river, providing access to Union Station and the Chicago and North Western Railway for commuters on their way from the Loop. The Daily News Building was one of the first privately built downtown structures to provide such an amenity for pedestrians.

Another important feature of the building is a two-story-high concourse (fig. 2), which enables Chicago and North Western Railway commuters to pass from the station to the Madison Street Bridge without entering traffic. The cathedral-like concourse features a heroic-scale, three-part ceiling mural by Chicagoan John Warner Norton (1876–1934), who employed semiabstract geometric forms to represent the way in which the newspaper gathers, prints, and distributes the news. Architects Holabird and Root often commissioned Norton and other artists to create paintings and sculptures that would be integrated into their skyscraper designs. Outside the concourse, on the limestone façade of the riverside plaza, the history of printing and the newspaper industry is told through a relief sculpture by Illinois artist Alvin Meyer (born 1892). The focal point of the plaza is a granite-and-stone fountain, set into the east wall, which is a memorial to Victor F. Lawson (1850–1925), founder of the

Daily News (see also no. 46). The west façade of the building was originally planned to face a double-decker superhighway above Canal Street, to have been called Avondale Avenue, but the street was never realized.

Although the building was commissioned by the *Daily News*, the newspaper occupied less than a third of the space. The first six floors housed the newspaper plant: the press room, offices, and newsroom; the seventh through the twenty-third floors were rented to outside tenants; the twenty-fourth floor contained recreation facilities for the *Daily News* staff; and the top two floors were rented to WMAQ radio station. On the rental floors, the Chicago and North Western Railway was the major tenant, leasing a third of the office space.

The building was dedicated on July 8, 1929, when President Hoover pushed a button in Washington, D.C., starting the presses rolling. The American Institute of Architects awarded the building its distinguished Gold Medal in 1930, and the same year the Holabird and Root firm won a Gold Medal from the Architectural League of New York for "the high architectural quality which they have achieved in the solution of the American office building." The *Daily News* occupied the building until 1960, when Field Enterprises purchased the newspaper and moved its entire production operation to the Sun-Times Building at 401 North Wabash Avenue. At that time, the Daily News Building was renamed the Riverside Plaza Building, as it is known today. —P.A.S.

53. Chicago Board of Trade Building, 1929–30

141 West Jackson Boulevard
Holabird and Root
Addition: Murphy/Jahn Architects, with Shaw and Associates
and Swanke, Hayden, Connell Architects, 1980
Second addition: Fujikawa Johnson, Architects, 1997

Fig. 1. Holabird and Root.
Chicago Board of Trade Building,
141 West Jackson Boulevard,
1929–30. View from the north

Fig. 2. Detail of Art Deco lobby
in Chicago Board of Trade
Building

The Chicago Board of Trade was founded in 1895 at a time when the young city was the center of the broad Midwestern grain belt, the hub of the nation's railroad network, and the country's most important inland port. Established by a group of Chicago businessmen, the Board of Trade was set up as a commercial grain exchange, and according to its charter it was intended "to inculcate principles of justice and equity to trade." The first Board of Trade building constructed on the 141 West Jackson Boulevard site was designed in 1885 by W. W. Boyington. It was demolished in 1929 to make way for the present limestone structure, designed by Holabird and Root, which was joined by a steel-and-glass addition in 1980.

The Board of Trade Building (fig. 1) is a striking, forty-five-story limestone tower prominently located at the foot of LaSalle Street, Chicago's primary financial artery. In response to changes in Chicago's zoning law of 1923, the architects designed a setback skyscraper characteristic of commercial structures of the period. Behind and set back from the building's nine-story base is a thirty-six-story tower flanked by symmetrical thirty-story wings. The setbacks carve out cavities in the mass of the building and give it the jagged, sawtooth façade and skyline profile associated with Art Deco skyscrapers. From the Board of Trade's completion in 1930 until the Prudential Building was finished in 1955, the Holabird and Root structure was the tallest in the city. The LaSalle Street façade features a large clock flanked by relief sculptures representing the institution's agrarian focus—a hooded figure holding a sheaf of wheat and an Indian holding a stalk of corn. The façade sculptures were designed by Illinois artist Alvin Meyer, who also created reliefs for the Daily News Building plaza (see no. 52). The pyramidal roof is topped by an aluminum statue of Ceres, the Roman goddess of agriculture, by prominent American sculptor John Storrs (1885–1956), whose commissions from Chicago architectural firms would include the imposing figure of Science for the Hall of Science at the Century of Progress Exposition in 1933.

The elegant, three-story lobby of the Board of Trade, a veritable celebration of Art Deco architecture, was described by historian Robert Bruegmann in *Chicago History* (Fall 1980) as "one of Holabird and Root's most dramatic interiors. The crispness of detail and streamlining make the lobby at once coldly efficient and warmly sensuous." The setbacks of the building's exterior are echoed in large, buff-colored marble cascades, which alternate with massive, black-marble piers (fig. 2). The stylized cascade forms outline doorways on the second level of the lobby, and the black piers connect with curved lintels to form an arcade on the same level. Storefronts on the first floor are faced with nickel panels. The same material, a silver-white metal often found in the décor of the period, was used in flat, stylized railings, vertical bands running up the black-marble piers, and relief panels of stylized ears of

corn and stalks of grain. Light dramatically articulates the lobby's sculptural volumes, particularly through the large backlit panel that runs in a continuous band across the ceiling and down the wall of the second-floor arcade. Dramatic accents of light project from wall sconces that repeat the cascade motif. Equally dramatic was the original trading room on the fourth floor. In order to support the weight of the tower above it, the room had six huge trusses to break its 110-foot clear span, which contained five "pits" for the trading of wheat, corn, and other commodities.

The lobby of the Board of Trade, one of Chicago's finest Art Deco interiors, provided inspiration for an equally intriguing recent addition to the historic limestone structure. In 1980, a twenty-four-story, steel-and-glass addition, designed by Helmut Jahn of the firm Murphy/Jahn, was constructed on the Van Buren Street side of the Board of Trade to provide a large trading floor and office space for the Chicago commodities exchange (fig. 3). Although the black-and-silver, steel-and-glass exterior of the addition contrasts sharply with the gray-limestone facing of the original building, the new is visually linked to the old by means of skillfully incorporated Art Deco references, including a setback, central tower, symmetrical projecting wings, pyramidal roof, and lobby design based on abstract cascades and scallops. This fusion of

Fig. 3. View of Chicago Board of Trade Building from the south with the 1980 addition by Murphy/Jahn in the foreground

Fig. 4. View of twelve-story atrium by Murphy/Jahn, in 1980 addition to the Chicago Board of Trade Building. Mounted on scaffolding is a restored mural of Ceres by John Warner Norton

historical and contemporary design prompted Andrea Oppenheimer Dean, critic for the *AIA Journal* (May 1983), to write: "As a radical transformation of its Art Deco forebear, the addition is far more intriguing than if it had been merely an updated copy." Defining the perimeter and shape of the building is the large, fourth-floor trading room, the scale requiring that the building be constructed to the edge of the sidewalk on the east and west sides, where at street level the architects designed arcades.

The lobby of the addition is a compact, contemporary version of the soaring Art Deco entry of the original Board of Trade. It is two stories high with a continuous, mezzanine-level arcade. The major design motif, reminiscent of the cascades in the earlier building, is a scallop, which recurs in varying scale from small wall sconces to the monumental two-story entryway. Also as in the lobby of the 1929 building, a large panel of recessed lights runs the length of the ceiling, and large sconces punctuate the piers. The entire structure, however, is given a contemporary flavor through the blue-green color palette used throughout.

Beginning at the twelfth floor of the addition is a spectacular, twelve-story atrium, which serves as a transfer point to rental office space above, incorporating variations of the blue-green color scheme and scallop shape used in the lobby (fig. 4). The atrium's north side is formed by the old building's exterior south wall, while offices and corridors form the atrium's other three sides. Its roof is a steel-and-glass skylight whose sheer structural beauty is reminiscent of nineteenth-century glass houses, such as the London Crystal Palace of 1851 and the large conservatories and train sheds found in other European cities. The view through the skylight is dominated by the soaring tower of the original Board of Trade Building. The historical and contemporary structures are so skillfully joined that Oppenheimer Dean, in the same issue of the *AIA Journal*, described their coming together as "a soaring tour de force.... The result is an adept visual connection between the mother building and its offspring."

The architect provided two additional focal points in the atrium—a monumental mural of Ceres installed on a freestanding steel armature and a bank of elevators whose exposed cabs look like kinetic sculpture as they move up and down, creating an ever-changing spectacle of reflections. The mural of Ceres, by Chicago artist John Warner Norton (1876–1934), had been removed years before from the original trading room when its ceiling was lowered. It is the architect's keen sensitivity to the historical context and his skillful reinterpretion of historical forms in contemporary materials that mark the Board of Trade addition as a high point in 1980s Postmodernism, just as the inspired use of limestone setbacks and marble cascades mark the original building as a high point in American Modernism of the 1920s. —P.A.S.

Fig. 1. Thielbar and Fugard.
Trustees Systems Service Building,
now 201 Tower, 201 North Wells
Street, 1930. Rendering by F.
Holcomb. The Art Institute of
Chicago

Fig. 2. View of Trustees Systems
Service Building, 1989

54. Trustees Systems Service Building, 1930

Later the Corn Exchange Building
Now 201 Tower
201 North Wells Street
Thielbar and Fugard

The firm of Frederick J. Thielbar (1866–1941) and John Reed Fugard (1886–1968), as well as its predecessor, Fugard and Knapp, had considerable experience in constructing Chicago high-rise buildings. Although the firm itself specialized in apartment houses, the partners acted as the associate architects on other commercial jobs, such as the Allerton House (1924, see no. 37) and Jewelers Building (1926, see no. 33). They also designed a commercial building in 1928—the Art Deco McGraw-Hill Building at 520 North Michigan Avenue. Their modernist work continued on a larger scale two years later in the Trustees Systems Service Building (figs. 1, 2), a twenty-story structure topped with an eight-story tower that features a setback, ziggurat top. The building housed an industrial bank until its conversion to the Corn Exchange Building in 1949. Soon after it was completed, the marble trade journal *Through the Ages* (April 1931) praised the mixture of red, gray, green, and gold marble in the lobby interior, calling it a "symphony in stone." The building was modernized in the 1980s and its top relit. —J.Z.

55. Foreman State National Bank Building, 1928–30

Later, American National Bank Building
Now 33 North LaSalle Street
Graham, Anderson, Probst and White

The Foreman family's dignified, thirty-eight-story skyscraper, completed in 1930, was the last new bank building to open in the Loop for thirty years. Its completion signaled the end of the steady march to the north of the city's financial institutions during the economic boom of the 1920s. In massing and setbacks, the bank is similar to its more distinguished, taller neighbor, the One North LaSalle Building (see no. 42), also dating from 1930. One can only speculate that the designers at Graham, Anderson, Probst and White conferred with their counterparts at Vitzhum and Burns, architects of One North LaSalle, since the two buildings create a uniform, block-long wall at street level and feature similar setbacks and fluted corners where the setbacks begin, although the latter is taller by eleven stories.

The symmetrical composition of the Foreman bank and its traditional, five-story base of polished granite, marked by oxidized-bronze spandrels and a sculptured relief above the entrance, restate its architects' long-standing commitment to classicism. Stressing the bank's verticality are four rows of ornamental bronze panels running up the center of each of the three towers, which are unified at the top by horizontal banding on the hipped roofs. The bank's rectilinear entrance presented a strong visual contrast to Adler and Sullivan's cavernous, arched entryway to the Chicago Stock Exchange of 1894 (now demolished; see introduction, fig. 13), directly opposite.

The Foreman State National Bank Building was completed soon after the Stock Market Crash of 1929, and the Foreman bank began to flounder shortly thereafter. When it merged with the First National Bank in 1931, the building at 33 North LaSalle Street briefly fell vacant. For the next two years it was occupied by the Straus National Bank and Trust Company, until that institution also met its demise. In the midst of this turmoil, the American National Bank was boldly formed and on December 4, 1933, opened to the public at 33 North LaSalle Street. The exterior has been carefully maintained and today retains its original character, while the lobby, originally faced in white marble, was paneled and the second-floor banking hall altered beyond recognition. The only remnants of past glory are the bronze elevator doors with chased, tree-of-plenty patterning.

Both this skyscraper and the One North LaSalle Building were occupied by the American National Bank until 1998 when the bank, now a wholly owned subsidiary of First Chicago NBD Bank, began a phased move down the street to the renovated 120 South LaSalle Street Building (Graham, Anderson, Probst and White, 1928). The Lurie Company, owner of both 120 South LaSalle and 33 North LaSalle, plans to renovate and upgrade the former bank building.—J.H.C.

Fig. 1. Graham, Anderson, Probst and White. Foreman State National Bank Building, now American National Bank Building, 33 North LaSalle Street, 1928–30

56. Merchandise Mart, 1923–31

Now Merchandise Mart Plaza
North bank of the river between Wells and Orleans streets
Graham, Anderson, Probst and White
Renovation: Graham, Anderson, Probst and White, 1986–91;
Beyer, Blinder Belle (conversion to retail stores of the first two
stories), 1989–91

Fig. 2. Detail of Merchandise Mart façade, 1989

By the early 1920s, Marshall Field and Company had outgrown its great Wholesale Store (1885–87) designed by Henry Hobson Richardson (1838–1886), and the firm's showrooms and sales offices were scattered throughout the Loop. To consolidate these operations, the company first planned to erect a ten- to twelve-story building exclusively for its own use. However, the immediate success of the American Furniture Mart in 1924 (see no. 36) prompted a decision to expand the plan and offer "space to leading concerns in allied lines of distribution," according to the prospectus. As a result, the Field interests built the $38 million Merchandise Mart (fig.1) with a floor area of nearly four million square feet, larger than any building in the United States until the Pentagon was constructed to house the War Offices during the Second World War.

The land acquired by Field was a five-acre site in the River District, on the Chicago River's north bank; it was the location of the Chicago and North Western Railway station of 1881 (demolished 1911) and in the 1920s still its major operations center. Sited over the North Western tracks, the Merchandise Mart was one of Chicago's earliest air-rights developments. When planning began by the architectural firm of Graham, Anderson, Probst and White, the LaSalle Street Bridge was under construction a block away. A new Merchandise Mart stop was to be built on the Elevated line, with a direct connection to the building's second floor. The North Western Railway planned to add a passenger stop at the Mart, extend its tracks to Michigan Avenue, and construct a new station on the grand boulevard. Both architects and investors believed that the River District would become a new business center, as part of an expansion for which no end was in sight.

Placement of the enormous Merchandise Mart Building followed recommendations in the 1909 Plan of Chicago; according to a caption in the building's prospectus, "in cooperation with the plan for a North Bank Drive to harmonize with Wacker Drive on the South Bank, the Merchandise Mart will be set back eighty feet from the River Edge." As built, a central tower rises seven stories above the eighteen-story mass, the whole supported by a steel frame sheathed in limestone with wrought-iron trim at the entrances. The blending of horizontal cornice lines (which appear at the third, fourth, fifteenth, sixteenth, eighteenth, and nineteenth floors) with the strong vertical lines of the shaft create an imposing, unified presence on the riverbank.

The design by architect Alfred P. Shaw (1895–1970) is far less classical in reference than were those for the Graham, Anderson, Probst and White buildings completed in the early 1920s. Ornament is skillfully integrated into the design—today shown to great advantage as the result of an ongoing $100 million renovation begun in 1986. Decorating the cornices are

Fig. 3. Night view of Merchandise Mart, c. 1931

bands of opposing chevrons that frame triangles of green-and-gold bronze set at regular intervals (fig. 2). These triangles, especially at the roofline, sparkle in the sunlight (at night, great horizontal bands of light illuminate the building along the fourth-floor cornice and at the levels of the two setbacks at the top; fig. 3). Completing the scheme are oxidized-copper turrets capping the central tower, the four corner bays, and the two small octagonal towers flanking the rooftop wings.

The wonder of the building was—and is—its interior, described before its opening by its General Superintendent, Frank F. Sengstock, in *Western Architect* (December 1930), as "intersected by spacious corridors, veritable business streets, extending for more than 650 feet on each floor." And, he added, a single floor of the Mart "will contain an area equal to the total floor space available in a ten-story building of the average Chicago skyscraper." The lobby was decorated with murals depicting markets around the world; painted by artist Jules Guérin, known for his renderings in the 1909 Plan of Chicago, these murals were undergoing restoration in the late 1980s.

Sengstock also described the ingenious methods originally employed for bringing in fuel to heat the vast spaces. Using North Western tracks, drop-bottom railway cars loaded with coal entered the building at ground-floor level, emptying the loads through grates into bunkers, which discharged the fuel onto conveyors (handling thirty tons per hour) leading to the stoker. Equally ingenious was the disposition of the ashes, which emptied directly into cars of the now defunct Chicago Tunnel Company, whose tracks ran under the boiler room. These loaded cars were then taken to the lakefront, where the ashes were used as landfill in preparation for the 1933 Century of Progress Exposition.

The Merchandise Mart was not the financial success the Field investors had expected. Although the wholesale division initially planned to occupy the second to the sixth floors on the building's south side, by the mid-1930s Field gave up its wholesale business and sold the Mart to the Boston entrepreneur Joseph P. Kennedy at a great loss. Although the Elevated stop had been built, the North Western passenger lines had not materialized, nor had North Bank Drive. In its place an esplanade was built along the river. Facing the entrance is the Merchandise Mart Hall of Fame, a series of eight busts including such merchant princes as Marshall Field, Montgomery Ward, and Frank W. Woolworth.

In the late 1980s, the River District, by then known as River North, had become a new business district, with the renovation of old buildings and the construction of new going on in all directions. Still owned by the Kennedy family, the Merchandise Mart expanded its furniture and design showrooms, as office tenants such as the National Broadcasting System moved out. The Mart continued to be a showcase for manufacturers from all over the United States and many foreign nations as well.

Furthermore, it was planned that by the summer of 1992, the Merchandise Mart would also be something the original investors had never expected: a retail shopping center. The first two floors were designated for conversion into a mall containing more than eighty-five stores and restaurants, a shopping hub its developers hoped would rival State Street and North Michigan Avenue. The anchor tenant is Carson Pirie Scott and Company, the Marshall Field store's old State Street rival. The plan called for an imposing entrance and lobby on the Mart's north side, and a new street-level entrance into the mall from each nineteen-story corner tower. The Merchandise Mart station on the Elevated line was renovated, and one of the new River North buildings, by Solomon Cordwell Buenz and Associates, was expected to be a seventy-story hotel and apartment tower, immediately to the north of the Mart. However, even in the future, as the prospectus stated prophetically, "the great southern façade of the building will be seen for blocks in a view permanently protected from obstruction by other buildings." —J.H.C.

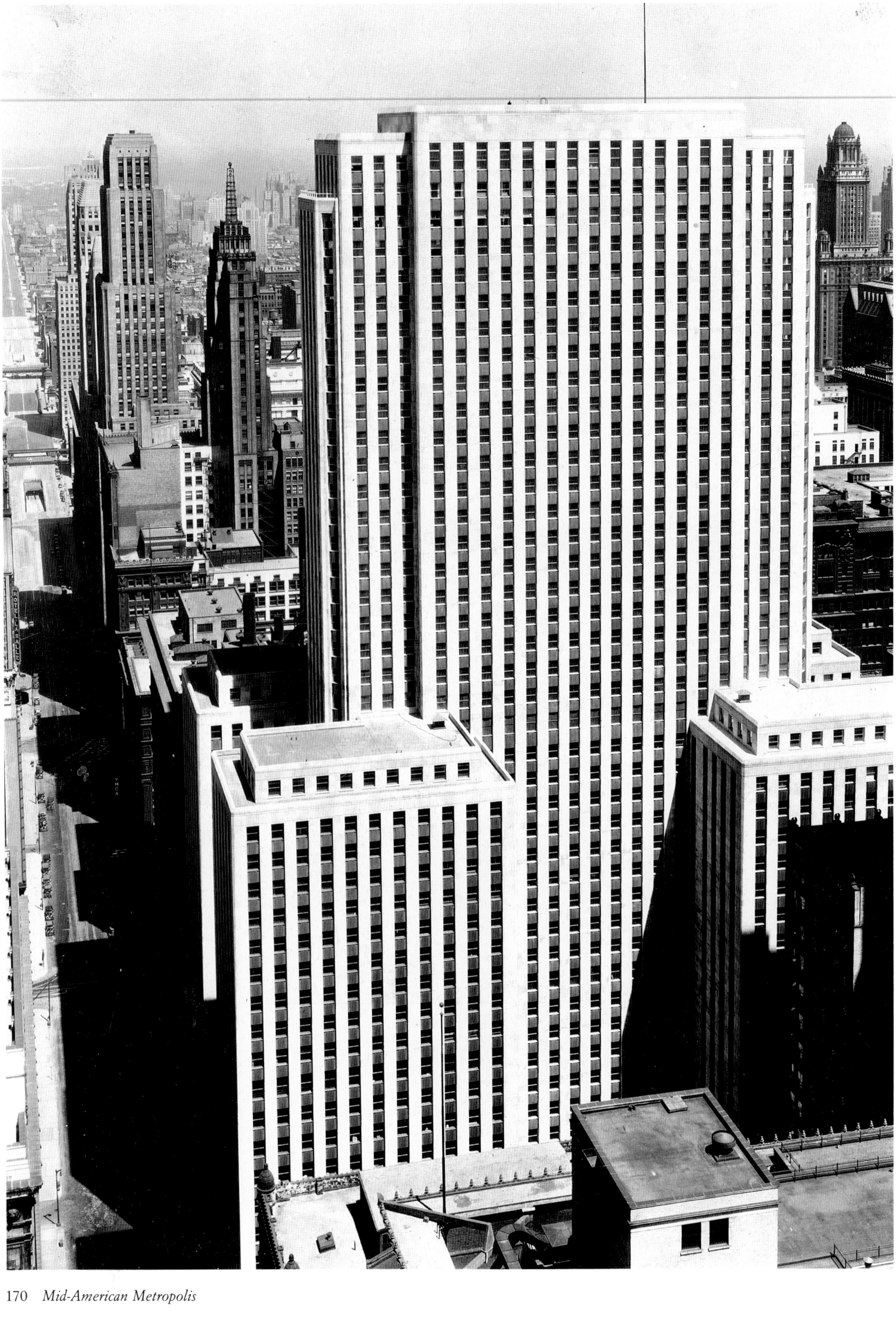

57. Field Building, 1928–34

Now LaSalle National Bank Building
135 South LaSalle Street
Graham, Anderson, Probst and White

Fig. 1. Graham, Anderson, Probst and White. Field Building, now LaSalle National Bank Building, 135 South LaSalle Street, 1928–34

Fig. 2. Clark Street entrance to the Field Building. Rendering by Henry Harringer, c. 1930–'31. The Art Institute of Chicago

The trustees of the Marshall Field Estate chose Graham, Anderson, Probst and White as architects for this skyscraper on LaSalle Street, just as they had selected them for the Pittsfield and Merchandise Mart buildings (see nos. 44 and 56) a few years before. Construction began on the Field Building in 1931, as the Mart was nearing completion. It was the Great Depression, when bricklayers and unskilled laborers were being paid $0.825 per hour, according to a survey in *Architectural Record* (May 1934), and carpenters and ironworkers were earning $1.3125. Despite these low wages, only an enterprise with resources as vast as those of the Field Estate could go forward with a skyscraper in the 1930s. Nor was it an ordinary high rise: it was intended to be the largest in the Loop and "dedicated to the future of LaSalle Street and Chicago," as the prospectus boldly stated, at a time when there was little faith in the future of either the city or the nation.

William Le Baron Jenney's Home Insurance Building (1884; see introduction, fig. 6), an icon in the history of Chicago architecture, was one of six buildings demolished to clear the site. In their place rose a forty-two-story tower flanked by four twenty-three-story wings (fig. 1), a complex that filled almost an entire city block in the "Canyon of Gold," as LaSalle Street was sometimes called. Left behind with the rubble of the Home Insurance was the classicism for which Graham, Anderson, Probst and White was renowned. The Field, like the Merchandise Mart, was designed for the firm by Alfred P. Shaw; he created a building of soaring verticals with sleek Art Deco lines, complementing Holabird and Root's masterful Chicago Board of Trade Building (1930, see no. 53) at the foot of LaSalle.

Simplicity and clarity characterize the Field Building design. Rock caissons support the steel frame, which is faced with Indiana limestone. Polished black granite and white bronze surround the identical entrances on LaSalle and Clark streets (fig. 2). Each doorway is five stories high, while a more modest entrance on Adams Street is only two. The five-story base is a continuous solid form; above it, deep recesses provide light wells outlining the four wings and the vertical tower.

Vertical set-ins above the twenty-third floor define the tower. Ornament is minimal and subtle: chamfered corners gradually open into fluted forms as they reach the horizontal banding at the top of each wing; rooflines of the two setbacks (facing LaSalle and Clark streets) at the thirty-eighth-floor level are angled, but all others are absolutely flat. Only tenants in the upper floors of the tower (or in that of the neighboring Board of Trade) could have observed an amenity described in the early prospectus: "All visible roofs of the Field Building are laid with quarry tile in attractive patterns." Today, undistinguished additions for the mechanical facilities have obscured most if not all of the tile roofs.

Figs 3–5. Three views of Field Building lobby and its appointments: from left, elevator indicator and mailbox, information desk, and Clark Street entrance with a mirrored bridge above

Figs 3–5. Three views of Field Building lobby and its appointments: from left, elevator indicator and mailbox, information desk, and Clark Street entrance with a mirrored bridge above

The Field Building's stripped form and Art Deco entrances signaled the modernity it offered prospective tenants: open floor space, high-speed elevators, recessed heating units, pure drinking water piped throughout the building, alternating electric current, aluminum window frames, both coal- and oil-burning furnaces, and rarest of all, "man-made weather," air conditioning, at least from the basement through the fourth floor. Still functioning behind the original semicircular information desk in the lobby is the famous elevator indicator, a bronze relief in the form of the building (figs. 3, 4). A shopping arcade and restaurants filled—and still fill—the basement. More shops lined the two-story passage connecting LaSalle and Clark streets (fig. 5). Elegantly finished, this east-west corridor was given creamy marble walls, sleek fluted columns, terrazzo floors, and mirrored bridges linking the

north and south balconies. Today, banking facilities have replaced the shops on the Adams Street side, but at the entrances the building's logo, back-to-back Fs, remain in the terrazzo floor.

The first unit completed, at the corner of LaSalle and Adams streets, opened on May 1, 1933. The final unit of the one-million-square-foot office complex opened on April 28, 1934, and with that event the great building boom of the 1920s had come to an end. When skyscraper construction resumed in Chicago's Loop more than twenty years later, new architects and new forms would shape the skyline.—J.H.C.

III. POSTWAR MODERNISM AND POSTMODERNISM

58. 860–880 Lake Shore Drive, 1948–52

Ludwig Mies van der Rohe with Pace Associates and
Holsman, Holsman, Klekamp, and Taylor

Although the German architect Ludwig Mies van der Rohe
(1886–1969) designed projects for high-rise towers in Berlin
and other cities during the 1920s, it was only after his move
to Chicago in 1938 that his high rises were actually
constructed. In contrast to the German projects, which were
plans for commercial buildings, his first executed American
towers were apartment houses. Built after the Second World
War, the apartments owed their genesis to the patronage
and friendship of the Chicago developer Herbert Greenwald.
The initial venture of the two men was the Promontory
Apartments Building in Chicago's Hyde Park (1946–49).
Although the Promontory was originally intended to be a
steel-and-glass building, it was executed in exposed reinforced
concrete and yellow brick to a height of twenty-one stories.
When Mies and Greenwald next worked together, it was to
produce 860–880 Lake Shore Drive (figs. 1, 2), a landmark in
apartment-house design.

The fireproof steel cladding of the underlying steel structure
in these twin towers owes much to Mies's earlier designs for
projects such as the Adam Building in Berlin and the
Landesbank Competition in Stuttgart, both in 1928. But it
was only in Chicago that Mies was able to take full advantage
of vertical expression, in the twenty-six stacked stories of the
Lake Shore Drive apartments. Although budgetary restrictions
led him to forego central air conditioning and the cubicular
traditions of apartment planning forced him to abandon a
more open, revolutionary space plan, he was able to exert
aesthetic control of the project's external appearance,
extending to such fine details as the consistent use of off-
white draperies throughout all the apartments. And even
though his aesthetic preference for steel over concrete made
the construction price of these buildings rise from $8.55 per
square foot for the Promontory to $10.38 for the Lake Shore
Drive apartments, the cost of either project was between five
and ten percent below that for comparable apartment houses
in Chicago.

When the buildings were completed they provoked a
variety of critical reactions. Frank Lloyd Wright dismissed
them as nothing more than "flat-chested architecture." A more
serious critical appraisal of the subtleties of their design was
offered by Peter Carter, in *Mies van der Rohe at Work* (1974),
where he called attention to the rhythmic relationship of the
glass bays, noting that the two central windows in each bay
were wider than those adjacent to the columns as opposed to
the smaller ones subdivided by the mullions.

Aesthetically, 860–880 Lake Shore Drive set the standard
for much of Mies's later high-rise work, including commercial
jobs such as the Seagram Building (1958) in New York, the
Federal Center (1959–75, see no. 61) in Chicago, the Toronto
Dominion Center (1963–69), and Westmount Square (1965–
68) in Montreal. Aside from the adjacent 900–910 Lake Shore

Drive (1953–56), his other apartments such as the
Commonwealth Promenade (1953–56) and 2400 Lakeview
(1960–63) in Chicago and Lafayette Towers (1963) in Detroit
use a variety of materials, departing from the restrained,
black-painted, steel exteriors of 860–880 Lake Shore Drive.
Aluminum in particular was used extensively as cladding for a
number of subsequent buildings. And as Mies began to
incorporate central air conditioning into his designs, his
architecture developed a very sophisticated surface plane that
covered the fireproof steel or concrete structure in what he
termed a "skin and bones" design. It was while the architect
was at work on an extension to the Commonwealth
Promenade Apartment Building that his friend and associate
Herbert Greenwald was killed in a plane crash in New York's
East River, on February 3, 1959. This disrupted the proposed
extension of that complex and ended a very fruitful
collaboration. At Greenwald's death Mies would remark:
"Herbert Greenwald began with an idea of the social
consequences of his work; along the way he also discovered
that he was a very good businessman." Together, the socially
conscious businessman and the architect created what has
become one of the world's great moments in architecture. —J.Z.

59. Prudential Building, 1952–55

Now Prudential Plaza Building
130 East Randolph Street
Naess and Murphy
Addition: C. F. Murphy Associates, 1968; Loebl Schlossman and
Hackl (lobby renovation and new building), 1988–90

The Prudential Building (fig. 1) was the first major office tower constructed in Chicago after the lean years of the Great Depression and the Second World War. It drew criticism even as it was getting underway. According to *Architectural Forum* (August 1952), it was "no design experiment, no Lever House [1952], no Alcoa [completed 1953], no UN Secretariat [1950]; . . . its emphatically vertical limestone and aluminum (or stainless steel) slab is contemporary with Rockefeller Center [begun 1931]." Although preliminary studies called for all-glass, curtain-wall schemes comparable to those of the famed postwar moderns mentioned by *Architectural Forum*, they were rejected because of potential glare problems and "Chicago's cold climate" (according to the same article), which would have meant "heavy heat loss with a continuous window treatment." Moreover, "in Chicago, more conservatism exists, and this conservatism was to some extent respected."

Although the Prudential's Indiana limestone and aluminum detailing harks back to a prewar era, it was the fifth largest office building in the world when it was planned, and at forty-one stories (about 600 feet high), it was the tallest building in Chicago when it was completed. Furthermore, it was the first building constructed on air rights of the Illinois Central railway yards, an eighty-acre tract bordering the Chicago River to the north, Lake Michigan to the east, Randolph Street to the south, and Michigan Avenue to the west. The Prudential Insurance Company negotiated with the railroad for eighteen months before acquiring the rights to under three-and-a-half acres of the land. Construction of the building along Randolph Street necessitated the laying of 187 foundation caissons among the railroad tracks. In first realizing the potential of the Illinois Central's air rights, the venture paved the way for the development of the extensive tract—a site six times as large as New York's Rockefeller Center—generally identified from the early 1960s through the present as Illinois Center (see no. 73).

The ground-breaking ceremony for the Prudential Building was held on August 12, 1952, and the dedication took place on December 8, 1955. In recognition of the insurance company's symbol, the Rock of Gibraltar, a chip from the historic site was presented to Prudential by the British Consul General at the dedication ceremony and used to seal a time capsule embedded in the lobby's middle column at the main entrance. The capsule, scheduled to be opened in the year 2000, contains memorabilia from 1955 and predictions about life in the twenty-first century. The lobby is sheathed in pink Canadian granite, and the columns are stainless steel; gold-anodized metal is used for decorations on the ceiling. On the exterior, sculptor Alfonso Ianelli (1888–1965), famed for his early work for Frank Lloyd Wright at Midway Gardens in 1913, created a sixty-five-ton sculpture of Prudential's trademark, the Rock of Gibraltar.

In subsequent years the building was extended to the north (1968) by the architectural firm of C. F. Murphy Associates, the successor firm of Naess and Murphy. The Prudential Building itself has gone through alternating periods of acclaim and neglect in the literature of Chicago architecture. Nevertheless, its importance to the skyline of postwar Chicago is indisputable. In the late 1980s, the building gained new life as the firm of Loebl Schlossman and Hackl began to make lobby renovations, and at the same time began work on a sixty-four-story addition. Having two tones of gray granite and silver glass, the addition (fig. 2) has a distinctive peaked roof thought reminiscent of 1920s towers and bears a resemblance, as well, to some designs of architect Helmut Jahn (now a partner of Murphy in Murphy/Jahn), particularly his unexecuted Bank of the Southwest Tower (1982), Houston, and his 1650 Market Street, Philadelphia (1984–87). —J.Z.

60. Inland Steel Building, 1954–58

30 West Monroe Street
Skidmore, Owings and Merrill

In the early 1950s, the architectural firm of Skidmore, Owings and Merrill was commissioned to build a skyscraper in Chicago—its first in the city and the first in the Loop since completion of the Field Building in 1934 (see no. 57). The client was the Inland Steel Company, one of the country's most powerful corporations. America's steel mills had been instrumental in the Allied victory in the Second World War, and in the 1950s they continued to flourish as they supplied the long-unfulfilled demands of both consumer and industry. A proud Chicago firm whose principal product was carbon steel, the Inland Steel Company was celebrating its eminence by building new headquarters in the center of the historic Loop.

The company's building committee opted for a structure that was costly, and justified its decision before the editors of *Architectural Forum* (May 1955): "The difference in investment between an exceptional building and an adequate commercial building is not sufficient, when considered over the useful life of the structure, to warrant anything but an exceptional type." The committee members cannily remarked that it "would provide a unique institutional identification for the company over an extended period of years." The Skidmore, Owings and Merrill building was indeed exceptional. Although the first postwar Chicago skyscraper, the Prudential Building (see no. 59), was relatively traditional, the Inland Steel Building was the design of a new generation of architects. Walter Netsch (born 1920) was the initial planner, but when he was called upon to develop the country's first Air Force Academy, in Colorado Springs, Colorado, Bruce Graham (born 1925) took over the project, with William Hartmann as partner in charge and with Andrew Brown and Sam Sachs as the structural and mechanical engineers.

Three factors account for the building's innovations: first, new technology developed during the construction industry's long hiatus; second, the influence of German émigré Ludwig Mies van der Rohe on American architecture; and third, the design program for Lever House (1952), Skidmore, Owings and Merrill's recently completed skyscraper in New York.

The properties of steel had been vastly improved during the war, and the Inland Steel was the first major building to be erected on steel pilings instead of concrete caissons. Commonplace today but remarkable for the time was the use of Miesian "clear-span" construction: supporting the entire building are fourteen exterior columns encased in stainless-steel jackets; suspended between these ribs are sixty-foot girders that support each floor. Through imaginative structural organization, all the elevators and utilities are placed in a twenty-five-story windowless core adjacent to the nineteen-story office tower, thus achieving Mies's ideal of unobstructed "universal spaces" on each 177-by-58-foot floor and separating, in Mies's words, the "served from the servant spaces."

In tribute to the company's major product, Graham planned a stainless-steel curtain wall, reminiscent of the design for Lever House. *Architectural Forum* commented on this obvious relationship:

In function, of course, Inland bears a fairly close family resemblance to New York's Lever House, also designed by SOM to house a particular company, particularly well, while suggesting the nature of its particular product. A Lever-shaped tower turned inside out, [Inland] shows off steel: the strength of long girders, the sculptural possibilities of columns, the luster and durability of sheet.

Graham further introduced green-tinted, dual glazing, its heat-absorbing qualities protecting office workers from the glare generated by the floor-to-ceiling windows of the office tower. Utilizing only sixty-six percent of its site, the Inland Steel Building offers passersby a small, protected plaza that flows naturally into the open, uncluttered lobby, where the aesthetic possibilities of steel are further celebrated in Richard Lippold's sculpture, *Radiant I* (1958), made of steel rod and wire.

To many critics, the Inland Steel Building's bold expression of a transparent steel skeleton made it the logical offspring of the Reliance Building (see no. 5) and thus the first skyscraper of the "Second Chicago School." The company did indeed receive "unique institutional identification" through its building, much as did Johnson Wax from the acclaim accorded Frank Lloyd Wright's innovative design for its corporate headquarters in Racine, Wisconsin, in 1939. The Inland Steel Building was given the Distinguished Building Honor Award in 1958 by the Chicago Chapter of the American Institute of Architects and its twenty-five-year award in 1983. On that occasion, M. W. Newman wrote in the *Chicago Sun-Times*: "Urbane, polished, open-looking... dapper but not brash, [it is] an elegant headquarters building that enlivens the streetscape." —J.H.C.

61. Federal Center, 1959–75

Dearborn Street between Jackson Boulevard and Adams Street
Ludwig Mies van der Rohe with Schmidt, Garden and Erikson;
C. F. Murphy Associates; and A. Epstein and Sons

Fig. 1. Ludwig Mies van der Rohe. Federal Center: Everett McKinley Dirksen Building, 219 South Dearborn Street, 1964. View of façade

Fig. 2. Model for addition to Federal Center, c. 1988. From left to right, Everett McKinley Dirksen Building, the single-story United States Post Office, and the John C. Kluczynski Building. At far right, the addition to the complex, designed by Fujikawa Johnson and Associates

In the 1960s, Ludwig Mies van der Rohe (1886–1969), continuing to pursue the solution to high-rise planning he first used in 860–880 Lake Shore Drive (1948–52, see no. 58), designed a series of office complexes in which twin towers were asymmetrically sited in a plaza, perhaps with other buildings, a park, or a fountain. These superblocks, which include the Toronto Dominion Centre (1963–69) and Westmount Square (1965–68) in Montreal, also owe something of their origin to his design for Chicago's Federal Center, begun in 1959.

That plan called for three buildings. The first was the thirty-story Everett McKinley Dirksen Building at 219 South Dearborn Street, completed in 1964 (fig. 1), which serves as a Federal courthouse and office building. The second phase of construction included the forty-three-story John C. Kluczynski Building across the street, at 230 South Dearborn Street, as well as the single-story post office in the plaza to the north. The Kluczynski Building, an office tower, occupies the site of the old domed Federal Building (1905), by Henry Ives Cobb (1859–1931), which was demolished to make way for the new complex.

After Mies's death in 1969, the two members of his office most actively involved in the project, Gene Summers and Bruno Conterato, brought it to completion, in 1975. In the same year they also installed Alexander Calder's red steel sculpture *Flamingo* between the office building and the post office.

Mies used light-gray granite to pave the plaza and lobbies of this four-and-a-half-acre site, thereby uniting the complex at the ground plane. He designed the lobby in each tower to match the height of the post office, thus giving visual unity and human scale to the spaces above the ground plane. Finally, the Mies buildings related in their boxy massing to that of the early-twentieth-century structures nearby. The steel exteriors of the Federal Center buildings were painted with graphite to produce a soft, velvetlike black; bronze-tinted glass was used to absorb some of the sun's heat, although that scheme met with mixed results, especially noticeable during the 1980s when cutbacks in energy consumption made temperature control of these glass towers somewhat problematic in the extremes of winter and summer.

Of working with Mies in realizing the courthouse, architect Karel Yasko, assistant commissioner for design and construction of the U.S. General Services Administration, commented in *Architectural Record* (March 1965): "It was an exciting experience. The Mies philosophy—that construction is design, is, in fact, everything—came clear as the intricate parts began to fit together with ease. Everything worked; there was no head scratching." In 1963 Mies was awarded the Presidential Medal of Freedom for his contribution to American architecture and, in part, for his work on the Federal Center. In the late 1980s, his successor firm, Fujikawa Johnson and Associates, planned with developer Stein and Co. a contexual addition to the complex for the southeast corner of Jackson Boulevard and Clark Street (fig. 2), which was completed in 1991. —J.Z.

62. Harris Trust and Savings Bank Additions

111 West Monroe Street, 1954–60
115 South LaSalle Street, 1975–77
Skidmore, Owings and Merrill

The deepening of the Depression in the 1930s forced hundreds of banks across the country to close their doors forever. By the next decade, however, the survivors were cautiously expanding into available spaces nearby, and by the 1950s they were responding to economic growth by building entire skyscrapers. In 1954, the family-owned Harris Trust and Savings Bank, located at 111 West Monroe Street, announced an ambitious plan to put up not one but two high rises, thereby becoming a pacesetter for Chicago's financial institutions. It would be the first bank in the Loop to erect a skyscraper since the Foreman State National Bank completed its building in 1930 (see no. 55).

According to the bank's three-phase master plan, the original midblock, twenty-story classical building of red brick and granite (Shepley, Rutan and Coolidge, 1910–11), guarded by the famous Harris lions in bronze relief, would remain as the centerpiece of the vastly enlarged complex. But the decision was made to demolish other buildings, replacing them with towers, first to the east and later to the west. By 1956, the bank had acquired the entire half block bounded by Clark and LaSalle streets to the east and west and by Monroe Street and Marble Court to the north and south. The first phase in the directors' long-range plan, the modernization of the original building (including air conditioning throughout), was accomplished without serious difficulty. Before the bank could proceed with phase two, breaking ground for its first new skyscraper, however, it was necessary to go to court. According to the zoning law as described in the *Chicago Tribune* on August 28, 1954, "the cubic contents of a downtown building can be only 144 times the square footage of the building site. Under this law, the Harris Trust addition could only be twelve instead of the twenty stories necessary to connect each floor with a corresponding floor in the [existing] twenty-story bank building." In time, the bank was granted a zoning variance, and demolition of a sixteen-story building at the corner of Monroe and Clark streets was completed in December 1957.

The thorniest problem faced by the Skidmore, Owings and Merrill design team—including design partner Walter Netsch, partner in charge William Hartmann, project manager John Schruben, and senior project architectural designer Pafford K. Clay—was, according to the firm's outline of the project, "to provide at all times, summer and winter, for continued occupancy of the existing building on each and every floor, [while] complying with fire regulations." The solution was to build core facilities at the juncture of the new and old buildings and place a public corridor on the western boundary of each new floor. This ingenious arrangement is similar in concept, although not in appearance, to the separate core building Bruce Graham had designed for Inland Steel (see no. 60), completed as the first Harris Trust addition was

beginning construction. The result was an uninterrupted, 75-by-160-foot rectangle on every floor of the new tower.

The choice of an exposed, stainless-steel skeleton in the Harris Trust and Savings Bank addition reflected the bank's wish for an enduring material with minimum maintenance costs, although the similarity to the Inland Steel Building is not purely coincidental. The bank directors made certain requests that resulted in other innovations. They wanted a boardroom and "guest dining suite unlike anything in Chicago" on the top floor. Thus, instead of placing an unsightly box of mechanical equipment on the roof, the architects provided a sculpture garden surrounded by elegant, glass-enclosed spaces for dining and meetings, a precedent followed in few other buildings. They installed the equipment in the middle of the building, on the eleventh and twelfth floors, setting back its louvered casings, as the descriptive outline states, "in line with the glass loggia walls of the first and twenty-third floors," breaking the exterior curtain wall and adding visual interest to the building.

In the end, this skyscraper reached a height of twenty-three stories because of the bank's compliance with the zoning law. A twenty-foot setback paralleling Marble Court on the south side not only permitted the increased height but also provided for a delivery dock at street level and, an even rarer bonus, natural light for the building's southern exposure. The lasting success of the elegant design was attested to when the Harris Trust and Savings Bank addition received the twenty-five year award from the Chicago Chapter of the American Institute of Architects in 1985.

The bank's most pressing need when planning its additions had been expanded banking facilities on the lower floors. In 1977, following its master plan, a thirty-eight-story skyscraper rose to the west, at the corner of Monroe and LaSalle streets. With its completion, an entire block at street level was opened for banking, the original multistoried lobby of 1911 remaining intact in the center. Not a trendsetter but an authoritative skyscraper, the 1977 addition repeats the stainless-steel framing and tinted-gray glass of its predecessor. Stainless-steel fixtures in the new banking halls link the exterior and interior. A recessed plaza on Monroe in front of the 1977 addition includes an antiqued-bronze fountain (1975) by Russell Secrest (born 1935), who provided a lively complement to the bronze lions at either end of the original building.

Founded in 1882 as the N. W. Harris investment banking firm, the institution had become the Harris Trust and Savings Bank in 1907 and was held by Harris family descendants until it went public in 1976. In 1984 the bank became wholly owned by the Bank of Montreal, which announced in January of 1998 a planned merger with Royal Bank of Canada. —J.H.C.

63. United States Gypsum Building, 1963 (now demolished)

101 South Wacker Drive
The Perkins and Will Partnership

Fig. 1. The Perkins and Will Partnership. United States Gypsum Building, 101 South Wacker Drive, 1963

When the United States Gypsum Building was completed in 1963, it was considered highly controversial. Two reasons were given: first, the building is turned at a forty-five-degree angle to the street, thereby breaking the regularity of the city's grid; and second, it is a faceted, eight-cornered tower considered "intricate and sentimental," an enigmatic design disengaged from the structural purity of the Chicago School of architecture and the building's Miesian contemporaries. Two years later, architect Philip Will, Jr., defending his design in relation to the recently completed Civic Center (see no. 65), was quoted in *Chicago Magazine* (Spring 1965):

I don't see Wright or Sullivan in the Civic Center ... [referring to the purists' choice of the Civic Center as the best new building in Chicago and the truest to the Chicago School]. There's more Wright in the Gypsum Building. Wright was a romantic. The Civic Center is essentially classic, not romantic. It is the end product of the most mathematical and geometric school. Our approach is a humanist approach.

The seventeen-story tower is the home office of United States Gypsum, miner of the eponymous mineral (also known as plaster of Paris) and the leading manufacturer of plasterboard and other building materials. At the company's request, the architects made use of its products wherever possible, incorporating United States Gypsum movable wall partitions and its wall, ceiling, and floor coverings throughout the interiors. In addition, renowned Chicago sculptor Edgar Miller was commissioned to design two white-gypsum relief panels for the lobby depicting the mining, manufacture, and use of the company's products.

The building's exterior consists of faceted columns that run from the plaza level to peaks projecting beyond the roofline. Their white-marble facing contrasts dramatically with the dark-gray-slate spandrels and gray-glass curtain walls. The roofline reflects the facet motif of the columns in triangular shapes that form a cornice. The use of reentrant corners transforms the plan from a square into an octagon, a design device that not only provided eight corner offices per floor but repeated the facet motif, as well. The crystalline faceting of exterior and plan is also used in numerous aspects of the interior, particularly in the lobby, where the twenty-foot-high ceiling is vaulted in diamond shapes.

In 1992 the United States Gypsum company moved its offices to the thirty-four-story tower that was constructed as the second phase of the AT&T Corporate Center Complex (see no. 103). U.S. Gypsum's distinctive 1963 headquarter building was later demolished with great care to encapsulate the asbestos that had been used throughout the structure. —P.A.S.

64. Marina City, 1964–67

*Between State and Dearborn streets on the north bank
of the Chicago River
Bertrand Goldberg Associates*

*Figs. 1, 2. Bertrand Goldberg
Associates. Marina City, north
bank of the Chicago River
between State and Dearborn
streets, 1964–67. Below,
reinforced-concrete towers under
construction*

*Fig. 3. Plan of central core and
petal-like apartment units in a
Marina City tower*

Chicago architect Bertrand Goldberg (born 1913) has not
only produced innovative architectural and engineering
solutions to common problems in the design of housing,
hospitals, and office buildings but also pioneered the concept
of the "city-within-a-city" in Chicago. First realized by the
architect in Marina City (fig. 1), a five-building complex
constructed on the edge of the Chicago River, it brings
together buildings for living, working, and recreation in a
dense urban complex, thereby allowing twenty-four-hour use
of expensive downtown land. Goldberg believes that, like
European cities, American urban centers are enriched by the
existence of high-density populations. The architect's intention
in creating a city-within-a-city was to stabilize the social and
economic erosion of Chicago's downtown area and to reverse
the postwar exodus of the city's population to the suburbs. It
is no coincidence that the construction of Marina City was
paid for by four union pension funds for janitors, a
constituency that relies upon a vital central city for its very
livelihood. In many respects, Goldberg proved to be a
visionary whose buildings have revitalized the aging urban
center, and Marina City has proved to be the design
prototype for virtually all of Goldberg's subsequent work.

Marina City consists of two cylindrical, sixty-story
apartment buildings facing the Chicago River; a slim, ten-story
rectangular office building to the north; and nestled in
between a dramatic-looking structure originally built to house
theaters. The saddle shape of the theater building is the result
of its engineering. Its sprayed-concrete roof is slung on
catenary steel cables supported by a curving concrete frame.
The four structures are unified by a horizontal base building
that originally housed a variety of recreational facilities,
including a bowling alley, a year-round swimming pool, an
ice-skating rink, and stores, theaters, and a marina with berths
for 700 boats—hence the complex's name. Like the Daily
News Building of 1929 (see no. 52), Marina City was one of
the first structures in downtown Chicago to take advantage of
the recreational potential of the Chicago River, rather than
simply using it as an industrial transportation artery.

When Marina City's two cylindrical towers were
constructed in the early 1960s, they were the tallest
reinforced-concrete structures in the world. The two cylinders
directly and poetically express the plasticity of reinforced
concrete, particularly when contrasted with the rectilinear,
steel-frame IBM Building (see no. 74) directly across the
street. But the real impact of the towers was their remarkable
engineering inventiveness. Their round utility cores (fig. 2)
were erected first by the innovative "slip-form" method of
construction, which Allan Temko described in the exhibition
catalog *A Guide to 150 Years of Chicago Architecture* (1985) as
"a system in which the cores acted virtually as their own
cranes, and then remained as armatures to which the rest of

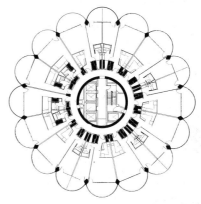

the buildings were attached, like petals to the center of flowers" (fig. 3).

As a result, the 900 apartments in the two towers (450 units per tower) are pie-shaped. An efficiency apartment occupies one "petal" and fans out from an eight-foot-wide wall near the core to one that is twenty-one feet wide at the balcony. The curving outdoor balcony beyond provides that rare commodity: personal outdoor space in the heart of downtown. Following the same model, one-bedroom apartments occupy one-and-a-half petals, with the same number of balconies, and two-bedroom apartments occupy two-and-a-half petals, with comparable balconies. When the towers first opened, potential tenants expressed concern that their furniture would not fit into the oddly shaped apartments. To allay their fears, original rental brochures included a space-planning kit with floor plans for the three types of apartments and tiny stickers of furniture in plan, to allow potential tenants to see for themselves whether their furniture would fit. In designing the towers, Goldberg reserved the first twenty stories for parking and service areas. As a result, every apartment has a spectacular

180-degree view, since the lowest apartments are situated on the twenty-first floor.

Goldberg returned to the example of Marina City time and time again, both in the use of cylindrical towers and the planning of a city-within-a-city. Notable among his later designs is the Raymond Hilliard Center, a public-housing complex of 1966 (fig. 4), located at State Street and Cermak Road. The Hilliard Center replaced aging South Side slums and set a high standard for successful low-cost, subsidized housing that has never been matched in Chicago. Following the city-within-a-city theory, Hilliard Center consists of two cylindrical towers designated for the elderly and two long, curving towers designated for families. The four buildings, whose curves visually complement one another, are located on landscaped grounds that create a parklike setting. Goldberg's achievement at the Hilliard Center is unique. As Allan Temko noted: "Goldberg, virtually alone among prominent American architects, deciphered problems with high-rise dwellings for poor families almost a generation ago with a penetration that was then matched, so far as I know, only by researchers in a few architectural schools, but characteristically, his solutions were less simplistic."

A more recent example of Goldberg's high-density housing concept is River City (fig. 5), located along the Chicago River at Harrison and Wells street. As in the design of Marina City, Goldberg again used the river as a focal point for urban redevelopment. Originally, the architect envisioned the first phase of the project as containing three cylindrical towers of seventy-two stories each, connected by sky bridges. The Chicago Planning Commission refused to approved that plan, and the first phase of the complex, completed in 1986, consists instead of two low-rise, concrete apartment buildings, serpentine in form, which echo the confluence at the river's south branch. Designed to connect with Dearborn Park to the east (see Franklin Building, no. 25) and Chinatown to the south, River City was intended to extend a mile in length and house 3,000 persons. —P.A.S.

65. Chicago Civic Center, 1965

Now Richard J. Daley Center
Bounded by Washington, Randolph, Dearborn,
and Clark streets
Jacques Brownson, Head Designer
C. F. Murphy Associates with Loebl, Schlossman and Bennett,
and Skidmore, Owings and Merrill

Fig. 1. C. F. Murphy Associates, with Loebl, Schlossman and Bennett and Skidmore, Owings and Merrill. Chicago Civic Center, now Richard J. Daley Center, 1965. View to the north along Dearborn Street

Fig. 2. Preliminary model (unexecuted) for Chicago Civic Center, 1960

Fig. 3. View of plaza with sculpture by Picasso in the foreground

This thirty-one-story tower (fig. 1), more than 650 feet high, was built to house 119 courtrooms of the Circuit Court of Cook County, two courtrooms of the Supreme and Appellate courts of the State of Illinois, and office space for the City of Chicago and Cook County, which had outgrown the adjacent City-County Building of 1905–11, designed by Holabird and Roche.

The architects were chosen in 1960 from among nineteen firms submitting proposals for the Center, including Ludwig Mies van der Rohe, Harry Weese and Associates, Holabird and Root, and Perkins and Will. As originally proposed, the plan called for two glass-and-steel buildings, approximately twenty-one and twenty-three stories high, set on a small plaza and flanked by the original City-County Building, which would have been comparably sheathed (fig. 2). It was subsequently decided, however, that a single, higher tower would be the most economical solution, enabling the city, county, and state to consolidate related functions in one building. This move enlarged the plaza, which, as reported in *Progressive Architecture* (October 1966), caused some to criticize the "vast granite" open space as "too much of a good thing." In 1966, the installation in the plaza of Pablo Picasso's monumental sculpture (fig. 3)—one of the first examples of modern public sculpture in the city—helped to alleviate that imbalance.

The Chicago Picasso originated in a visit to the artist's studio by architects William Hartmann of Skidmore, Owings and Merrill, Charles Murphy of C. F. Murphy Associates, and Norman Schlossman of Loebl, Schlossman and Bennett. They were accompanied by Picasso's friend and biographer, Sir Roland Penrose, then organizing an exhibition of the artist's sculpture that would take place in London in 1967. Their presentation of the plans to the artist was followed by a personal visit by Hartmann, who brought Picasso such gifts as a Sioux Indian war bonnet and sports trophies of the Chicago White Sox, Cubs, and Bears. The artist was won over, beginning work on a design for the sculpture in 1964 and completing a forty-one-inch-high, welded-steel maquette the following year (in the collection of The Art Institute of Chicago). Although Picasso's design was a gift by the artist "to the people of Chicago," the enlarged sculpture was fabricated with funds from the Woods Charitable Fund, Inc., the Chauncey and Marion Deering McCormick Foundation, and the Field Foundation of Illinois. The finished sculpture, fifty feet high and weighing 162 tons, is made of Cor-Ten steel, the same material that is used to cover the fireproofed steel skeleton of the building.

The tower uses a module of four feet ten inches by nine feet eight inches, and the structural bays are eighty-seven feet long and almost forty-eight feet wide. Although the Civic Center's exterior proportions and appearance are not Miesian in the strict sense, they bear an essential relationship to the work of that Chicago master, and the detailing, furnishing, and design of the interiors are closely related to, say, the Mies interiors of the courts in the Federal Center (see no. 61).

At completion the building was published internationally, but a quote from the review in *Progressive Architecture* (Greenwich, Connecticut, October 1996) best summarizes the building's place in Chicago architecture:

The Chicago Civic Center does dignified justice to its site in the birthplace of the skyscraper. The attention to structure would have pleased Major Jenney; the expression of structure and function would have won the praise of Sullivan; and it is easy to imagine Mies smiling benignly from his apartment not far away.

Early in 1977, the building was renamed the Richard J. Daley Center for the city's well-known mayor, who served from 1955 to 1976. In 1996, architect Howard Decker and landscape architect Peter Schaudt added benches and trees in a skillful renovation of the plaza. —J.Z.

66. Brunswick Building, 1961–65

69 West Washington Street
Skidmore, Owings and Merrill

*Fig. 1. Skidmore, Owings and
Merrill. Brunswick Building, 69
West Washington Street, 1961–
65. At right, the Chicago Temple
Building (see no. 30)*

*Fig. 2. Exterior view of
Brunswick Building lobby*

It was on the site of the Brunswick Building, at the southwest corner of Washington and Dearborn streets, that on the day after the disastrous Chicago Fire of 1871 a real estate man named William D. Kerfoot erected a shanty and put up a hand-lettered sign that read: "All gone but wife, children, and energy," and was back in business. Kerfoot's entrepreneurial spirit was justified, for the site continued to grow in value and importance over the years. In 1961, it was a logical target for redevelopment as the nation's postwar building boom belatedly overtook Chicago.

One of the chief beneficiaries of the boom was the architectural firm of Skidmore, Owings and Merrill, whose designers' and engineers' creative use of advanced technology brought them an ever-increasing number of corporate commissions. In the Chicago School tradition, they had clearly expressed the exterior frame in their Inland Steel Building (see no. 60) and the first Harris Trust and Savings Bank addition (see no. 62); they followed the same tradition in framing the thirty-seven-story Brunswick Building (fig. 1), but here the Skidmore team of designers, Bruce Graham, Myron Goldsmith, and Joseph Yohanan, in conjunction with the engineer Fazlur Khan, selected reinforced concrete rather than steel and utilized a tube-in-tube system. Tall buildings must withstand both the vertical force of gravity's load and the lateral stress of wind shear. In the Brunswick Building, the outer tube is the concrete, load-bearing, screen wall, and the core housing the service elements forms the interior tube, or shear wall. The tubes, connected by concrete floor framing, interact to resist wind pressure; and the result is a building with minimum sway and column-free, flexible interior spaces.

The extremely unstable subsoil of the Brunswick site necessitated a further structural innovation. At the third-floor level, a massive, two-story-deep, concrete ring girder transfers the load from the screen wall to ten concrete perimeter columns that act as footings. In the tradition of the first Chicago School, this structural system is clearly visible, and its inward curve above the base recalls the gently curving profile of the Monadnock Building (see no. 8) only four blocks south on Dearborn. However, in the Brunswick, as Carl W. Condit noted in *Chicago, 1930–1970* (1974), the unity of those concrete elements is "denied by covering the girders and the piers with materials that are not only misleading but inharmonious; the piers are clothed in the ubiquitous travertine and the great girder in a high-density paneled concrete that looks like limestone of inferior quality."

If the effect was somewhat strained, it may have been chosen because the Brunswick and the new Chicago Civic Center (see no. 65) were going up simultaneously across Washington Street and the two teams of architects were attempting to create structural forms that would relate to one another. The Brunswick Building columns below the ring girder form a covered arcade on Washington Street (fig. 2), acting in counterpoint to the stiltlike, Cor-Ten steel pilotis of the Civic Center; and the transparent lobby of the Brunswick may refer to the openness of the Civic Center Plaza.

Although the aboveground connections between the two buildings may not be totally successful, below ground the Brunswick Building and the Civic Center were pioneers. Linked by underground shopping arcades, the two were joined as well to a subway station, in one of the initial stages of a Pedway, a system of passageways that by the late 1980s would spread in the directions of the compass as the North Loop Redevelopment finally began to take shape.

A small plaza to the west of the Brunswick Building was designed for a sculpture by the Spanish artist Joan Miró; finally funded and installed in 1982, it is part of an outdoor art gallery that includes the Civic Center's monumental Picasso sculpture, which the Skidmore, Owings and Merrill architects were instrumental in bringing to Chicago. —J.H.C.

67. Equitable Building, 1962–65

401 North Michigan Avenue
Skidmore, Owings and Merrill

Fig. 1. Skidmore, Owings and Merrill. Equitable Building, 401 North Michigan Avenue, 1962–65. At left, the Wrigley Building (see no. 29)

Fig. 2. Staircase leading from Pioneer Court to the riverbank

When the Equitable Life Assurance Society of New York bought a choice site on the Chicago River near the important Michigan Avenue Bridge, it accepted the stringent conditions imposed by the seller, the Chicago Tribune Company. To maintain the high visibility of the Tribune Tower (see no. 32), the new building had to be set back 135 feet from the Michigan Avenue right of way and could be no taller than the Tower. The deed also required that the space between the two buildings be developed as a plaza, and the Tribune agreed to share in its cost.

These restrictions, in addition to the romantic styles of the neighboring 1920s skyscrapers and the Equitable's requirement that the building be as large as zoning laws would allow, presented Skidmore, Owings and Merrill design partner Patricia Swan, partner in charge Roy Allen, and project manager Robert Cutler with their parameters. Their solution was to design an anomaly, a highly visible background building. Bruce Graham, the firm's senior design partner, described the Equitable in the *Architectural Record* (October 1965) as "the most sophisticated office building this office has done." The thirty-five story, continuous-weld, orthotropic-steel structure (fig. 1) is clad in gray-green aluminum, dark-gray granite, and bronze-tinted glass above the base. This simple sheathing reflects the rigid metallic frame and provides a strong but quiet presence, which is in harmony with the masonry structure of the Tribune Tower. The three-bay, narrow end of the rectangular building overlooks the river, and the longer side, five bays wide, defines the eastern edge of Pioneer Court, the required plaza. The building's clear glass at the recessed base, according to Graham, allows the outdoors "to flow through and beyond the lobby."

Pioneer Court realizes a recommendation of the 1909 Plan of Chicago to provide public spaces along the riverbank, here completing an urban ensemble begun in the 1920s by the Wrigley (see no. 29) and Tribune buildings. And it also commemorates the historic significance of the site. Two bronze plaques and a central fountain honor, among others, the area's first permanent resident, the Haitian Jean-Baptiste Pointe du Sable, who in the 1780s settled at the river's edge somewhere nearby to trade with the Indians, and Cyrus Hall McCormick (1809–1884), who in 1847 built his first reaper plant 150 feet to the east of the Equitable Building's site.

Further capitalizing on the location, the Skidmore, Owings and Merrill landscape architects linked Pioneer Court with the riverbank below. A public staircase spirals down in a sweeping curve (fig. 2), circling a tree before reaching a landscaped plaza, which in the summertime offers an outdoor restaurant and temporary mooring for pleasure boats. For more than twenty years this pleasant oasis of greenery contrasted sharply with the riverbank on the opposite side, which until 1987 the developers of Illinois Center (see no. 73)

made no attempt to improve. At river level, the Equitable's plaza contains not only greenery but also a shopping arcade, parking concourse, and loading dock, the latter invisible from above but accessible from the lower level of Michigan Avenue which was developed in 1920 when the double-deck bridge was built.

Although the river offered obvious advantages to the Equitable, the consequent high water table also provided an obstacle to construction. The architects found that the caissons needed to support the thirty-five-story building would have to be sunk 120 feet through gravel, rubble, and sand to reach bedrock. The general contractor, the A. L. Jackson Company, employed a unique method to counteract the unstable, wet subsoil. As described in an Equitable building report, old railroad tank cars—their ends cut off and welded together to form a pipe—were used to line and support the holes for the caissons. The lowest cars remain in place today, adding structural strength to the caissons.

During its first two decades, the Equitable Building marked the eastern boundary of development along the north side of the river, but in the late 1980s a complex called Cityfront Center was begun (see NBC Tower, no. 102) east of Columbus Drive. Redeveloped nineteenth-century pier terminals and new towers in what is now known as River East follow the river's course to Lake Michigan. Walkways and plazas link an expanded Pioneer Court with the new area and integrate the Equitable and its site into the eastern development. —J.H.C.

68. United Insurance Building, 1962

1 East Wacker Drive
Shaw, Metz and Associates

Mid-Continental Plaza, 1969–72

55 West Monroe Street
Alfred Shaw and Associates

Fig. 1. Shaw, Metz and Associates. United Insurance Building, 1 East Wacker Drive, 1962. At left, the Jewelers Building (see no. 32)

Fig. 2. Alfred Shaw and Associates. Mid-Continental Plaza, 55 West Monroe Street, 1969–72

The United Insurance Building (fig. 1) and the Mid-Continental Plaza (fig. 2), separated by almost a decade, are the work of architectural firms headed by Alfred P. Shaw (1895–1970). Boston-born and trained, Shaw entered the prestigious firm of Graham, Anderson, Probst and White during the 1920s, and as a junior partner there designed two of Chicago's most famous limestone-clad buildings, the massive Merchandise Mart (1923–31, see no. 56) and the Art Deco Field Building (1928–34, see no. 57). During the late 1930s and into the next decade, he was a partner in Shaw, Naess and Murphy before joining civil engineer Carl Metz and mechanical engineer John Dolio in a partnership in 1947. The firm of Shaw, Metz and Dolio designed a number of buildings clad in masonry, a reflection of Shaw's lifelong interest in such materials. Examples include the Bonwit Teller Store (1949, altered and now occupied by retail shops), at 830 North Michigan Avenue, and apartment buildings at 1540 North State Parkway (1953) and 3950 Marine Drive (1954). Comparable buildings by successor firms Shaw, Metz and Associates and Alfred Shaw and Associates include an apartment building at 777 North Michigan Avenue (1964) and the Continental Plaza Hotel (1963, addition 1972; now the Westin Hotel), at 909 North Michigan Avenue.

The United Insurance Building is, in a sense, the ultimate monument to Shaw's interest in masonry, particularly marble. When it was built in 1962, at forty-one stories, or 522 feet, high, it was the tallest marble-clad building in the world. That record was superseded within the decade, however, by the Standard Oil Building (1974, see no. 77) and Water Tower Place (1976, see no. 81), and perhaps for this reason it rarely appears in Chicago architectural guidebooks.

By contrast, the fifty-story, 580-foot Mid-Continental Plaza is faced with aluminum. Begun in 1969, a year before Shaw's death, and completed in 1972, it was designed by the architect in partnership with his son, Patrick, who had joined his father's firm in 1961. As in the United Insurance Building, the vertical lines of the facing material predominate in the overall appearance. Masonry, however, is used extensively inside the main lobby. Its floors and walls are lined with gray marble throughout their length, stretching from Monroe Street on the north side to Adams on the south.

Patrick Shaw trained at Harvard University and joined the firm after working with, among others, Holabird and Root, the New York office of Skidmore, Owings and Merrill, and John Carl Warnecke. Under the younger Shaw, the firm's commitment to the high rise continued when he was associate architect for the Board of Trade addition (1980, see no. 53) and 190 South LaSalle Street (1983–87, see no. 104), as well as design architect for President's Plaza (1980), near O'Hare Airport, and the Drake Office Building in Oak Brook, Illinois (1981). —J.Z.

69. Blue Cross–Blue Shield Building, 1968

Later Ryan Insurance Building
Now 55 West Wacker Drive Building
C. F. Murphy Associates

*Fig. 1. C. F. Murphy Associates.
Blue Cross–Blue Shield Building,
now 55 West Wacker Drive
Building, 1968*

*Fig. 2. Detail of lobby staircase of
the Blue Cross–Blue Shield
Building*

This fifteen-story, 256-foot-high structure (fig. 1), built with bush-hammered concrete, was designed by Otto Stark of C. F. Murphy Associates, as were the similarly detailed Library at DePaul University in Chicago and the Will County Courthouse in Joliet, Illinois, both concrete structures built in the 1960s. The interiors of the Blue Cross–Blue Shield Building were designed by William E. Monahan of the C. F. Murphy Associates interior-design division, and executive offices were designed by Harper Richards Associates. The building's large lobby and textured appearance, as well as its soaring exterior columns, caused many to liken it to Frank Lloyd Wright's Larkin Building of 1903 and the work of Louis Kahn and Paul Rudolph—although, according to the *Inland Architect* (December 1969), others complained that from the exterior it resembled a parking garage. But when the headquarters building was occupied by Blue Cross–Blue Shield, the insurance company's 1,600 employees seemed to find it congenial. As the *Inland Architect* put it: "No, at Blue Cross–Blue Shield, they're not all blue."

At opening, the lobby of the building was especially attractive, with its free-standing staircase (fig. 2) and spacious, sixty-foot service counter, built from the core, which originally permitted assistance to hundreds of visitors each day. Although a sculpture by American artist Louise Nevelson (1905–1988) was commissioned for the space as part of the corporate art collection, the work has been removed. The building was dedicated on November 26, 1968, but it functioned as the corporate headquarters for Blue Cross–Blue Shield only until 1972, when the company moved to the Illinois Center (see no. 73). However, the concrete building of 1968 remains an individualistic expression within the work of an architectural firm whose design tendencies otherwise leaned heavily toward Miesian Modernism. —J.Z.

70. Time and Life Building, 1966–68

Now 541 North Fairbanks Court Building
Harry Weese and Associates

By the late 1960s, corporate headquarters designed in the Miesian idiom were the norm in Chicago's Loop, so this example, constructed for the subscription services of Time and Life, the New York-based news-magazine empire, came as no surprise. It was a surprise, however, to find the name of Harry Weese (born 1915) as the architect. From a firm that had followed an independent path, whose principal was the spokesman for the less orthodox endeavors of the profession during Ludwig Mies van der Rohe's heyday, this office building was unexpected. As the exhibition catalog *100 Years of Architecture in Chicago: Continuity of Structure and Form* (1976), by Oswald W. Grube, Peter C. Pran, and Franz Schulze, stated: "Weese is not customarily associated with the second Chicago School. . . . In the [Time and Life Building], however, [he] affirmed the rectilinear character of the frame as candidly and as vigorously as any other Chicago designer of his time."

The Time and Life Building (fig. 1), conservative by the standards of its decade, follows the direction set by the Federal Center (see no. 61) and uses Cor-Ten steel to sheathe the reinforced-concrete frame and ubiquitous pilotis at the base, which generate arcades protecting the Ohio Street and Grand Avenue entrances.

The infill of bronze-tinted mirror glass, unusual in a tall office building, is highly functional. It deflects the sun's ultraviolet rays, saving on air-conditioning costs. Another efficiency of the thirty-story building is a true first: double-deck elevators that stop at two floors simultaneously. Entered from the appropriate level in the split-level lobby, the two-story elevators also cut down on the number of shafts required, allowing for especially generous spaces in the building's lobby. These spaces are sometimes used for exhibitions, while a still lower level contains a retail concourse, expanded in 1989 when the building was renovated by Perkins and Will. —J.H.C.

Fig. 1. Harry Weese and Associates. Time and Life Building, now 541 North Fairbanks Court Building, 1966–68. View from Grand Avenue

71. Lake Point Tower, 1968

505 North Lake Shore Drive
Schipporeit-Heinrich
Associate architects: Graham, Anderson, Probst and White

Fig. 1. Schipporeit-Heinrich, with Graham, Anderson, Probst and White. Lake Point Tower, 505 North Lake Shore Drive, 1968

Fig. 2. Ludwig Mies van der Rohe. Model for an unexecuted glass tower (destroyed), 1921

The elegant Lake Point Tower (fig. 1) is often called the world's tallest apartment building; seventy stories, or 645 feet, high, it has 900 units within its cloverleaf shape. It was commissioned by William Hartnett, a developer who had been employed by Herbert Greenwald during the years that that innovative real estate man was working with Ludwig Mies van der Rohe on various high-rise projects (see 860–880 Lake Shore Drive, 1948–52, no. 58). For the design of his tower, Hartnett hired the architectural firm of Schipporeit-Heinrich, composed of George Schipporeit and John Heinrich, who had been students of Mies at the Illinois Institute of Technology in the mid-1950s. They placed the tall, residential building on a slab that houses parking and commercial services for the tenants.

According to the *Architectural Record* (October 1969), this glass skyscraper was intended to be one of three similarly designed towers, two of them uncompleted (that project prefigured the expansion planned for the 1990s by two developers, Chicago Dock and Canal, and Broadacre). It was the *Architectural Record*'s contention, as well as that of numerous guides to Chicago, that the building's plan and overall appearance derive from a 1921 glass skyscraper (fig. 2) designed by Mies for an imaginary site. Although in certain respects Lake Point Tower bears a strong resemblance to Mies's project, in certain others it does not. Lake Point Tower's plan is Y-shaped and symmetrical, whereas Mies's is asymmetrical in form. Moreover, in elevation Mies's project suggests greater transparency than is found in the Schipporeit-Heinrich tower, with its somewhat opaque, bronze-tinted glass. Finally, the Y-shaped plan may have derived from several other Chicago apartment buildings of the time, notably 2626 Lakeview Avenue, completed in 1969, and 1130 South Michigan Avenue, c. 1962–65, both by Loewenberg and Loewenberg.

Although the architects chose the Y over a cross-shaped building because the greater angle of the Y plan afforded better views to the occupants, according to the *Architectural Record*, the cross plan for apartment buildings would have been more in keeping with projects by Mies's colleagues, such as Ludwig Karl Hilberseimer (see introduction, fig. 24). Indeed, it seems that Schipporeit-Heinrich did adapt the shape of previous Chicago apartment houses to their stylistic vocabulary—although some have suggested that the plan was the contribution of associate architects Graham, Anderson, Probst and White to the project. In any event, Lake Point Tower stands as a very large reminder of Mies's influence on his disciples within Chicago. The glass skyscraper's contribution to the cityscape is far greater than that of later adaptations of the form, such as 115 North Harbor Point Drive (1975), by Solomon Cordwell Buenz and Associates.
—J.Z.

Fig. 1. C. F. Murphy Associates, with The Perkins and Will Partnership. First National Bank Building, now One First National Plaza, Madison Street between Dearborn and Clark streets, 1964–69

Fig. 2. View of sunken plaza of the First National Bank Building

Fig. 3. Charles William Brubaker, The Perkins and Will Partnership. Page of sketches for proposed roofline of the First National Bank Building (detail), 1964

72. First National Bank Building, 1964–69

Now One First National Plaza
Madison Street between Dearborn and Clark streets
C. F. Murphy Associates, with The Perkins and Will
Partnership

Active planning for this 850-foot-high headquarters of the First National Bank of Chicago (figs. 1, 2) began in 1964, when representatives of two architectural firms, C. F. Murphy Associates and The Perkins and Will Partnership, had a series of meetings with bank officials. What resulted is principally the design work of Stanley Gladych, Carter H. Manny, Jr., and Charles Rummel of C. F. Murphy Associates and of Lawrence Perkins, Philip Will, and Charles William Brubaker of The Perkins and Will Partnership. The planning records kept by several of those participants document the design process (fig. 3). For example, in an early sketch for this sixty-story building, its façade was cast in contrasting light and dark tones, much as in the United States Gypsum Building by Perkins and Will (see no. 63), but the executed version is a monochromatic, buff granite over steel, with vertical shafts balanced by horizontal spandrels. Even in the earliest schemes, however, the building had a curved façade.

This curve was in part dictated by the need at the lower floors for large spaces to accommodate public-access functions of a bank, whereas the tenants on the floors above had a greater need for natural light and panoramic views. Space analyses led to the construction of a curve that would meet the requirements of all users. As a consequence, a large, double-storied banking hall was constructed on the main level. Its interior was designed by a team of architects from both firms in cooperation with ISD Inc., and the office interiors of the bank's fourth through twenty-first floors were designed by Ford and Earl Design Associates. Elevators to the upper floors were housed in cores at either end of the building so as not to disrupt the banking hall at street level. Although the curved form grew out of a literal interpretation of functional needs, it provided this large bank with a distinctive architectural image, which *Architectural Record* (September 1970) whimsically likened to a "huge ribbed sail caught in the Chicago wind."

By 1972, the adjacent D. H. Burnham and Co. First National Bank Building (1896) was demolished to make way for a sunken plaza and fountain (fig. 2). At the street level overlooking this plaza can be seen the celebrated French artist Marc Chagall's *Four Seasons*, a mosaic mural mounted on a wall that measures ten feet high by seventy feet long. Its design was a gift to the city from the artist, and its construction was made possible by a gift from Mr. and Mrs. William Wood Prince. The plaza itself has proved to be one of the most popular in the city, especially during the warm summer months when large crowds gather at lunchtime to relax on the steps.

In the 1970s and 1980s, two other buildings were added to the First National Plaza complex, including Two First National Plaza (1968–73), by C. F. Murphy Associates and The Perkins and Will Partnership, and Three First National

Plaza (1981), by Skidmore, Owings and Merrill. The latter is one of the more interesting new buildings in the city. Its granite-clad, fifty-seven-story tower and adjacent eleven-story building have bay windows that bear a resemblance to those in Chicago School office buildings from the late 1800s. Connecting the two structures is a nine-story glass atrium containing a twenty-two-foot-high bronze sculpture by Henry Moore (1898–1986). —J.Z.

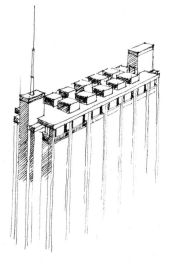

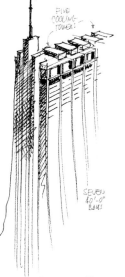

Fig. 1. *View of Illinois Center looking southeast toward Wacker Drive, c. 1981. From left to right: Three Illinois Center (1980), 233 East Wacker Drive (1980), Hyatt Regency Hotel (1974), and One Illinois Center (1970). The corner building, 333 North Michigan Avenue (1928, see no. 41), and the Bell Building (1925, see no. 42) to the south of it, are not part of the complex. Boulevard Towers (1981) is visible on Michigan Avenue south of the Bell Building*

73. Illinois Center, begun 1967

Bounded by Wacker Drive, Lake Michigan, East Lake Street, and Michigan Avenue
Office of Ludwig Mies van der Rohe, with buildings by other firms

Fig. 2. Fujikawa Johnson and Associates. Boulevard Towers, 225 North Michigan Avenue, 1981/1985

Illinois Center is the world's largest mixed-use project, as well as the world's biggest air-rights development. The site consists of some eighty acres of obsolete railroad yards once operated by the Illinois Central Railroad, later part of IC Industries, that bordered on Wacker Drive from Michigan Avenue east to the lake, extending as far south as East Lake Street. The project dates back to the 1920s, when the electrification of the Illinois Central lines along the lakefront spurred proposals to make use of the air rights. Architects such as Eliel Saarinen and the firm of Holabird and Root (see Introduction, figs. 21, 22) were among those who responded. But the Great Depression of the 1930s and Second World War of the 1940s prevented economic development of the area until 1952, when the Prudential Insurance Co. built its mid-America headquarters on the fringes of the Illinois Central land. The success of the Prudential Building (see no. 59) as an air-rights project prompted private development of Illinois Center in the 1960s and 1970s, despite some municipal claims to ownership of those rights.

The first building constructed at that time was 111 East Wacker Drive, also called One Illinois Center (1967–70, fig. 1), designed by the office of Ludwig Mies van der Rohe, with Joseph Fujikawa as head designer. Although final approval for the larger development of the air-rights land was still pending, this first tower was built on property not technically above the railroad tracks. Standing thirty stories high, it was nevertheless meant as the keystone of this development. Fujikawa, who was made a partner in Mies's firm before the founder's death in 1969, continued work on the development of Illinois Center, designing Two Illinois Center between 1969 and 1973, and then preparing a master plan in collaboration with Solomon Cordwell Buenz and Associates.

Preliminary renderings from 1967 reveal plans for the complex to have been connected by a series of underground courts, as well as to have had a terraced riverwalk, but those features, which would have unified the development and alleviated the sterility and boredom of the enclosed passages and shops, were never executed. Between the late 1970s and early 1980s, Mies's successor firm, Fujikawa, Conterato, Lohan and Associates (later Fujikawa Johnson and Associates), executed several more buildings in like form and scale, including Three Illinois Center (1980), at 303 East Wacker Drive, and Boulevard Towers (1981/1985, fig. 2), at 225 North Michigan Avenue. *Splash*, a public sculpture by Jerry Peart, was installed at Boulevard Towers in 1986.

But other buildings within the complex are intrusive in scale and materials. These include the Hyatt Regency Hotel (1974/1979–80), a brick structure by A. Epstein and Sons; Columbus Plaza (1980), at 233 East Wacker Drive, a concrete apartment building by Fujikawa, Conterato, Lohan and Associates; the rose-colored-granite Fairmont Hotel (1987), at

200 North Columbus Drive, by Hellmuth, Obata and Kassabaum; and the triangular Swiss Grand Hotel (1988–89), at 323 East Wacker Drive, by Harry Weese and Associates. Only the Sporting Club of 1989 by Kisho Kurokawa relates to the fine proportions and detailing tradition of Mies's work. And it stands as a small jewel box within this cacaphony of high rises.

As executed, Illinois Center turned out to be a lost opportunity. In the words of Paul Gapp, architecture critic of the *Chicago Tribune*: "Illinois Center is fast becoming a textbook example of how not to develop downtown land. It is a cold, insular, sterile collection of structures." Perhaps if Mies had lived things might have turned out differently, but its realized condition adds little to the aesthetic experience of the city. —J.Z.

74. IBM Building, 1969–71

Wabash Avenue and State Street on the north bank of the Chicago River
Ludwig Mies van der Rohe, with C. F. Murphy Associates

Ludwig Mies van der Rohe (1886–1969) received the commission for the IBM company's regional headquarters in 1966, and even though he was confined to a wheelchair, he insisted on being driven to the site. When he arrived, according to the *Inland Architect* (July 1972), he observed the irregular plot, a little more than an acre and a half in area, and inquired in a somewhat perplexed tone: "Where's the site?" His colleague, Bruno Conterato, partner in charge of the project, concurred: "The site appeared to us as almost nonexistent. Especially when you consider the extensive program requirements of IBM." So began the story of Mies's last American building, started in 1969, the year of his death, and completed in 1971.

A rectilinear, dark-aluminum and bronze-tinted-glass slab, typical of Mies's buildings, the IBM Building (fig. 1) rises to a height of 695 feet (670 feet from the entrance plaza) and fifty-two stories. The sides of the slab are set parallel to Chicago's street grid, but the plaza on the riverside conforms with the angle of the riverbank. Although the critics charge that the site turns its back on the river by placing a large granite wall alongside it, the architects were hampered by some existing problems: they had to contend with railroad tracks running beneath the plaza and to provide storage space for the smaller *Chicago Sun-Times* headquarters across Wabash Avenue. Moreover, Mies set his slab far back in the plaza in order to provide views of the contrasting, curvilinear towers of Marina City (fig. 2). According to Conterato: "Since we are at the axis of the river, we placed the structure on the north end of our site, enabling us to overlook the newspaper's building, and to look down the river, and on out to the lake."

The building is technically superior to many of Mies's other works in one respect: he incorporated a sophisticated temperature-control system; it has a heat-reclamation system, double-glazing, a thermal barrier between the exterior and interior layers of glass, and a procedure to equalize pressure within that two-inch-thick skin to reduce air loss. Structurally, the steel bays are thirty feet by forty feet, with columns spaced in five-foot modules. The lobby is among the tallest in a Mies building, being almost twenty-six-feet high. It contains a fitting tribute to the architect, a commemorative bust by the renowned Italian sculptor Marino Marini (1901–1980). The Cor-Ten steel garage to the north of the building was added by a Mies disciple, George Schipporeit, in 1972. —J.Z.

Fig. 1. *Ludwig Mies van der Rohe, with C. F. Murphy Associates. IBM Building, between Wabash Avenue and State Street on the north bank of the Chicago River, 1969–71. At left, a tower of Marina City (see no. 64)*

Fig. 2. *View of IBM Building, with Marina City in the background and the Chicago Sun-Times Building in front. At left, the London Guarantee and Accident Building (see no. 31)*

75. John Hancock Center, 1965–70

875 North Michigan Avenue
Skidmore, Owings and Merrill

Fig. 1. Skidmore, Owings and Merrill. John Hancock Center, 875 North Michigan Avenue, 1965–70

Fig. 2. View of sunken plaza of the John Hancock Center, on Michigan Avenue, c. 1970

Artist Claes Oldenburg compares it to a funerary obelisk. Critic Robert Bruegmann calls it a successful gamble. Bruce Graham, one of its designers, calls it gutsy. Many Chicagoans call it Big John. It is the John Hancock Center (fig. 1), the 100-story skyscraper that upon completion immediately became a symbol of Chicago. Expressing structure is a concept synonymous with the Chicago School of the 1880s and 1890s; and the Hancock, rising almost a century later, expressed its structure by putting its innovative diagonal braces on the exterior for all to see. Its black skin saluted the giant of its own era, Ludwig Mies van der Rohe, whose first buildings in the downtown area, the splendid apartment towers at 860–880 Lake Shore Drive (see no. 58), are only a few blocks away.

More than one gamble was involved. The first was to place a 1,145-foot tower (only New York's Empire State Building was taller) on North Michigan Avenue at the edge of an affluent residential district. The second was to create a multiuse structure that combined retail stores, offices, and apartments. And the third was the construction system itself.

To counteract the anticipated traffic problems generated by such a large building, the Hancock includes six floors of parking reached by a ramped structure resembling Frank Lloyd Wright's Guggenheim Museum in New York. In architecture critic and historian Bruegmann's words (*Design Book Review*, Fall 1988): "Not only did [the ramp] solve the parking access problem . . . it served as a piece of sculpture," which he found much more convincing than "the often perfunctory pieces of metalwork . . . placed on plazas during this era." The Hancock's taper on all four sides seems to lessen its massiveness. The tower occupies only fifty percent of its site, and at its base on Michigan Avenue there is a sunken plaza (fig. 2), intended to serve the nearby community as well as the building's occupants. However, the plaza provides neither an impressive entrance to the building nor a lively gathering place. One of Chicago's most acrimonious architectural debates erupted in 1988 when the building's management tried—and failed—to win City approval to enclose the plaza in a highly inappropriate atrium.

The gamble of mixed use in part lay in the location, far from commuter railroad terminals, where the only form of mass transit is the bus system. The Skidmore, Owings and Merrill design team—Bruce Graham, design partner, and Robert Diamant, studio head, with Albert Lockett as partner in charge and Richard Lenke as technical coordinator—stacked retail stores on the first five floors, offices in the twenty-seven floors above, and apartments or condominiums in the forty-nine floors at the top. They interspersed lobbies and floors of mechanical equipment, and placed a restaurant (ninety-fifth floor), observatory, radio and television facilities, and more mechanical equipment in the uppermost stories.

The flowing, tapering form is eminently suited to this mix, providing the widest spans on the lower floors where they are needed for the retail stores and the parking garage. The midlevel office floors are flexible and open. Above, five apartment designs take into account the diminishing floor area. Residents can live, work, and shop without ever leaving the building—a neighborhood encapsulated. The financial gamble paid off. From the beginning, the John Hancock Center was considered a prestigious address, attracting tenants for both offices and apartments. However, in time, as shopping meccas such as Water Tower Place (see no. 81) and 900 North Michigan Avenue (see no. 101) were built nearby, the competition adversely affected the retail floors and generated additional pressure to enclose the plaza. The solution accepted in 1992 and completed in 1995 by Hiltscher, Shapiro and Associates was to reshape the sunken court into an ellipse, rename it the Garden Level Plaza, and link it with Michigan Avenue by staircases descending from the north and south.

The gamble with the highest stakes was the Hancock tower's braced-tube structure. As described by Andrea Dean in the *AIA Journal* (October 1980), it is like "a bridge standing on end." The building's taper cut down on the sail effect from the wind; and according to Bruce Graham, in *Real Estate Forum* (November 1969), "the [diagonal braces] . . . distribute the gravity load to all exterior columns," which formed "the equivalent of rigid external bearing walls on all four sides." This concept, devised by Fazlur Khan, the Skidmore, Owings and Merrill engineering partner on the project, was an economical solution to the problem of constructing such a tall building. According to Graham in *Real Estate Forum*, the diagonal braces saved $15 million, because no high-cost, rectilinear Vierendeel trusses were necessary. Delays due to faulty caisson work slowed progress on the building, but it finally topped out in May 1968 and opened two years later.

Almost twenty years went by before the dire predictions of traffic jams and pedestrian congestion in this neighborhood came true, for by then a plethora of towers surrounded the Hancock on Michigan Avenue. But perhaps it is this density that gives a city its vitality—a thesis advanced by William H. Whyte in his book *City: Rediscovering the Center* (1989). This skyscraper was the precursor of numerous other complexes that "live twenty-four hours a day" and return people to the urban center. In drama and ambition, it recalls the Adler and Sullivan Auditorium Building (1889, see no. 3), which encompassed hotel, offices, and theater all in one. And perhaps it succeeds, as Graham himself suggests, because it projects "the gutsy masculine tradition of Chicago where structure is of the essence." —J.H.C.

Fig. 3. John Hancock Center, with Water Tower Place (see no. 81) at right

76. McClurg Court Center, 1971

333 East Ontario Street
Solomon Cordwell Buenz and Associates

Fig. 1. Solomon Cordwell Buenz and Associates. McClurg Court Center, 333 East Ontario Street, 1971

Fig. 2. L. R. Solomon and J. D. Cordwell and Associates. Sandburg Village, between Clark and LaSalle streets, from Division Street to North Avenue, 1960–72

Fig. 3. Solomon Cordwell Buenz and Associates. Presidential Towers, 555, 575, 605, and 625 West Madison Street, 1985–86

McClurg Court Center (fig. 1) is a variation on the "city-within-a-city" concept pioneered by architect Bertrand Goldberg in Marina City (1964–67, see no. 64), in which a self-sufficient, mixed-use apartment complex is located within the heart of downtown Chicago. McClurg Court Center was named for one of the streets on which the square-block complex is located. Its twin forty-six-story towers, which contain 1,028 apartments, were sited at a right angle to one another in order to provide each tower with the best views of the lake and city. To further maximize the views, the towers were constructed with curved, columnless glass corners. The rest of the complex contains a number of amenities that make it self-sufficient, including parking facilities, a grocery store, movie theaters, tennis courts, and a health club.

The city-within-a-city is an urban housing model in which the architects of McClurg Court Center specialized. Their predecessor firm, L. R. Solomon and J. D. Cordwell and Associates, designed Sandburg Village (1960–72, fig. 2), the huge complex of high-rise apartment buildings, town houses, and studios located on a landscaped site between North Clark

Sandburg Village, 1960–72

Bounded by Clark and LaSalle streets, from Division Street to North Avenue
L. R. Solomon and J. D. Cordwell and Associates

Presidential Towers, 1985–86

555, 575, 605, and 625 West Madison Street
Solomon Cordwell Buenz and Associates

and LaSalle streets and between Division Street and North Avenue. A central pedestrian mall links the various buildings. Named for Chicago poet Carl Sandburg, the complex was part of a vast urban-renewal effort called the Clark-LaSalle Redevelopment Project. At the time of construction, the complex was severely criticized, primarily because it displaced dozens of inner-city families who could no longer afford to live there. In addition, the wholesale land clearance diminished the diversity that gives the city its vitality, demolishing historic structures located in the area, such as Chicago's most famous German restaurant, The Red Star Inn (1899).

Another example of a self-sufficient apartment complex designed by Solomon Cordwell Buenz and Associates is Presidential Towers (1985–86, fig. 3), which consists of four identical, forty-nine-story apartment buildings arranged in a northeast-to-southwest diagonal covering two city blocks. The buildings contain a total of 2,346 apartments and are connected by an atrium and arcade bridges. The forty-foot-high skylit atrium acts as the main entrance and links an

80,000-square-foot shopping mall with a winter garden and pedestrian arcade; this in turn links the towers so one can travel from building to building without going out of doors. The towers are constructed of cast-in-place concrete, painted brown, and of tinted glass.

Like Sandburg Village, Presidential Towers received stiff criticism for its gigantic scale and its displacement of the urban poor, which has had tremendous impact on its immediate surroundings. As critic Catherine Ingraham wrote in the *Inland Architect* (November–December 1986): "Like blotting paper it is soaking up the area around it and leaving its signature everywhere. In both of these movements—the concentration inward and the radiation outward—Presidential Towers exerts an unavoidable influence on the West Loop and the city as a whole." The same criticism has been leveled against other large, mixed-used apartment complexes, which present unique problems to architects, developers, and urban planners faced with the task of redeveloping the city in such a way that its vitality is enhanced rather than diminished, and its varied populations are cared for. —P.A.S.

77. Standard Oil Building, 1974

Now Amoco Building
200 East Randolph Street
Edward Durell Stone and Perkins and Will
Addition: Perkins and Will (north entryway), 1985
Plaza redesign: Voy Madeyski, Architects, Ltd.,
Holabird and Root Architects, and
Jacobs/Ryan Landscape Architects, 1994

Fig. 1. *Edward Durell Stone, with Perkins and Will. Standard Oil Building, now Amoco Building, 200 East Randolph Street, 1974*

Fig. 2. *View of Standard Oil Building*

Constructed as the corporate headquarters for the Standard Oil Company of Indiana, the Amoco Building (fig. 1), as it is now known, is the tallest marble-clad structure in the world and one of the five tallest buildings ever constructed. The eighty-story building has a slender silhouette owing to its vertical bands of white marble, reentrant corners, and absence of horizontal features. Because the structure is sited on a block-square plaza located at the northern end of Grant Park, where it will never be obstructed by newer buildings, it will always maintain a prominent position in Chicago's skyline.

The square building (measuring 194-by-194 feet) was designed with an innovative "tubular" structural system in which closely spaced, V-shaped columns on the periphery of the building form a hollow tube that absorbs tremendous wind loads and provides the offices with column-free interiors and flush window walls. To link the building more directly with the surrounding area, in 1985 the firm of Perkins and Will designed two gatelike pavilions on the north side of the building, providing a new entryway for pedestrians and anchoring a new oval driveway for automobile traffic. The pavilions, each with a triple-gable glass roof, are sheathed in red and white polished granite.

When the Amoco Building was being constructed, it was roundly criticized. Many faulted its huge scale, for it dwarfs its nearest neighbor, the Prudential Building (see no. 59). More prophetically, many felt that cladding an eighty-story building in white Carrara marble, one of the most expensive and fragile materials in existence, was absurd and wasteful. It ignored all the structural developments of the last half century, when innovations in curtain-wall construction produced some of the finest architectural monuments of our time, including the Chicago Civic Center and the IBM Building (see nos. 65 and 74).

The use of marble cladding later proved questionable on practical grounds. In March 1988 Amoco Oil Company revealed that the marble slabs on the southeast face of the building were in danger of breaking loose and crashing to the pavement. Apparently because of Chicago's extreme temperatures and high winds, as well as the thinness of the marble cladding, the panels on the southeast corner below the forty-third floor had begun to bow and show signs of weakness. As a precautionary step, stainless-steel straps were bolted to the face of each marble panel to hold it in place. However, on March 6, 1989, Amoco announced plans to strip the tower of its marble skin and replace the panels with salt-and-pepper-colored granite from North Carolina. In order to cover the $60 to $80 million cost of recladding, Amoco instituted a lawsuit against the building's architects, construction company, general contractor, marble installer, and marble supplier.

Commenting on the architect's choice of materials, in an article in the *Chicago Tribune* (March 18, 1988), titled "Amoco Tower Faces Facelift," Michael Arndt stated: "No marble-clad building as tall as Amoco has ever been tested by high winds at great heights and thermal expansion and contraction over a period of years." In the same article, Shelby Pierce, Amoco's manager of engineering, remarked: "This could be one of the cases in which technology shot itself in the foot." —P.A.S.

78. William J. Campbell United States Courthouse Annex, 1973–75

Also the Metropolitan Correctional Center
71 West Van Buren Street
Harry Weese and Associates

A cell with a view is guaranteed each detainee held in this prison without bars. The twenty-seven-story Chicago Correctional Center (fig. 1) is noted for the excellence of its design and for the humanitarian guidelines that governed its planning. When dedicated on October 15, 1975, it was one of only three Metropolitan Correctional Centers in the United States, and its primary purpose is to house Federal detainees awaiting trial.

Skyscraper prisons are a rarity. Constructed of reinforced concrete, this structure is triangular in shape, and its cream-colored surface and decorative window pattern are visually arresting, the very antithesis of the fortress image presented by many prisons. It was praised by Paul Gapp, architecture critic for the *Chicago Tribune*, who described it as "an urban high-rise prison with a distinctive urban form," and found that "it exemplified the type of creative solution to urban problems for which Harry Weese is known."

The interior organization of the correctional center reflects an awareness of inmates' needs. The lower floors contain administrative and social services, and the upper sixteen house the detainees and prisoners in multipurpose core spaces, each serving forty-four persons. Within each core are an exercise area, lounge, kitchenette, dining and visitors' rooms, and forty-four individual cells. This modular prison-within-a-prison format allows for the separation of men from women, old from young, and first-time offenders from repeaters. The triangular form is also practical, permitting maximum perimeter area where the cells are placed and minimum corridor length, which is highly advantageous to the guards. Each cell contains a window that is five inches wide, the maximum width allowed without bars by the Bureau of Prisons's standards, which governed the program of the correctional center. The windowless corners contain stairwells and elevators, and the flat roof is the site of a walled and landscaped exercise yard for prisoner use.

The building is entered at the street level through a triangular space enclosed by floor-to-ceiling plate glass and outlined by the building's eight supporting columns painted a bright blue. The square-block site includes a seven-story parking garage and, at the skyscraper's base, a polygonal landscaped plaza, which softens this gritty corner of the Loop bordered by the Elevated structure. —J.H.C.

Fig. 1. Harry Weese and Associates. William J. Campbell United States Courthouse Annex (Metropolitan Correctional Center), 71 West Van Buren Street, 1973–75

79. Gateway Center, 1963–83

10–300 South Riverside Plaza
Bounded by Madison and Van Buren streets
along the Chicago River
Skidmore, Owings and Merrill

Fig. 1. Skidmore, Owings and Merrill. Gateway IV, 300 South Riverside Plaza, 1981–83. At right, MidAmerica Commodity Exchange, 1971

Fig. 2. Skidmore, Owings and Merrill. Gateways I and II, 10–120 South Riverside Plaza, 1963–68

Despite the plentiful supply of property on the west bank of the Chicago River, development of the area has proceeded fitfully, as the twenty-year Gateway Center project, designed by Skidmore, Owings and Merrill, amply testifies. Constructed over the railroad tracks leading to Union Station, it consists of several buildings that are relatively modest in scale, lacking the grandiosity of the monumental skyscrapers originally proposed for this air-rights project in 1961.

The first two Gateway buildings (fig. 2), designed by Bruce Graham and Robert Diamant, face the river immediately to the south of the Art Deco Daily News Building (see no. 52), now known as Riverside Plaza. Gateways I (1963–65) and II (1965–68) are identical, twenty-two-story rectangles of black steel and sea-green glass, executed as Miesian counterparts to the twin Butler Brothers Warehouse buildings on the north side of the Daily News. Those splendid examples of Chicago commercial architecture originated in the D. H. Burnham office and were ranked by Lewis Mumford in 1926 as two of the four "best modern buildings in Chicago." The northernmost, now called One Northwestern center, was the first completed, in 1913. Its twin, to the south, now known as River Center, was built in 1922 by the Burnham office, then under the direction of the founder's sons. Both warehouses were built of red brick with classically detailed cornices and imperial entrances. The two buildings have since been converted to offices and in 1997, One Northwestern Center was renamed Randolph Place and conversion to luxury housing began. Regrettably, the erection of the Morton International Building (see Epilogue) in 1990 obscured River Center's river view and destroyed the symmetry of what had been a harmonious riverfront from three different architectural periods.

Between 1984 and 1986 Gateways I and II benefited from an improved plaza and esplanade commissioned by Tishman Speyer Properties, which in the 1980s acquired the two buildings (and their successor, Gateway III) from the Equitable Life Assurance Society. The design for the river walk by Skidmore, Owings and Merrill included more varied foliage, outdoor seating, iron railings instead of a wall overlooking the river, and two belvederes extending seven and a half feet over the water's edge.

The structure of Gateway III (1970–71), also by Graham and Diamant, has no connection with its neighbors or its site. It is an ordinary, thirty-five-story commercial building with concrete bearing walls over a steel frame. Its undistinguished appearance is made all the more regrettable because its construction brought about the demolition of the great vaulted concourse of Union Station (1916–25).

The three-block river walk ends in front of the commuter entrance to Union Station. Cantilevered above it is a five-story box that is the home of the MidAmerica Commodity Exchange (fig. 1), easily identified by its single row of exterior X-braces. Its green-glass sides link it to Gateways I and II to the north and to the most recent building in the complex, Gateway IV, to the south.

Gateway IV (1981–83, fig. 1), located directly across Jackson Boulevard from Gateway III, is an example of Skidmore, Owings and Merrill's sleek brand of Postmodernism. This building, developed by Tishman Midwest Management and the Equitable Life Assurance Society, was designed by James DeStefano, Diamant, and Fred Lo of Skidmore, Owings and Merrill. They have retained the green glass of its predecessors, but here the skin is reflective, giving no hint of the underlying structure. Constructed about the same time as 333 Wacker Drive (see no. 93), Gateway IV, like that building, has a curved façade that echoes a bend in the river. Here the river view and outdoor walkway are reserved for patrons of a first-floor restaurant entered from a spacious lobby faced in green marble. On the west side of the building there is a generous public plaza that is slated to be replaced by a tall tower. —J.H.C.

80. Sears Tower, 1968–74

233 South Wacker Drive
Skidmore, Owings and Merrill
Addition: Skidmore, Owings and Merrill
(atrium on Wacker Drive), 1984–85

Fig. 1. Skidmore, Owings and Merrill. Sears Tower, 233 South Wacker Drive, 1968–74

Fig. 2. Nimmons and Fellows. Sears Merchandise Building, Arthington and Homan avenues, 1904

The Sears Tower (fig. 1), a 110-story, 1,454-foot-high structure, became the tallest building in the world upon its completion in 1974. It was the symbol of the vast merchandising empire of Sears, Roebuck and Company, which had been based in Chicago since 1893. The city's earliest Sears tower had been built in 1904, when Nimmons and Fellows designed the company's five-building headquarters at Arthington and Homan avenues. From its Merchandise Building rose a tower that was a then-imposing height of fourteen and a half stories (fig. 2). The complex, which still stands, was "very likely the largest single commission in the history of Chicago building up to that date," according to Carl W. Condit in *The Chicago School of Architecture* (1964). Similar towers were part of Nimmons's designs for numerous later Sears buildings, including the one attached to the Sears, Roebuck and Company pavilion at the 1933 Century of Progress Exposition in Chicago. But none, of course, was of the magnitude of the building that topped off at 110 stories on May 3, 1973, at South Wacker Drive and Adams Street.

In 1970, when construction began, the Sears Tower was the largest single building commission of the year. As Donald Katz reported in *The Big Store: Inside the Crisis and Revolution at Sears*, then-chairman Gordon Metcalf boasted to *Time* Magazine: "Being the largest retailer in the world, we thought we should have the largest headquarters in the world." Sears required a building to house 6,500 employees, consolidating offices scattered across the city. The company chose the site on Wacker Drive because of its proximity to commuter railroad stations, the Elevated, CTA bus routes, and expressways from the north south, and west. To acquire the necessary land, Sears even bought a section of Quincy Court, which bisected the site, and paid the city $2.7 million for it in 1969.

An interior design firm, Saphier, Lerner, Schindler, studied Sears's operations and analyzed its space needs, estimating future demands up to the year 2003. The prime requirements were enormous office floors to serve the Merchandise Group, which commanded armies of clerks, as well as income-producing space to lease to tenants. Based on the Saphier report, Sears first expected, and its architects, Skidmore, Owings and Merrill, first considered, two towers, or one gigantic cube. The architects' final proposal, however, was to build a single tower of unprecedented height, limited only by what the Federal Aviation Authority would permit, which was 1,450 (finally 1,454) feet.

The building could not have attained this record-breaking height without the participation of many members of the Skidmore, Owings and Merrill firm, led by partner in charge, William Dunlap, project managers Alan Hinklin and Neil Anderson, design partner Bruce Graham, studio head William Drake, and engineering partner Fazlur Khan. This

Fig. 3. *Sears Tower, view of atrium entrance on Wacker Drive, 1984–85*

extraordinary team adapted technology devised for earlier Skidmore buildings, in particular the John Hancock Center (1965–70, see no. 75).

The basis of the Sears structure is the bundled tube. A tubular building is one in which perimeter columns brace the building against the natural enemy of all skyscrapers, the wind. The taller the building, the faster the speed of the wind and the greater the wind stress, both in its horizontal force and downward thrust known as wind shear. According to Mario Salvadori in *Why Buildings Stand Up* (1980), "the Sears Tower must resist wind effects four times as large as those on the [fifty-five-story] Woolworth Building (Cass Gilbert, 1913)."

In the Sears Tower, nine contiguous tubes, in essence nine towers seventy-five-feet square, make up the fifty-story base of the building. Their frames are interlocked; thus each tube helps to support its neighbor. The density of the building decreases as tubes drop off, two at the fiftieth floor, two more at the sixty-sixth, and three at the ninetieth, leaving only two to reach the 110-story apex. The setbacks at those levels help to deflect the horizontal wind stress, and further wind bracing comes from "bundling" the tubes with belt trusses at the levels of the twenty-ninth, thirty-first, sixty-sixth, and ninetieth floors. The result of this structurally sound design is a setback profile of immense power on the skyline, visible from great distances as one approaches the city by land, air, or water. The plan was eminently practical as well, requiring only thirty-three pounds of steel per square foot instead of the usual for skyscrapers of fifty to sixty, thus making the tower economically feasible.

The steel columns of the building's frame channel the wind shear and gravity load down to bedrock caissons, where they are transferred to the soil, as *Engineering News Record* (August 26, 1971) explained: "All tower caissons are connected by a 5-foot-thick mat, the floor of the lowest of the three basement levels. The mat transfers the wind shear forces to the clay because the caissons only take vertical loads and not bending. On this mat the building's steel rises."

The steel rose in less than three years, in part owing to the use of prefabricated modules called "Christmas trees." These were two-story-high columns to which one or two fifteen-foot-wide spandrels had been welded off-site. Probably the largest construction crew in recent times erected the tower; over 2,000 members of the building trades were at work at the peak period, solving problems builders had never before faced, and finally sheathing the tower in black, anodized aluminum and bronze-tinted window glass.

The large office floors in the base building were originally occupied by Sears, and the upper floors were and still are rented, with the highest stories being the most desirable. "We worked ourselves up, starting on the 45th floor, then the 86th floor and two years ago, the highest you can go, the 99th floor," a representative of a law firm commented in a 1988 interview in the *Los Angeles Times*. Elevator service to deliver the building's approximately 12,000 occupants to appropriate destinations is of paramount importance. High-speed, double-deck express elevators, introduced by Harry Weese and Associates in the Time and Life Building (see no. 70), as well as sky lobbies for transfers to local elevators, are part of the system.

Although an extraordinary feat of architectural and engineering skill and an aesthetic triumph on the skyline, the Sears Tower has not been a complete success. Despite Khan's claim that he was seeking a humane skyscraper architecture, nothing is less so than the granite-paved plaza surrounding the base of the Tower. It is a wind-swept, cheerless space, virtually devoid of seating or landscaping and generally devoid of people. It is often chained off in winter because of the hazards of falling ice, but in any season there is danger from falling windows during high winds. Furthermore, at street level the entrances were almost invisible, making the building seem forbidding.

Ten years after the Tower opened, Skidmore was invited to provide a more gracious connection with the street. A four-story, vaulted atrium was added (fig. 3), welcoming arrivals on Wacker Drive. The atrium gave higher visibility to the motorized mobile by Alexander Calder (1974) one flight up and a more attractive entrance to the retail concourse one flight down. A major entrance was added on Jackson Boulevard, and more retail spaces and better traffic patterns were designed for the lower four floors in this $25 million renovation.

The bombshell that exploded in the financial world in 1991 when Sears announced it would leave its lofty tower and move its headquarters to the suburb of Schaumburg vastly increased the amount of empty office space in an already glutted market. Between 1992 and 1994, De Sefano and Partners repositioned the public spaces in a $70 million dollar project that made the building more attractive to prospective tenants. New monumental lobbies were added at both the Franklin Street and Wacker Drive entrances. A new Skydeck Pavilion on Jackson Boulevard separates tourists headed for the Skydeck from the building's commercial users. In 1994 new owners, Aldrich, Eastman, and Waltch, took possession of the building, but Sears Tower retains its name, if not the title of the world's tallest building. Officially surpassed in 1996 by twin towers in Kuala Lumpur, Malaysia, Sears still provided the highest occupied floors, a fact somewhat grudgingly conceded by the Council on Tall Buildings and Urban Habitat. Thus, as the millennium approaches, this monument to twentieth-century engineering is neither the Sears headquarters nor quite the world's tallest building, but it remains the dominant tower on Chicago's skyline. —J.H.C.

81. Water Tower Place, 1976

845 North Michigan Avenue
Loebl Schlossman Dart and Hackl,
with C. F. Murphy Associates

Fig. 1. Loebl Schlossman Dart and Hackl, with C. F. Murphy Associates. Water Tower Place, 845 North Michigan Avenue, 1976

Fig. 2. View of interior elevators in the eight-story vertical shopping mall of Water Tower Place

This spectacular multiuse project is the world's tallest reinforced-concrete building (fig. 1). Facing Michigan Avenue is a low-rise, twelve-story building containing a shopping mall with office spaces on top; it is attached to a sixty-two-story, 859-foot tower that houses the twenty-two-story, 400-room Ritz-Carlton Hotel and 260 luxury condominiums. The vertical shopping mall on the first seven floors is wrapped around a large atrium with flanking courts (fig. 2), bringing what was commonly considered a suburban form into an urban location. Although detractors were at first skeptical of this experiment—and critics such as Paul Gapp of the *Chicago Tribune* called it an "animated mausoleum"—it has been very successful with the public, attracting over twenty million visitors each year to the shopping center alone. The interiors of the mall, named for the nearby Old Chicago Water Tower of 1869, were designed by Warren Platner Associates of New Haven, Connecticut, with Edward Dart of Loebl Schlossman Dart and Hackl as head designer; C. F. Murphy Associates was in charge of certain engineering aspects of the building. Both the interior and exterior make extensive use of marble, gray on the outside and tan on the inside. But, because of the mall's need to maximize retail space, and, as Gapp puts it, cram "10 pounds of building into a 9-pound box," the walled, fortresslike exterior turns its back on the city and Michigan Avenue, making the Magnificent Mile "a little less magnificent." However, the practical success of this large multiuse project inspired a comparably scaled building up the road at 900 North Michigan Avenue (see no. 101), completed in 1989. —J.Z.

82. 444 North Michigan Avenue, 1976

Perkins and Will

Two North LaSalle Street, 1979

Perkins and Will

200 North LaSalle Street, 1984

Perkins and Will

Fig. 1. Perkins and Will. 444 North Michigan Avenue, 1976

Fig. 2. Perkins and Will. Two North LaSalle Street, 1979

Fig. 3. Perkins and Will. 200 North LaSalle Street, 1984

Between 1976 and 1984, a Chicago architectural firm, Perkins and Will, produced a series of downtown office towers: at 444 North Michigan Avenue, Two North LaSalle Street, and 200 North LaSalle Street. Functional, mainstream modern structures, all were constructed as speculative office buildings, designed for efficiency. During the same period, Perkins and Will was also collaborating with the New York firm of Kohn Pedersen Fox on the design of the elegant 333 Wacker Drive (1979–83, see no. 93) and 900 North Michigan Avenue (1983–89, see no. 101). And between 1984 and 1986, the firm would produce a distinctive tower at 123 North Wacker Drive (see no. 99), which responds to its historic context, incorporating forms from the great skyscrapers of the 1920s.

The thirty-five-story building at 444 North Michigan Avenue (fig. 1) is in close proximity to two renowned Chicago towers—the Wrigley Building (see no. 29) to the south and the Tribune Tower (see no. 32) across the street. The 444 North Michigan Avenue Building, designed with small and medium-sized companies in mind, was constructed of poured-

in-place concrete, both for reasons of economy and because in color and texture the material complements the Wrigley and Tribune towers. Floor-to-ceiling windows of gray-tinted glass provide the building's tenants with views of the Magnificent Mile. Originally, the building had an arcade at the base, but it has been filled in with a storefront and entrance that extend to the lot line. The street-level renovation, designed by Himmel Bonner Architects, was completed in 1988.

An office building that filled its entire site from its inception is Two North LaSalle Street (fig. 2). The twenty-seven-story structure departs from what has become a Chicago tradition—the office tower set within a plaza, as in the John Hancock Center, Sears Tower, and Madison Plaza (see nos. 75, 80, and 90). Instead, Two North LaSalle, located on the site of the old LaSalle Hotel, has been constructed up to its lot line and contains commercial space at ground level. As the architect and client intended, the building was designed to be efficient, uncomplicated, unsubtle, and utilitarian. As described in *Chicago since the Sears Tower* (1988):

The building encases a structural system of concrete columns and flat plate floor slabs with a skin of alternating ribbons of dark-gray, double-glazed windows and rigid, structural, aluminum-sandwich wall panels. Corners are rounded to emphasize the "continuity" of the skin.

A 1984 Perkins and Will building that has been described as "one of the last monuments to modernism" is 200 North LaSalle Street (fig. 3). Designed for the firm by Wojciech Madeyski, this thirty-story office building has a serrated profile that evenly locates ten corner offices around the perimeter of each floor, thereby allowing a greater number of small companies to lease these desirable spaces. Like its nearby contemporary at 203 North LaSalle, the tower at 200 North LaSalle features a green-glass curtain wall. The lower floors on the south side of the building feature four-story atriums, thus providing views of the lobby rather than the Elevated trains. —P.A.S.

83. Xerox Centre, 1977–80

55 West Monroe Street
C. F. Murphy Associates

The Xerox Centre is a reinforced-concrete structure clad in white-painted aluminum and reflective glass. More than forty stories high, the building was intended to be one of two curvilinear towers connected by a concave entrance in midblock on Monroe Street. As a composition, these rounded forms would have made an impressive statement. However, only one tower was executed, and the entrance was shifted to the base of that tower. According to some observers, the source of inspiration for this single, curved tower, located on a corner, may have been Louis Sullivan's Schlesinger and Mayer Store of 1904 (see no. 14). But this ignores the twin-tower phase in the structure's design. Moreover, the Xerox Centre's glass and enameled-aluminum planes, arranged in alternating horizontal bands, have more direct prototypes in Modern movement designs such as Erich Mendelsohn's Schocken Store of 1928 in Chemnitz (now Karl Marx Stadt, East Germany), the Luckhardt Brothers' proposal for remodeling the Alexanderplatz in Berlin from 1928, and, much closer to home, the designs of Chicago's Bowman Brothers of the 1930s, which were featured in the *International Exhibition of Modern Architecture* at The Museum of Modern Art, New York, in 1932.

Comparisons with Expressionist architect Mendelsohn may be especially apt, since the lobby's entrances, as well as the original bank counters (now demolished), are organized in Expressionist curves. Even the diagonal patterns of the lobby floor and of the roof (fig. 1) add to that design feeling. The Xerox building is in many ways an important transition in the career of its designer, the German-born Helmut Jahn. The building draws on the traditions of the Modern movement as he must have absorbed them in his training at the Illinois Institute of Technology and in his early work with C. F. Murphy Associates in the late 1960s and early 1970s; but more importantly, the Xerox Centre is the first in a long series of Jahn buildings to draw on the imagery of 1920s Modernism as a starting point for contextual references (see especially his Board of Trade addition, One South Wacker Drive, and the Northwestern Atrium Center, nos. 53, 84, and 87). His reflective-glass façade also acknowledges Chicago's own contributions to the history of Modernism in the 1950s and 1960s, in the nearby Inland Steel and First National Bank buildings (see nos. 60 and 72). —J.Z.

84. One South Wacker Drive, 1979–82

C. F. Murphy Associates

Fig. 1. C. F. Murphy Associates. One South Wacker Drive, 1979–82

Fig. 2. View of lobby interior of One South Wacker Drive

This forty-story, speculative office building went through a series of design stages, involving both curvilinear and trapezoidal forms, before achieving its completed shape. Evoking Art Deco imagery of the 1920s, One South Wacker Drive (fig. 1), designed by Helmut Jahn, features striped black masses, a ziggurat motif that recurs throughout its two tones of reflective glass, and setbacks at the entrance on Wacker Drive and adjacent arcade along Madison Street. Atrium spaces are housed in the angular transitions that mark the setbacks. A two-story-high lobby connects the Wacker Drive and Madison Street entrances, and in its polished stone walls and the patterning of its fluorescent lights, continues the Art Deco references (fig. 2).

In 1981, before the building was constructed, its designs were featured internationally in the exhibition *New Chicago Architecture* at the Castelvecchio Museum in Verona and published in the Deutsches Architekturmuseum's *Jahrbuch für Architektur*, in Frankfurt. Yet when the building was completed, it was said by architecture critic Paul Gapp in the *Chicago Tribune* (January 9, 1983) to be Helmut Jahn's "first sharply disappointing performance." Gapp found the reflective-glass exterior disorienting, and remarked on its poor detailing, especially in the joints; he called the Wacker Drive façade "simultaneously dull and intrusive, like a dolt at a party." Despite those harsh criticisms, the building holds its own within the city's skyline through its references to the 1920s cityscape. It is also, according to Gapp, an example of the variety of the architectural forms within Jahn's repertory relating to the 1920s and 1930s: "Jahn has so far shown no signs of mindlessly repeating himself. He is unpredictable." —J.Z.

85. Fulton House, 1979–81

345 North Canal Street
Harry Weese and Associates

200 South Wacker Drive, 1979–81

Harry Weese and Associates
Addition: Quincy Park, 1987–88

Fig. 3. Harry Weese and Associates. 200 South Wacker Drive, 1979–81

Over the years, Chicago architect Harry Weese has proposed numerous long-range plans for the preservation, improvement, and development of the banks of the Chicago River. An admirer of Daniel Burnham's Plan of Chicago and of his often repeated maxim: "Make no little plans; they have no magic to stir men's blood," Weese has been a contemporary maker of "big plans." His imaginative drawings, maps, diagrams, and models for the riverbank have been exhibited, published, and praised—and generally ignored. For more than thirty years after the completion of the Merchandise Mart in 1931 (see no. 56), river sites were largely overlooked by architects and developers alike. At the end of the 1970s, however, Weese himself began work on two riverfront projects.

Fulton House (fig. 1), at 345 North Canal Street, is one of the earliest examples in Chicago of both adaptive reuse and contemporary riverfront development. When completed in 1908, the former North American Cold Storage Warehouse (fig. 2) had been one of the first steel and concrete structures in downtown Chicago. A building with clean, classical lines, it was converted between 1979 and 1981 into a home for 104 loft-style condominiums and 20,000 square feet of commercial space. Because of its original cold-storage function, the walls of the shaft were ten to twelve inches thick and largely windowless. The greatest challenge for Weese and his associates was to punch openings through these walls for more than five hundred windows and sliding-glass doors without endangering the building's structural integrity. According to the architects, this was accomplished "by using a system of scaffolding and swing stages and puncturing the masonry from both the inside and outside." The original porthole windows below the cornice line now illuminate duplex apartments, while a row of Palladian windows enhances the block of penthouses added to the roof. A veteran sailor, Weese included moorings for private boats in front of Fulton House, and did the same when River Cottages, a group of townhouses immediately to the north, were completed in 1988.

The river itself affected the plan of 200 South Wacker Drive (fig. 3), a thirty-eight-story speculative office building designed for the John Buck Company between 1979 and 1981. The small site and its location at the angle of the river, plus the client's requirement that the typical floor plan be the maximum size, dictated the unusual configuration of the tower. It is an asymmetrical, four-sided polygon comprised of a right triangle joined at the hypotenuse with its mirror image. The triangular form undoubtedly was influenced by Weese's studies for the Metropolitan Correctional Center (see no. 78), completed in 1975. The office building, like the Correctional Center, is constructed of reinforced concrete, and its corners are rounded, recalling those of the Monadnock Building of 1891 (see no. 8). The sides of 200 South Wacker Drive are

sheathed in aluminum paneling painted white; for energy efficiency, only forty percent of the façade is glass. At the street level, a glass-roofed arcade overlooks the river and continues around the entire building. An exterior walkway flows into the lobby, where triangular walls frame the reception area and elevator foyers, echoing the building's basic shape.

The building's connection with the river was made complete in 1988. The John Buck Company commissioned Weese's firm to design a small park at the river's edge. Landscaped and connected to the street above by a wide staircase, the court was a gift to the city by the developer—another link in a growing chain of parks bordering the river.
—J.H.C.

Fig. 1. Murphy/Jahn, with Lester
B. Knight and Associates. State of
Illinois Center, 100 West
Randolph Street, 1979–85. In the
foreground, Monument with
Standing Beast, by Jean Dubuffet

86. State of Illinois Center, 1979–85

Now the James R. Thompson Center
Bounded by Randolph, LaSalle, East Lake, and Clark Streets
Murphy/Jahn, with Lester B. Knight and Associates

Fig. 2. State of Illinois Center, view from the east along Lake Street

Since completion in 1985, the State of Illinois Center (fig. 1) has been called many things. *Chicago Sun-Times* writer M. W. Newman dubbed it Chicago's "Eyeful Tower." Robert Benson, in the *Inland Architect* (March–April 1987), likened it to "a modern equivalent of the Baths of Caracalla," and the jury for the Chicago Chapter—American Institute of Architects Distinguished Building Award for 1986 called it the "Pantheon of Chicago." Guidebook writer Ira Bach referred to it as "our local Taj Mahal." *New York Times* architecture critic Paul Goldberger termed it "one part Pompidou Center, one part Piranesi, and one part kitsch 1950s revival," whereas Kevin Close of the *Washington Post* said that it was "one of the wildest and craziest new buildings this side of Katmandu." Illinois governor James R. Thompson, who commissioned the project, asserted that this would be the "building for the year 2000," but Paul Gapp of the *Chicago Tribune*, along with many other citizens, called it "Thompson's folly." Whatever one's opinion, it has been one of the most striking and controversial buildings constructed in Chicago, if not America, in the past century. Although the State of Illinois Center is not a true skyscraper in today's terms (the building is only seventeen stories high), a book about commercial and public buildings in Chicago would be incomplete without it.

The final design was one of eight by architect Helmut Jahn presented to the governor for review. In an interview with Lisa Goff in *Crain's Chicago Business* (June 6, 1988), Jahn noted that the governor "picked the low building," and, the designer concluded, "the building had to create this controversy, because it's a provocative design." He continued: "But eventually, the storm dies down, and the building remains [for serious investigation and analysis]"—which in fact has taken place in a few of the articles about the project.

The steel structure with its blue and salmon glass panels houses a cylindrical atrium, with floors of State offices ringing that core. The outside colors have been likened to those of 1950s cars. The boxy form of the exterior has been widely criticized, as have the salmon and gray masonry piers (fig. 1) that follow the Chicago street grid like a contemporary version of Stonehenge. According to *Progressive Architecture* (December 1985), these piers "were far more bewitching as a paper concept than as reality. There is something about a stone ruin supported by lollipop-stick columns that disappoints." Yet the piers also refer indirectly to the polychromed masonry of the Sherman Hotel, which stood on the site until it was demolished for the State building. Still the inclusion of the piers as sculptural elements tends to make the Jean Dubuffet plaza sculpture (1985) superfluous. The building's exterior, however, is very effective at its curved main entrance, where its clear-glass façade addresses the Chicago Civic Center (see no. 65) diagonally across the street: an image of the State making a gesture to City Government.

Figs. 3, 4. *Views of interior atrium in State of Illinois Center, looking into the well (below) and toward the roof (right)*

It is the effect of the interior, however, on which most critics agree. Just about everyone finds it spectacular!

To even the most jaded visitor, the view from the top floor down into the rotunda (fig. 3)—with its classically patterned marble and granite floor at the main concourse—is breathtaking. The 160-feet-in-diameter, cylindrical form and truncated roof (fig. 4) consciously derive from the tradition of large central spaces found in state capitols and county courthouses throughout America. And this rotunda specifically refers to the Henry Ives Cobb Federal Building (1905), which was demolished to make way for the Mies van der Rohe Federal Center (see no. 61) in the 1960s. Moreover, in the transparency of the glass at the entry corner and in the open spaces around the atrium, there were conscious references to the ideals of "openness" and "accessibility" in government, on the part of the governor as well as the architect. The firm of Vickrey-Ovresat-Awsumb Associates planned the offices, not only the commercial spaces on the first two floors but also those used by the State agencies and their three thousand employees who work higher up in the building. Although there were complaints about the noise from the atrium, Paul Gapp has aptly noted that the "steady background sound in and near the atrium will soften into the almost surflike rustle heard in the rotundas of countless capital buildings, monuments, and churches." But it is the climate control of those populated spaces that has proved most controversial.

An ice-making system was intended to generate 800,000 pounds of ice each night when electricity rates were lower than in daytime. The ice was supposed to chill water in the air-conditioning system during the day to keep the temperature at 78 degrees. But during the summer, temperatures in this glass greenhouse soared to 110 degrees. In the words of Lisa Goff in *Progressive Architecture* (July 1987): "Some frustrated employees working along the building's sun-drenched perimeter erected large, colorful beach umbrellas over their work stations in an effort to beat the heat. In the winter [when the temperature dropped to 60 degrees], they worked in gloves." This situation prompted State Attorney General Neil Hartigan to file a $20 million lawsuit against the architects and their associates. The system was repaired by Flack and Kurty, consulting engineers from New York, but the suit was still in litigation some years later. Paul Gapp's conclusion to his *Chicago Tribune* (August 10, 1986) review of the building went to the heart of the matter when he claimed that it "would be foolhardy" to predict what architectural historians will say about the building a half century or so from now, but "it seems likely that the great air cooling fiasco will be forgotten by then. Architecture is a science and a business as well as an art—but who talks about how the inside of the Pantheon still gets wet every time it rains?" —J.Z.

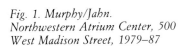

Fig. 1. Murphy/Jahn.
Northwestern Atrium Center, 500
West Madison Street, 1979–87

Fig. 2. View of the lobby of
Northwestern Atrium Center

87. Northwestern Atrium Center, 1979–87

Now Citicorp Center
500 West Madison Street
Murphy/Jahn

The Northwestern Atrium Center (fig. 1) is a thirty-seven-story office tower that rises over the terminal of the Chicago and North Western Railroad at the southwest corner of West Madison and Canal streets. Designed by Helmut Jahn of the architectural firm of Murphy/Jahn, the tower began life in a design for his 1980 addition to the Board of Trade Building (see no. 53) and relates to one of his preliminary sketches for One South Wacker Drive (see no. 84) of 1982. The design itself is a triple-curved form reminiscent of an inverted light fixture from the original Board of Trade, the Holabird and Root building of 1929–30. After the waterfalling curve was rejected as a scheme for One South Wacker, it was amplified and refined here to create a tripartite façade with vertical striations to emphasize the height of this streamlined office block. The tower rises over an atrium that is more than a hundred feet high (fig. 2) and leads to the Chicago and North Western commuter terminal. The steel and glass building in various tones of blue would seem to relate not only to modern skyscrapers of the 1920s and 1930s but also to streamlined transportation imagery of that period. One need only recall the curvilinear machined forms of trains such as the Burlington Zephyr (1934) and airplanes such as the Douglas DC–3 (1936) to realize this connection. This curvilinear motif appears in decorative elements throughout the interiors, including lobby furnishings such as the office directories and trash receptacles. The large concentric entry arch on Madison Street is an overt reference to doorways in works by Adler and Sullivan, such as their Chicago Stock Exchange (see

introduction, fig. 13) and their Transportation Building at the World's Columbian Exposition, both 1893 (and both demolished).

Despite the apparent success of the executed design, it created a controversy when it was first announced, in part because it precipitated the demolition of an enormous Baroque railroad terminal of 1906–11 designed by Frost and Granger. Although Jahn's design did not incorporate the main terminal, it preserved the train sheds, which are being restored by Harry Weese and Associates. The transition from the new space to the old is handled with barrel vaulting reminiscent of that used in Jahn's United Airlines Terminal at O'Hare International Airport in 1988. With the references to glass arcades of the nineteenth century, the atrium makes an appropriate entrance to the actual station. And, as architecture critic Paul Gapp noted in the *Chicago Tribune* (August 16, 1987), Jahn's spaces here are "grandly scaled partly in recollection of monumental old-time railroad stations such as the demolished North Western." Although Gapp praised the spaces, he criticized the building for an "appearance of insubstantiality" that is incompatible with its spatial grandeur. In his review Paul Goldberger, architecture critic of the *New York Times* (April 17, 1988), added that it is "slick" and "hard edged." Yet he praised the way in which a railroad station has been incorporated in a new office-building design, comparing it very favorably to New York's Pennsylvania Station project and concluding that Chicago "has not fared so badly at all." —J.Z.

88. 320 North Michigan Avenue, 1983

Booth Hansen and Associates

Designed by Laurence Booth, 320 North Michigan Avenue (fig. 1) is a slender, twenty-six-story building wedged into a narrow site. Its distinguished neighbors include the London Guarantee and Accident and the Carbide and Carbon buildings (see nos. 31 and 47), which helped establish the tradition of the richly ornamented 1920s skyscraper. In an admirable attempt to respond to the building's context, Booth's design incorporates such references to historic Chicago architecture as three-part Chicago windows, which compose the Michigan Avenue façade. Architecture critic M. W. Newman praised the building in the *Chicago Sun-Times* (September 5, 1982) for being so respectful of its context. He described it as "so modest that it is radical. Booth has set out to fit a decent building into an existing setting rather than ignore or upstage everything around, which is the usual flash-in-the-panic solution."

The façade features simplified moldings, curves, and column capitals that add depth, variety, and interest to what could have been a flat, mundane elevation (fig. 2). Owing to budget constraints, the moldings were made of poured concrete rather than sculpted stone. Nevertheless, the façade detailing may be counted successful on either an aesthetic or a practical level. According to architecture critic Paul Gapp, writing in the *Chicago Tribune* (March 13, 1983): "The effect of such meticulous shaping of elements is a building that proclaims quite appropriately the plasticity of concrete and whose detailing casts interesting shadows that hide weathering and other imperfections."

From the outset, 320 North Michigan Avenue was designed to accommodate a variety of uses: it has two levels of below-grade parking, retail space on the ground floor, offices on floors two through thirteen, and condominium apartments in the rest of the building. Because eventually it may well be hemmed in by taller structures on either side, its north and south façades were constructed as windowless walls of solid, prefabricated panels. However, many of the panels have since been punctured by windows, providing the tenants with dramatic vistas of the Magnificent Mile. At the top, the wall of Chicago windows gives way to three setbacks with outdoor terraces. A two-story penthouse with a gabled roof provides a dramatic terminus to the building.

In his *Sun-Times* article, Newman eloquently summed up 320 North Michigan's significance: "It deliberately picks up the thread of Chicago's building history, culture and long-range values. It is a work of clear structure, quietly decorative. That is Chicagoesque. Booth has used available present-day techniques to reclaim the past, freshen the present and set a direction for the future." —P.A.S.

89. The Associates Center, 1983–84

Now the Stone Container Building
150 North Michigan Avenue
A. Epstein and Sons

Since completion in 1984, The Associates Center (fig. 1) has become an icon in Chicago's skyline. Like the Sears Tower, the John Hancock Center, and Marina City, it is a building whose skyline profile is so distinctive and so highly visible that it has become emblazoned in the public memory (and on souvenirs) as a unique symbol of Chicago. What makes the skyscraper so distinctive is that it sits at a forty-five-degree angle to the street, has been bisected into two triangular towers, and has a sloping-glass roof that slices diagonally through the top ten floors. What makes the building so visible is that it is located on one of the most prominent sites in downtown Chicago, at the northwest corner of Michigan Avenue and Randolph Street, across from the northern edge of Grant Park, which assures it a wide-open vista in perpetuity. At night it is etched into the dark sky by a string of white lights that outline its diamond-shaped top.

The forty-one-story tower was commissioned as a speculative office building by Collins Tuttle and Company, a New York real-estate developer. When the Associates Commercial Corporation, a commercial finance company, leased five and a half floors, thereby becoming the major tenant, the building was named for the organization. A. Epstein and Sons, the sixty-six-year-old firm that designed the building, is best known for its cost-effective, speculative office towers, such as the Borg-Warner Building, at 200 South Michigan Avenue; 10 North Clark Street; and 300 South Wacker Drive. The Associates Center was planned by the firm's chief designer, architect Sheldon Schlegman.

Despite the high regard with which it is viewed by the public, The Associates Center has been severely criticized by architects and the press since its steel framework began to rise in 1983. Reasons for the controversy are threefold. First, critics find the building unresponsive to its context. The Associates Center replaced the John Crerar Library (1920), designed by Holabird and Roche, which complemented the Chicago Public Library Cultural Center across Randolph Street to the south. In scale and in style, the fourteen-story Crerar Library, with its classical masonry exterior, related well to the four-story, Beaux-Arts Public Library, whereas, critics allege, The Associates Center disregards its immediate context in its far larger scale and its curtain wall of reflective silver glass and paneling of white aluminum and stainless steel.

Second, rather than aligning with either Michigan Avenue or Randolph Street, The Associates Center is turned at a diagonal, so that it is on axis with Grant Park across the street. The shift in axis is significant: when the Plan of Chicago was adopted in 1909, Michigan Avenue was envisioned as a wide boulevard lined with classical buildings of uniform cornice height, all aligned with the city's rectangular street grid. Since 1909, every other building constructed on Michigan Avenue has respected that planning

principle, and the result is a wall of buildings facing Grant Park and providing a view that is magnificent and unique in all the world. By shifting The Associates Center on an angle to the grid, the continuity of that wall of buildings is disrupted. David Greenspan, writing in the *Inland Architect* (May–June 1984), summed up critical opinion by describing the building as "an aggressive intruder." However, according to Paul Gapp, in the *Chicago Tribune* (January 1, 1984), architect Schlegman "regarded the site as a portal to the Loop and thus appropriate for a visually strong building instead of a neutral one."

Third, the exterior design, consisting of forty-one floors of horizontal ribbon windows and a top that has been shaved off at a sharp angle, has been the subject of the stiffest criticism. In the *Inland Architect*, Greenspan quoted architecture critic Nory Miller, who found the building "top heavy by virtue of what's *not* there," with which opinion the architect would agree, since the proportion of the slice would have been significantly altered had the five additional floors of the original plans been constructed. From a functional standpoint, the bisecting of the building into two triangular towers provides six corner offices on most floors, which is important in a speculative office building. Also, the sloping top provides the two-story atrium offices on the top ten floors with unobstructed views of Grant Park and Lake Michigan. Paul Gapp's article in the *Chicago Tribune* gave an aesthetic rationale for those two design characteristics: they express the building's closeness to the lake—hence the sail-like appearance of the structure's top planes—and they provide an ever-changing view to passersby. —P.A.S.

90. Madison Plaza, 1980–83

200 West Madison Street
Skidmore, Owings and Merrill

The dramatic, sawtooth front elevation of Madison Plaza (fig. 1), a forty-five-story tower located at the northwest corner of Madison and Wells streets, represents a departure for Skidmore, Owings and Merrill from its gridded forms of the 1970s. The skyscraper reflects, as well, the energy crisis of the 1980s. Foregoing the all-glass skin, the architects faced sixty percent of the exterior with polished Luna Pearl granite, alternating it with bands of silver reflective glass framed in aluminum, which together form an energy-efficient curtain wall whose glittering surface provides a striking contrast to the Elevated train structure running along Wells on the building's east side.

The inventive entrance elevation (fig. 2) of Madison Plaza, designed by Bruce Graham with Chris Cedargreen as studio head (the Skidmore team also included Robert Diamant as partner in charge and William Larson as project manager), effectively sliced off a corner of the building, allowing for the siting of a plaza in front of it. And the façade's accordion fold provided the developer with eight corner offices per floor instead of the usual four. The structure of Madison Plaza is composed of a variation on the Skidmore, Owings and Merrill tube system; an exterior framed tube is joined to a full-height braced steel core.

Located in the plaza is the sculpture *Dawn Shadows*, by American artist Louise Nevelson, who officiated at its unveiling in May 1983. Upon receiving the commission she had visited the site and immediately altered her design, increasing the height of the sculpture so that it would be plainly visible from the passing trains. Promised at the time of construction was a glass-enclosed bridge linking the building with the Elevated, but that did not materialize.

The developer, Miglin-Beitler, also planned to build a second Madison Plaza on the southwest corner of Madison and Wells, envisioning the towers as forming a gateway to the new "West Loop," beyond the original boundaries formed by the circular path of the Elevated. The gateway concept was abandoned by the developer in 1989, and instead he announced plans to construct what was called the tallest building in the world, the Miglin-Beitler Tower, designed by Cesar Pelli (see Epilogue). —J.H.C.

91. Chicago Mercantile Exchange Center, 1983–87

10 and 30 South Wacker Drive
Fujikawa Johnson and Associates

After Chicago architect Alfred S. Alschuler designed and built the London Guarantee and Accident Building (see no. 31), he received two commissions for tall office buildings. The first, dating from 1926, was a Gothic Revival high rise at 180 North Michigan Avenue, which is still standing, although its entrance and lobby have been altered. The other is the more impressive Chicago Mercantile Exchange, at 110 North Franklin Street, which was begun in 1927 and finished within a year. That elaborately detailed, classical building of seventeen stories in height housed the successor to the Old Chicago Butter-and-Egg Board—hence the relief sculptures of cows and chickens on its façade. Although the Exchange cost some $3 million to build, trading in 1928, the year of its completion, amounted to more than $500 million—a far cry from Butter-and-Egg Board transactions of less than a century before, in 1829, when a Chicago trader would have paid $.24 a pound for ten pounds of butter and $.12½ for a dozen eggs.

In 1981, a new Chicago Mercantile Exchange Center (fig. 1) was completed, attesting to the growth of Chicago as an international center for the trade of stocks, securities, commodities futures, and a great variety of other speculative instruments. The new building appeared to be a straightforward pair of forty-story towers (one on Monroe Street, the other on Madison), connected by a low, eleven-story building. However, the complex structure was actually made possible by innovative engineering solutions. The developers, Metropolitan Structures and JMB Realty Corporation, gave the architects and engineers several restrictions to work with: the complex not only had to include the two forty-story towers, but also had to contain 30,000 square feet of office space per floor; further, two clear-span trading floors were required, one 40,000 square feet in area and the other, to be held in reserve for expansion, some 30,000 square feet in all. And in order to make the project financially feasible, construction of the second tower had to take place after the first tower was leased.

Ordinarily, these restrictions would not have posed special problems, because three independently supported but connected buildings could have been constructed. But since the developers wanted a building whose footprint was 100,000 square feet while the river site measured only 83,000, a substantial area of the tower floors had to be cantilevered over the trading rooms in order to provide the required space. This logical, even simple, solution demanded new and creative engineering systems: because the trading rooms have no interior columns to support the weight of the towers above, it was necessary to divert that weight around the open trading floors and shift it to the ground by means of a system of thickened walls and wide columns. Huge steel trusses support the ceilings of the trading rooms. This solution, devised by Alfred Benesch and Company, an engineering firm, also made

it possible to build the Madison Street tower four years after its Monroe Street twin had been filled with tenants.

However, if no other compensations had been made, this rather unusual thickened wall system would have caused the towers to tilt under their own weight. The solution is that each tower is slightly arched. In an article in the *Chicago Tribune* (March 25, 1984), architecture critic Paul Gapp described the carefully calculated process of allowing the weight of each tower to straighten itself:

From ground level to the 21st story, each floor was poured so that it protruded an eighth of an inch farther outward than the floor below. Above the 21st story the pattern was reversed and the floors were poured in tiny inward setbacks. Exactly as figured, the curve created to prevent a tilt straightened itself as the weight shifted. The tower is absolutely plumb.

The exterior of the building is rather conservative and reveals nothing of the complex structural system within. The carnelian-red granite skin, which the developers requested, is an unexpected stylistic departure for Mies disciples Joseph Fujikawa and Gerald Johnson, who produced such steel and glass classics as the 1970 One Illinois Center (see no. 73). Each of the two towers contains 1.1 million square feet of office space, most of it leased to firms with businesses related to the Mercantile Exchange. The corners of the towers are serrated, providing sixteen corner offices per floor. The lobby, clad in granite, features an eight-story escalator well. The public promenade along the Chicago River reflects contemporary concern for developing the waterfront as a major recreational resource. However, the two trading floors of the Chicago Mercantile Exchange are the building's most impressive features. The 40,000-square-foot trading room includes twenty-one trading pits, none of which is obstructed by interior support columns. The second trading room, 30,000 square feet in area and located directly above, is likewise column-free.

Commenting on the importance of the Mercantile Exchange, critic Paul Gapp wrote in the *Chicago Tribune*:

Because it makes no flamboyant design statement, the CMEC clearly comes off as an engineering and construction triumph before all else. Yet it is also a signal from Fujikawa Johnson that modernism is not dead in Chicago any more than it is in New York, São Paolo or Hong Kong. Even though it has lost ground to other philosophies of form-giving, the International Style is still international. —P.A.S.

92. One Magnificent Mile, 1978–83

940–80 North Michigan Avenue
Skidmore, Owings and Merrill

Fig. 1. Skidmore, Owings and Merrill. One Magnificent Mile, 940–80 North Michigan Avenue, 1978–83. The John Hancock Center (see no. 75) is at left

Fig. 2. Site plan for One Magnificent Mile, c. 1980

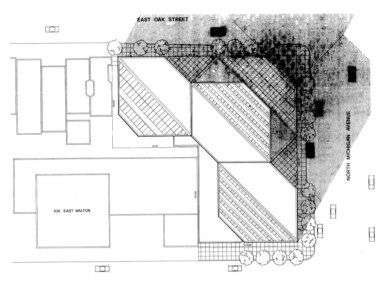

Some years ago, Michigan Avenue north of the bridge was named the Magnificent Mile by an optimistic real-estate developer. In the early 1980s, before this multiuse building at 940–80 North Michigan Avenue was finished, one of the prospective retail tenants began to call it "One Magnificent Mile," signifying its position at the end—or the beginning—of the mile of condominium, shopping, and office towers that line Michigan Avenue from the Chicago River to Oak Street, and the name stuck.

The cramped, angular site and the requirement of its developer, the Levy Organization, for a mixed-use structure led to the decision by Skidmore, Owings and Merrill's Bruce Graham and Fazlur Khan, the design and engineering partners on the project, to use again the bundled-tube concept they exploited in the Sears Tower (see no. 80). In this case, instead of nine tubes they used three, which rise twenty-one, forty-nine, and fifty-seven stories respectively (fig. 1). The towers, faced in pink granite, break no height records, but they are unusual in other respects. They are made of reinforced concrete, not steel, and are hexagonal, not square. As Cynthia Davidson-Powers noted in the *Inland Architect* (May–June 1984): "The height of the building was determined by the maximum loading on hard pan caissons. The casting of afternoon shadows on the beach, which SOM studied with a computer, determined the placement of the tallest tube."

The importance and the difficulties of the site led to other design decisions: for example, to place a bustlelike entryway at the base of the central tower. On line with the corner (fig. 2), it offers a clearly visible entrance and a low-scale presence at street level that is not overpowering. The choice of granite for the exterior was made to complement the limestone façade of the Drake Hotel (see no. 28) across Michigan Avenue. Clear-glass shop windows are used at street level, but on the shaft a variety of window shapes denotes the building's interior uses: commercial spaces in the lower three floors, offices in the midsection, and luxury condominiums on the upper floors.

The towers boast some of the most spectacular views in the city, but whether One Magnificent Mile can hold its own against the pioneer multiuse building in this prestigious area, the John Hancock Center (see no. 75), also designed by Graham and Khan, remains to be seen. Powers's statement in *Inland Architect* sums up a consensus: "The real symbol of North Michigan, the black monolith of the Hancock Tower, . . . remains unsurpassed." —J.H.C.

93. 333 Wacker Drive, 1979–83

333 West Wacker Drive
Kohn Pedersen Fox
Associate architects: Perkins and Will

Fig. 1. Kohn Pedersen Fox, with Perkins and Will. 333 Wacker Drive, 1979–83. The Elevated track is at right

Fig. 2. View of 333 Wacker Drive from the Chicago River

Fig. 3. Typical floor plan

The problematic configuration of many sites along Wacker Drive, which follows the course of the Chicago River, is nowhere more challenging than at 333 West Wacker, where the river curves sharply to the south. There, on a triangular lot, this elegant, thirty-six-story skyscraper, emblematic of the river in the spherical shape and water-green tint of its reflective glass skin, was completed in 1983. Yet 333 Wacker Drive (figs. 1, 2), so uniquely suited to its Chicago site, was designed by a New York architect, William Pedersen (born 1938) of Kohn Pedersen Fox; his senior designer was Alexander Ward.

The New York firm is noted for its careful study of context, and this structure's relationship to the city extends beyond the river. Following the concept of the skyscraper as originated by Louis Sullivan and other architects of the nineteenth-century Chicago School, this high rise contains the tripartite form of base, shaft, and capital. The three-story marble and granite base is of great significance: distinctive arcades at either end link the river with the historic Loop itself and are framed by octagonal columns of black granite and green marble, trimmed in stainless steel, which echo the octagonal towers of the Merchandise Mart (see no. 56) across the river. According to Pedersen, as quoted in the *Inland Architect* (May–June 1984): "The Vermont marble and polished granite at the base of 333 are totally different in texture than that sheer glass wall, and much richer in detailing. We hoped the base would echo the robustness of the Rookery, and the end arcades [would] relate to the Merchandise Mart."

As a deliberate visual contrast to the vertical lines of the Mart, 333 Wacker Drive stresses its own horizontality. The mullions almost disappear, their aluminum surfaces tinted a soft green to match the glass skin. Pedersen said of this aspect of the design (*Progressive Architecture*, October 1983): "With the bowed face and the acute corners, the front looks as if it's stretched. To accentuate that stretching, we developed the horizontal bullnoses at six-foot intervals to give a sense of that horizontal gripping of the building."

Just as the shapes of base and shaft differ, so do the building's two faces. The taut curve of the river wall defies the city's grid, but the Loop façade, a truncated triangle (fig. 3), follows the line of the street. The entrance here, centered on the façade as exactly as any Beaux-Arts doorway, is approached by a sweeping, semicircular flight of stairs from the corner of Lake and Franklin streets. The curving motif as repeated in the lobby (fig. 5) spatially unites exterior and interior, and the marble and stainless-steel fixtures give this space visual unity with the arcades. Not a taut skin, the Loop façade is notched in the center, at the ends, and repeatedly at the top. A penthouse rises out of the end notches, set back from the building's curve, forming a "signature on the sky— its skyscraper image," as Pedersen put it in the *Inland Architect*.

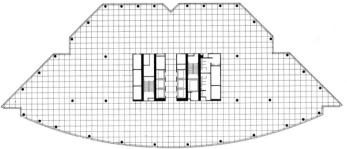

Fig. 4. Detail of street level
arcade of 333 Wacker Drive

Fig. 5. Interior detail of Lake
Street lobby

An unobstructed view of the building obtains from Wacker Drive, but the Elevated is its neighbor on Lake Street (fig. 1). To diminish this disadvantage, the architects placed the mechanical facilities on the third floor at the level of the Elevated and encased the air vents within decorative, grilled portholes (fig. 4), turning a liability into an asset. These medallions recall the porthole windows of a famous nearby building that bears the same door number, 333 North Michigan Avenue (see no. 41). Despite the contextuality of 333 Wacker Drive, one aspect of the building is atypical of Chicago: it does not reveal its structure. Invisible behind the reflective-glass curtain wall are the diagonal steel cross braces that withstand wind stress and give the building its stability.

Kohn Pedersen Fox is a relatively new firm, dating only from 1976, and this thirty-six-story skyscraper was its first big building, representing a gamble for the developer, Urban Investment and Development Corporation, which commissioned the tower. But the bigger gamble for this company was the location, as problematic as the site's configuration. No one considered Wacker Drive part of the Loop in the late 1970s, and surrounding buildings were old, many of them in disrepair. And since 333 Wacker Drive was completed in the middle of a recession, the financial investment in this peripheral area did not pay off at once. *Crain's Chicago Business* (June 4, 1984) quoted a prospective tenant (who had opted for another location): "I couldn't get a taxi. And when I couldn't get a taxi, I thought 'Where am I going to have lunch?' " A second problem was and is the building's form. The structural steel is not hidden on the interior: it intrudes into office spaces that also have odd corners because of the building's curving shape.

As architecture, however, the gamble paid off handsomely in critical reviews and awards. The building's very distinction stimulated the revival of Wacker Drive; and at the beginning of the 1990s, the mirror glass of 333 Wacker Drive reflected new construction and the renovation of older buildings on both sides of the Chicago River, some influenced by this powerful design. Most tenants of 333 Wacker capitalized on the odd floor plan (fig. 3) through good interior design.

The American Institute of Architects gave the building an award in 1984, stressing its "sculptural elegance." David Greenspan, writing in the *Inland Architect* (May–June 1983), made a more telling comment:

333 Wacker Drive is . . . a building of our time. It is a *modern* building. But . . . its design challenge[s] the reductivist impulses of Modernism. To borrow a political cliché from the late '60s, it is working for change from within the system, rather than dropping out and joining the Postmodernists.

It is a building of our time, and probably one that is timeless as well. —J.H.C.

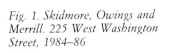

Fig. 1. Skidmore, Owings and Merrill. 225 West Washington Street, 1984–86

Fig. 2. Skidmore, Owings and Merrill. 303 West Madison Street, 1985–88

94. 225 West Washington Street, 1984–86

Skidmore, Owings and Merrill

303 West Madison Street, 1985–88

Skidmore, Owings and Merrill

Skidmore, Owings and Merrill, which in 1957 brought Modernism to the Loop with the Inland Steel Building (see no. 60) and worked within the Modernist tradition for a quarter of a century, bent to the winds of change in the early 1980s. According to architecture critic Paul Goldberger, writing in *Chicago History* (Winter 1983–84), it had been the fate of Modernist architecture to have appealed to a set of values (those of the corporation) other than the architect's own; moreover, "it looked so easy to make glass boxes, it seemed anyone could do so, and many did." The omnipresent glass boxes by this firm and others, although often characterized by detailing of high quality, began to pall on the public, clients, and architects alike. In the late 1970s, there appeared in the Skidmore, Owings and Merrill studios new designers with inclinations toward Postmodernism, Poststructuralism, and even Mannerism—and they helped form, in *Chicago Tribune* critic Paul Gapp's all-encompassing term, "the New Mainstream."

The skyscrapers 225 West Washington (fig. 1) and 303 West Madison (fig. 2), modest in scale at, respectively, twenty-eight and twenty-six stories high, are examples of work by the firm's new generation. Both buildings include decoration and historical reference, two architectural expressions particularly abhorrent to Modernist practitioners and notably absent from such Skidmore, Owings and Merrill classics of the 1950s and 1960s as Inland Steel, the Harris Trust and Savings Bank additions, the Brunswick and Equitable buildings, and the Sears Tower (see nos. 60, 62, 66, 67, and 80).

When Steven Fifield, developer of 225 West Washington, announced plans for the building, he was quoted in the *Chicago Sun-Times* as saying: "It will have traditional design elements with a pitched roof, arches and other classic features. We'll use granite and have bay windows like Three First National Plaza and One Financial Place [see nos. 72 and 95]," both by Skidmore, Owings and Merrill. Another model for Fifield, according to the *Inland Architect* (May–June 1988), was the arched entrance to the Neiman Marcus store in the new Olympia Centre (see no. 96). His admiration for this detail led Fifield to request Adrian Smith, the Olympia tower's designer, as his architect; John Burcher was the studio head.

The completed 225 West Washington has all the features Fifield requested, as well as a richness of color that refers to such nineteenth-century Chicago School office blocks as the Rookery and Marquette buildings (see nos. 2 and 11). Precast concrete spandrels, lightly sand-blasted to simulate limestone, are framed by narrow, red-granite inserts, and the two-story base is polished red and black granite. Both criticized and admired are the two versions of the Chicago window: oriel windows form the corners, giving offices in those important locations wide expanses of glass, as requested by Fifield, while punched Chicago windows form the bays.

*Fig. 3. View of entrance to 303
West Madison Street*

*Fig. 4. Interior view of the lobby
of 225 West Washington Street*

Joseph Gonzalez, another member of the Skidmore, Owings and Merrill firm's second generation, was studio head for 303 West Madison, with Bruce Graham as design partner. This building, commissioned by the developer Jaymount Properties, backs up to Helmut Jahn's One South Wacker Drive (see no. 84). Instead of taking a cue from Jahn, Gonzalez appeared to be working in counterpoint to him. Jahn's building has a glittering glass curtain wall; Gonzalez used granite and punched windows. Jahn's building is removed from the street, set back at its Wacker Drive entrance and raised above it on Madison; Gonzalez built out to the lot line and included strong entrances on both Franklin and Madison streets. In addition to making reference to the Chicago School office buildings, Gonzalez alluded to Frank Lloyd Wright and the Prairie School through his use of geometric-patterned stained glass to frame the Franklin Street entrance (fig. 3).

These two speculative office buildings by Skidmore, Owings and Merrill add color and variety to the cityscape. They are human in scale, a welcome contrast to the giantism of other projects on Franklin, one of the main paths of development in the city's new frontier, the West Loop. —J.H.C.

95. One Financial Place, Chicago Board Options Exchange, and Midwest Stock Exchange, 1981–85

400–40 South LaSalle Street
Skidmore, Owings and Merrill
Addition: Skidmore, Owings and Merrill
(sky bridge over Van Buren Street), 1987

Fig. 1. Skidmore, Owings and Merrill. One Financial Place (center), Chicago Board Options Exchange (left), and Midwest Stock Exchange (right), 400–40 South LaSalle Street, 1981–85

Fig. 2. View of the plaza of One Financial Place, with San Marco II *(1985) by Ludovico de Luigi*

Gateway buildings have had a place in the Chicago imagination since the 1920s, when the completion of the Wrigley Building and the Chicago Tribune Tower (see nos. 29 and 32) flanking Michigan Avenue signaled the city's development to the north. In the mid-1980s, the concept again came into focus with the building of One Financial Place (fig. 1), a complex on LaSalle Street between Van Buren Street and Congress Parkway. It is a new expression of an idea from the 1909 Plan of Chicago: Daniel Burnham and Edward Bennett's vision of Congress as the east-west axis of the center city. According to the plan, the artery was to connect the lakefront and all its possibilities for recreational pleasures with the densely populated West Side. U.S. Equities Realty, the developer of One Financial Place, envisioned this tower and its attendant exchanges as the first step in the belated realization of that scheme, also a key recommendation of the Chicago Central Area Plan of 1983.

The complex is aptly named. The forty-story, steel-frame office tower (1981–85) is centered between the ten-story building of the Chicago Board Options Exchange (1981–83), bordering Van Buren Street to the north, and the five-story trading facility of the Midwest Stock Exchange (1981–85), built over Congress Parkway to the south. Interior passages link the three buildings, which are visually tied by the Imperial Red granite cladding the tower and the bases of the two exchanges. A glass-enclosed fourth-floor bridge over Van Buren Street connects the Options Exchange with the Board of Trade (see no. 53) and thus with the traditional financial world of LaSalle Street. The new complex replaces the LaSalle Street railroad station of 1903 (demolished in 1982), by Frost and Granger; a minimalist substitute was provided for Rock Island Line commuters, who daily head for their trains through a covered passage in the building bridging Congress Parkway.

The rippling bays of the One Financial Place tower are reminiscent of those in Chicago School buildings such as the Monadnock of 1891 (see no. 8); but at the request of the builder, the granite-clad tower is more closely related to Skidmore, Owings and Merrill's Three First National Plaza of 1981, which also presents a profile of varying heights to the skyline. The Skidmore design team for the complex included Bruce Graham, design partner, and Alan Bombick, studio head, with Robert A. Hutchins as partner in charge and Don Ohlson as project manager. Last minute, very expensive additions to the Midwest Stock Exchange building spanning Congress were the double arches, dramatic forms that stress the importance of the street and also salute the Chicago School, in particular Louis Sullivan and the entryway of his famous Stock Exchange Building of 1894 (demolished in 1972).

In the Miesian idiom, the buildings are separate from but defined by a block-long plaza (constructed over a large underground parking lot). Facing due west, this grand, open space is expressly designed for residents of the rapidly expanding South Loop; a former industrial neighborhood, the area south of Van Buren and east of Dearborn is now a mixture of new office buildings, apartment towers, residential lofts, and shops. Richly varied plantings, numerous places to sit, and a fountain and reflecting pool (surrounding Ludovico de Luigi's sculpture in tribute to one of the four horses of San Marco in Venice, fig. 2), make this the most attractive new urban space since the 1972 plaza of the First National Bank Building (see no. 72). The landscape design for One Financial Place earned Skidmore, Owings and Merrill an award for excellence from the American Institute of Landscape Architects in 1987.

In the belief that Congress Parkway will gain in importance as the South Loop develops, U.S. Equities has expressed the intention of completing the gateway concept by building Two Financial Place on another former railroad property immediately to the south of Congress—and of extending the plaza, as well. If this project goes forward and Congress itself becomes a landscaped parkway as recommended in both the Chicago Plan of 1909 and the 1983 Central Area Plan, perhaps the thoroughfare truly will become the city's prime east-west axis, suitably guarded by two gateway towers.
—J.H.C.

96. Olympia Centre, 1978–86

737 North Michigan Avenue (Neiman Marcus)
161 East Chicago Avenue (office and residential tower)
Skidmore, Owings and Merrill

Fig. 1. Skidmore, Owings and Merrill. Olympia Centre, 161 East Chicago Avenue, 1978–86

Fig. 2. View of the arched entrance to Neiman Marcus Department Store, 737 North Michigan Avenue

Chicago shoppers may have been elated in the early 1970s when rumors began to circulate that Neiman Marcus, the fashionable Dallas store, was opening a Chicago outpost on Michigan Avenue, but they had a long wait. The developer of the proposed site changed, financial problems arose, and designs were altered many times before the store's grand opening on November 6, 1983.

Olympia Centre is the third mixed-use complex designed by Skidmore, Owings and Merrill for the upper end of Michigan Avenue; completed in 1986, it follows the John Hancock Center of 1970 and One Magnificent Mile of 1983 (see nos. 75 and 92). The complex is built on an L-shaped site. The four-story retail area, occupied only by Neiman Marcus, fronts on Michigan Avenue, at the corner of Superior Street (on an east-west axis), and is joined to a sixty-three-story office and apartment tower, which extends northward to Chicago Avenue where its main entrance and lobby are located (fig. 1). Following the Hancock's example, the Olympia's tower tapers as it rises, narrowing on the north and south sides between the eighth and thirty-fourth floors. As in the Hancock, the inward slope serves to reduce the building's mass and to provide greater floor space for offices on the lower levels and more congenial, compact spaces for residences on the floors above.

The dramatic, two-story arched entrance of Neiman Marcus (fig. 2) is the design of Adrian Smith, Skidmore, Owings and Merrill's design partner on the project, in collaboration with Diane Legge, studio head (Robert Diamant was partner in charge, and Neil Anderson was project manager). Rejected by the store's management in its original, larger scale, the arch has in time become a symbol of the store.

Although Smith's associations in choosing the arch are historical, they go back not to Roman architecture but to the Chicago buildings of H. H. Richardson and Louis Sullivan (see introduction, figs. 13 and 14). Although not structural in any sense, the Neiman Marcus arch is carefully integrated into the design by a glass slit—some describe it as a keystone—that runs up the façade to the roofline, where it meets the arched skylight, which perhaps alludes to the great glass galleries of the nineteenth century. Another historical allusion exists in the low scale of the Neiman Marcus store, recalling that of Michigan Avenue in the 1920s.

There may be a historical allusion as well in the building's framing. Neiman Marcus has a conventional steel frame, and the tower is a reinforced-concrete tube; both are sheathed in alternating layers of flamed and polished granite, the former roughening the surface and the latter bringing it to a shiny smoothness. The rusticated base of the tower relates it to the 1920s limestone and red-brick apartment buildings nearby, as well as to such landmark Chicago School buildings as the Rookery (see no. 2).

At the suggestion of the contractor Paschen-Newburg Joint Venture—and the urging of the developer, the Toronto firm of Olympia and York—the building cut construction time by engaging in what has been called the "up-down" method, which had been used in Europe but never before in the United States for a building of this scale. As described in the *Guarantor* (March–April 1984), the system works like this: "The builders dug down just one level and poured a concrete slab. From that base they began building the superstructure while at the same time continuing to excavate and pour the lower levels underneath." Expedited by this system, Olympia Centre—under discussion since 1969, in the design phase from 1978, and under construction since July 1, 1981—was finally topped off and completed in late 1986. —J.H.C.

97. 203 North LaSalle Street, 1982–85

Skidmore, Owings and Merrill
Addition: Skidmore, Owings and Merrill
(underground passage to CTA subway station), 1989

This twenty-seven-story building is a rare specimen: a parking garage topped by an office tower. It was the first building completed in the North Loop Redevelopment project, an urban-renewal plan announced by the city of Chicago in 1973. Almost a decade of controversy followed; but in September 1981, the city accepted the joint-venture bid of developer Richard Stein and of Myron Warshauer of the Standard Parking Corporation for this mixed-use building. They commissioned Skidmore, Owings and Merrill to design it, and the team of Adrian Smith and Peter Ellis produced a lively structure that takes a cue for its exterior design from the State of Illinois Center (1985, see no. 86), its neighbor to the south. The very complex program of 203 North LaSalle (fig. 1) resulted in a building described by David Greenspan of the *Inland Architect* (November–December 1986) as "a paradigm of late-20th-century mannerism."

Horizontal bands of concrete and of reflective and tinted glass ring the structure, concealing ten levels of parked cars above ground (two underground levels serve rental-car agencies). Slotted insets in the façade read as decoration but actually ventilate the garage. The narrow bands are repeated above the garage floors to give unity to the design. What appears to be a massive glass column on the Clark Street façade contains the elevator that delivers drivers to their parked cars, the passengers clearly visible from the street below. To assist drivers in finding their cars, each parking level is identified by a distinct wall-tile color, the name of a city, and the continuous broadcast of a song related to that city. On one floor the tiles are burgundy-colored, the city is New York, and the song is "New York, New York," sung by Frank Sinatra.

The elevator is entered from a small, elegant foyer off the two-level concourse, a handsome, streamlined interior that extends from LaSalle to Clark Street. An urban plus is that some concourse shops also open onto the street. A break in the exterior profile begins above the fifteenth floor, where slanting skylights create two interior atriums and provide spectacular views for office tenants (fig. 2). This break corresponds roughly to the roofline of the State of Illinois Center. The 203 North LaSalle exterior color scheme, blue-gray concrete and tinted glass, is a subdued version of the glittery blue and silver of the State building.

In its preliminary stages, 203 North LaSalle was called the Loop Transportation Center, a reference to its plan to concentrate on businesses related to travel and to its location near the "train to the plane," the CTA extension to O'Hare Airport. However, the developers changed the name to correspond to its prestigious LaSalle address, spurring lagging office rentals—and the parking concession as well.

The city's North Loop Redevelopment guidelines require developers to provide pedestrian links to public

transportation. A street-level concourse running through the building from LaSalle to Clark continues from Clark to Dearborn through the residential building, 200 North Dearborn. Subway access was completed in late 1989, when a new street entrance on Lake Street connected 203 North LaSalle with the Elevated and also with the CTA subway station below. The renovation of the station includes a link with the growing underground system of pedestrian passageways. —J.H.C.

Fig. 1. Skidmore, Owings and
Merrill. Onterie Center, 446
Ontario Street, 1979–86

98. Onterie Center, 1979–86

446 Ontario Street
Skidmore, Owings and Merrill

The Onterie Center (fig. 1) is a sixty-story, mixed-use tower named for two of the streets on which it borders, Ontario and Erie, on the Gold Coast east of Michigan Avenue. Although this building is one of many complexes that proliferated in that neighborhood after the John Hancock Center (1970, see no. 75) pioneered the genre there, the Onterie is also both a first and a last. It is the first concrete-tube building in Chicago and the last skyscraper designed by Fazlur Khan, the brilliant structural engineer long associated with Skidmore, Owings and Merrill. The firm's first engineering partner, he and Bruce Graham, design partner, are responsible for two of Chicago's most famous skyscrapers, the John Hancock Center and the Sears Tower (1974, see no. 80). According to the *Architectural Record* (August 1981), which published a detailed examination of the Onterie's design, the building "takes structural innovations from each: the cross-bracing of John Hancock, but the more closely spaced columns of Sears."

The tower consists of two cross-braced, reinforced-concrete tubes and a center core without diagonal bracing. The tubes are formed of reinforced-concrete panels that create a rigid, wind-resistant shell through interaction with the perimeter columns. "The entire stability of the building is on the outside," Khan explained to *ENR News* (April 1981). "The middle sections will literally be held up by the outer tubes, as if by two arms."

The exterior system is highly visible, creating a decorative pattern of diagonals and crosses recognizable from a great distance. However, unlike the X-braces on the John Hancock Center, the Onterie's are invisible from the interior, where they read as part of the wall; each apartment simply loses one window to a concrete panel. Since the closely spaced exterior columns of the upper floors also provide rigidity, the interior floor plans are flexible: "Supports are strictly gravity columns to hold up the floors," in Khan's words, according to *ENR News*. This flexibility was of great importance to the developer, Chandra Jha of PBM International, who first chose the site and then selected the architect.

The mixed-use components are similar to the Hancock's, with shops at street level, parking and offices on the next floors, and residences above. At the base a twelve-story office building joins the sixty-story tower, and slanted roofs provide two atriums and a pedestrian arcade through the building; the latter has a glazed ceramic tile floor with diagonal patterns that mimic the building's structural braces. This floor is one of the many examples of Skidmore, Owings and Merrill's inclusion of work by outstanding contemporary artists in buildings it designs. The ceramist is Joan Gardy-Artigas (born 1938), who followed in the footsteps of his famous father, Josep Llorens Artigas (1892–1978?), who frequently collaborated with Spanish artist Joan Miró. The younger Artigas also created the ceramic insets for the Miró sculpture in the Brunswick

Building plaza (see no. 66). In addition to finding art underfoot, residents in Onterie Center enjoy an unusual amenity described by *Chicago Tribune* critic Paul Gapp shortly after the building was completed in 1986: "A laundry room on the uppermost floor where—while your sheets are drying—you can stroll around a broad terrace and get a smashing 360-degree view of the city."

Construction of the Onterie Center was held up for several years, and Khan did not live to see the ground-breaking in December 1983. But he summed up the building's design as succinctly as would any critic, in *Architectural Record* (1981): "This is very much a Chicago building, one in the tradition of the Chicago School. The inherent character of the structure is expressed, just as the columns and beams of the early 1900s buildings in the Loop are expressed clearly, while the windows are infill." Few if any other buildings are dedicated to their designers and perhaps none to their engineers, but a memorial plaque on the wall as well as a mural by Artigas in the atrium of the main entrance dedicate Onterie Center to the memory of "Dr. Fazlur Rahman Khan (4/3/29–3/27/82)." —J.H.C.

99. 123 Wacker Drive, 1984–88

123 North Wacker Drive
Perkins and Will

Fig. 1. Perkins and Will. 123
Wacker Drive, 1984–86

Fig. 2. View of the lobby of 123
Wacker Drive

Nearly every building that rose on North and South Wacker
Drive in the 1970s and 1980s responded in some manner to
the 1929 Civic Opera Building (see no. 50). The arcade for a
1980 office building at 101 North Wacker Drive by Perkins
and Will is an example. However, in other ways this structure
is a basic exercise in steel-frame, curtain-wall Modernism. The
thirty-story skyscraper at 123 North Wacker Drive (fig. 1) by
Ralph Johnson of Perkins and Will, completed eight years
later, however, is a richer example of contextualism. This
tendency has been a consistent theme of Johnson's work, and
here the setbacks, punched windows, exterior masonry,
pyramidal top, and arcade on Wacker Drive are directly
related to the opera house.

With its clearly defined base, shaft, and top, the 1988 high
rise also stands firmly in the Chicago School tradition, while
the central bay of each façade reflects the curtain-wall style of
the Modern movement, characteristic of the nearby Sears
Tower (1974, see no. 80). As Richard Jay Solomon aptly
commented in the *Inland Architect* (May–June 1988), the
diverse elements in 123 Wacker Drive "tend to relate to each
other and to the whole. The building is not textured; rather,
it is an assemblage of formal components."

Polished red and black granite form the five-story base and
decorate the three-story atrium lobby (fig. 2). The clear-glass
enclosure of this space, in Johnson's words, allows the lobby to
become an "urban room tied to the activity of the streets."
The dramatically lit top adds another touch of bravura to this
highly visible tower. Buildings such as this, which address
Wacker Drive and make a powerful architectural statement,
have finally brought about the often-discussed landscaping of
the street's center island, so that Wacker Drive now has the
appearance of what it is in fact: one of the city's most
important boulevards.

Although 123 Wacker Drive looked from the beginning like
a corporate headquarters, it was in fact commissioned by a
development firm, Rubloff, as a speculative office building.
The individuality of its design was so strong that a single
tenant leased almost the entire building, transforming the
image into reality. —J.H.C.

100. Riverfront Park: Quaker Tower, 1983–87

321 North Clark Street
Skidmore, Owings and Merrill

Hotel Nikko Chicago, 1985–87

320 North Dearborn Street
Hellmuth, Obata and Kassabaum

A three-block area on the Chicago River's north bank, between Clark and Dearborn streets, is called Riverfront Park by its developers. The first two projects of a possible five are the Quaker Tower and Hotel Nikko Chicago (figs. 1, 2). Skidmore, Owings and Merrill initially had overall responsibility for the planning and landscaping of the area, but in time two different developers became involved, resulting in two different architects and two dissimilar buildings, which architecture critic Paul Gapp, in the *Chicago Tribune* (April 10, 1988), dubbed "the odd couple."

Quaker Tower, the thirty-five-story office building developed by JBCE Development Properties, is a welcome reprise of Modernism, resembling the 1965 Equitable Building (see no. 67). As Gapp wrote of Quaker Tower: "The developer wanted a simple box with a flat roof. Bruce Graham of Skidmore, Owings and Merrill vowed to deliver an elegant box, and that is what he did." Studio heads for this project were Diane Legge and Richard Tomlinson. The polished stainless steel of the curtain wall reflects sunlight. Its blue-green glass has a shimmering quality appropriate for the river setting, but also acknowledges 333 Wacker Drive (see no. 93) on the south bank. Quaker Tower's spacious lobby has two-story walls of clear plate glass, set back far enough to provide covered walks around the building.

The developers of the Hotel Nikko—Japan Air Lines and Tishman Realty—wanted a "contemporary Japanese" appearance and high-quality accommodations for guests. The St. Louis architectural firm of Hellmuth, Obata and Kassabaum designed the twenty-story hotel. Vertical bands of light granite frame banks of bay windows, their dark, tinted glass neither reflecting the river nor blending with it. However, as Gapp pointed out, "the summit of the hotel . . . is suggestive of a Japanese roof without crossing the line into kitsch." The roofline is repeated on the low, almost tea-house-size annex that houses the hotel's lobby and registration desk on the north side, as well as on the glassed-in passage between Quaker Tower and the hotel to the south.

A Japanese concern for providing the pleasing view led to a joint project of the hotel and the City of Chicago: the Hotel Nikko Riverfront Park, a block-long site directly across the river and at its edge. The well-known Japanese architect Kenzo Tange (born 1914) designed it, based on the early-thirteenth-century garden for the Ryoan-ji Temple in northwest Kyoto. Completed in June 1988, Riverside Park includes a walkway, a crushed marble "dry garden," seating, and night lighting.

The one unifying design element for the two buildings is the landscaping. Public river walks were built at both street level and water's edge, and private terraces were designed for Quaker tenants and Nikko guests at midlevel. Staircases at the east and west ends bracket the landscaped terraces. Skidmore,

Owings and Merrill enclosed the elevator giving access to the river walk from Quaker Plaza in a miniature version of a Chicago bridge house.

What progeny "the odd couple" will produce for the rest of the site is unknown, but the immediate public gain is landscaped promenades on both sides of the river. —J.H.C.

101. 900 North Michigan Avenue, 1983–89

Kohn Pedersen Fox
Associate architects: Perkins and Will

Fig. 1. Kohn Pedersen Fox, with Perkins and Will. 900 North Michigan Avenue, 1983–89

Fig. 2. View of the eight-story base of 900 North Michigan Avenue, northwest corner of Delaware Street and Michigan Avenue

Although the sixty-six-story skyscraper at 900 North Michigan Avenue (fig. 1) is officially known by its street address, it is known to the general public by another name: Bloomingdale's. The success of Water Tower Place (1976, see no. 81), a vertical shopping mall below a mixed-use skyscraper, led Urban Investment and Development to attempt its duplication ten years later on the opposite side of the Magnificent Mile. The 1989 building's components are the same as those of Water Tower Place: an atrium mall, parking and office floors, a hotel, and condominium apartments.

As an engineering achievement, the skyscraper is remarkable. As a retail venture the returns are somewhat mixed, as are reviews of the design by the New York firm Kohn Pedersen Fox, for which William Pedersen acted as design partner and Sudhir Jambhekar as senior designer. James Allen, partner in charge for the Chicago firm Perkins and Will, supervised construction. Architecture critic Paul Gapp reported in the *Chicago Tribune* (September 18, 1988) that the tube structure of 900 North Michigan Avenue was complicated. "Steel framed both the boxy retail base building and the office space in the bottom twenty floors of the tower section. . . . [Concrete supports] the top thirty-six floors of the building." These two structural systems come together at the thirtieth floor, where "the heavy duty splice was made at 700 points . . . by thermally fusing together the steel frame and the steel reinforcing bars embedded in the concrete. . . . The technical wizard . . . is R. Shankar Nair, who was chief engineer for Alfred Benesch & Co. at the time." Another modest but practical innovation is in the basement: a motorized turntable that lines up trucks with twelve loading docks.

Relating to the urban fabric is the basis of Pedersen's design philosophy. In *Kohn Pedersen Fox: Buildings and Projects 1976–1986* (1987), he states: "We intended to 'gather' the meaning of our buildings into, hopefully, an artistic unity . . . a large building could be more sensitively scaled to the city if it was made up of distinct pieces; . . . we intended to introduce the complexity of the modern city into the individual building." However, too many pieces may have been gathered here.

The eight-story base (fig. 2) is intended to lessen the impact of the building's enormous bulk and to recall the height and scale of Michigan Avenue buildings in the early 1920s. Here, however, the variety of classical forms lacks coherence. The slim tower rises from the base with setbacks that relate to Holabird and Root's nearby Palmolive Building (1927, see no. 40) and with punched windows like those of the Drake Hotel (1919, see no. 28). The simple curtain wall in the central bay is given a handsome, even charming closure in the four lanterns capping the tower. To install them it was necessary to lift parts to the roof of one of the upper setbacks, where the four pavilions were assembled and then hoisted into place.

The separation of the Michigan Avenue entrance to the atrium mall from the lobbies on the side streets for the hotel, apartment, and office segments has been widely praised, as has the arrangement of interior spaces on the lower floors. Bloomingdale's became a magnet to shoppers upon the building's opening. However, smaller retailers in the six-story atrium have found the level of traffic disappointing. If this complaint is valid, it defies planning that took into account a major flaw of Water Tower Place: 900 Michigan Avenue has placed the entrance to Bloomingdale's deep within the mall, forcing shoppers to pass the boutiques and specialty stores before reaching the department store's doors.

The office floors were all leased before the building was finished, underscoring the success of mixed use at the north end of town. Success has continued in the 1990s despite the opening of two similar complexes at 678 and 700 North Michigan (see Epilogue). —J.H.C.

Fig. 1. Skidmore, Owings and
Merrill. NBC Tower at Cityfront
Center, 454 North Columbus
Drive, 1985–89. Michigan
Avenue elevation

102. NBC Tower at Cityfront Center, 1985–89

454 North Columbus Drive
Skidmore, Owings and Merrill

A century and a half after Chicago was founded, Cityfront Center was emerging on the site where settlement began, the north bank of the Chicago River east of what is now Michigan Avenue. From the mid-nineteenth century to the late 1920s, the area was a thriving shipping and manufacturing center. But the long, slow decline of river transport and the departure of manufacturers in more recent years left decaying wharves, warehouses, and railroad sidings, as well as scattered plots of vacant land. Like Michigan Avenue north of the river before 1920, the derelict site was without a bridge to connect it to the city. In 1983–84, Columbus Drive, located a block east of Michigan Avenue and south of the Chicago River, was extended to the north and bridged the river.

This site, some sixty acres in area, is bounded by Lake Shore Drive, Michigan Avenue, Grand Avenue, and the Chicago River. Most of the property is owned by the Chicago Dock and Canal Trust, founded in 1857 by William B. Ogden, who had been Chicago's first mayor. In 1983, the trust formed a joint venture with the Equitable Life Assurance Society, owner of the Equitable Building (see no. 67) and its adjacent property. To gain the necessary zoning variances, the developer submitted a Planned Unit Development (PUD) to the City Plan Commission. A PUD is a comprehensive site plan following guidelines set up by the city. To draw it up, Chicago Dock Equitable Venture had organized a master team consisting of urban designer Alexander Cooper, formerly of Cooper-Eckstut, planners of a similar project, Battery Park City in New York; a developer, Tishman-Speyer Properties; and the architectural firm of Skidmore, Owings and Merrill. After modifications required by the city, the PUD for Cityfront Center was accepted in 1985. The Chicago Plan Commission's prime concern was that the area be integrated into the city and not be an island or fortress set apart, and that new streets follow the city's grid. The Cityfront plan allows for buildings of varying heights, but they must be clad in stone, masonry, or precast concrete. "No flat-topped glass boxes here," as Mark Jannot commented in *Chicago* magazine (January 1989). As in Battery Park City, residential, office, commercial, hotel, and entertainment use is encouraged, and designated open spaces must be landscaped by the developers.

The joint venture was dissolved late in 1985, with Chicago Dock retaining control of the forty-nine acres east of Columbus Drive and Equitable of the eleven acres to the west. Lohan Associates assumed responsibility for carrying out the PUD-approved plan in the Chicago Dock area and Skidmore, Owings and Merrill in the Equitable area. Tishman-Speyer Properties continued as developer of the Equitable property, and Broadacre Development Company took over for Chicago Dock. Despite this division, the two completed projects seem to indicate that Chicago would fare better with Cityfront Center than it had with Illinois Center

(see no. 73) on a similar site just across the river. The comprehensive planning would also serve as a model for Central Station, a seventy-two-acre development proposed in 1989 for the Near South Side on air rights over Illinois Central tracks along the lakefront.

The first achievement of Cityfront was Chicago Dock's redevelopment of a long, low shipping terminal (1909–20), designed by Christian Albert Eckstrom. Rehabilitated by Booth Hansen and Associates and renamed North Pier Chicago, it opened in 1988 with shops and restaurants on the lower levels and offices above. A thirty-foot-wide, landscaped esplanade, reminiscent of the one along the Hudson River at Battery Park City, runs the length of North Pier, with plans for its extension to the full length of Cityfront as other projects are finished. In 1990, the sixty-one-story North Pier Apartment Tower immediately to the east of the renovated terminal, by Dubin, Dubin and Moutoussamy and Florian/Wierzbowski, was readied for occupancy.

The second project completed was Skidmore, Owings and Merrill's forty-story NBC Tower (fig. 1) of 1989, designed by Adrian Smith, with John S. Burcher and Leonard Claggett as studio heads. Here again the model was New York, in this case the streamlined RCA Building in Rockefeller Center (1931–40) designed by Raymond Hood and a consortium of architects. The program for NBC was to design a building that would complement its close neighbor, the Chicago Tribune Tower (see no. 32), also a Hood design. The NBC Tower's sleek vertical lines, setbacks, decorative crown, tall spire, and even the suggestion of flying buttresses below the crown accomplish this objective. The final contextual element is NBC's limestone cladding. This veneer was achieved by bonding natural stone to precast-concrete panels, a technique used on a massive scale for this building. A typical panel may contain 100 pieces of limestone and cover an area of 125 square feet.

A four-story building joined to the north wall of the NBC Tower provides television studios for NBC productions. Major entrances to both buildings glitter with bronze ornament and face the new Cityfront Plaza to the west, which sets the stage for the tower. Walkways lead into the existing Pioneer Court (see Equitable Building, no. 67), which is to be redesigned and enlarged, as well as to the lower level of NBC on Columbus Drive. Garages for NBC's minicam trucks are expediently placed at this lower level, giving them quick access to city streets. The developer provided the infrastructure for a new upper-level Illinois Street, as well as a new Cityfront Plaza Drive, linking Columbus Drive (the former East Water Street) and Cityfront Plaza, the first of the planned public spaces. Chicago has waited years for a major development that showcases the river, makes open spaces a priority, and sets a high architectural standard. Cityfront Center may finally be that project. —J.H.C.

103. AT&T Corporate Center, 1985–89

227 West Monroe Street
Skidmore, Owings and Merrill

When the American Telephone and Telegraph Company (AT&T) was forced to divest itself of its local phone companies in 1982, doomsayers predicted it would fade away. But to the contrary, it would continue to make its presence known during the following decade, in no small way by means of new buildings it would erect across the country. The sixty-story AT&T Corporate Center (fig. 1) in Chicago is among the most prominent. On April 1, 1985, the company had invited proposals from developers for a Chicago headquarters building. Among the eleven realtors responding was Stein and Co., which approached Skidmore, Owings and Merrill for a design only four weeks before the deadline. The developer did not want a glass box for the site bounded by Adams, Franklin, and Monroe streets; rather he wanted a building with a distinctive skyline that would separate it from the Sears Tower (see no. 80) only a half block away.

The Skidmore, Owings and Merrill proposal, a complex consisting of two towers, sixty and thirty-four stories high, linked by a sixteen-story base building, was accepted, and the historicist, sixty-story AT&T tower at the corner of Monroe and Franklin streets was begun. According to design partner Adrian Smith, who had been working in the area (see 225 West Washington Street, no. 94), "the concept came naturally"; as described by studio head Peter Ellis (partner in charge was Robert Diamant and project manager, Neil Anderson), the design has "the strong massing and verticality of the 1920s, and the solidity of the Board of Trade."

References to earlier skyscrapers include setbacks at the twenty-ninth and forty-fourth floors, a decorative top, monumental entrances with Gothic detailing, and prominent lighting at crucial elevations. Inside, the forty-foot vaulted lobby evokes a European great hall. Characteristic of Skidmore's work in the 1980s is the granite sheathing, deep red at the five-story base, lighter as the building rises.

Aluminum spandrels imprinted with decorative patterns by a new photographic technique recall decorative ironwork of the turn of the century. The language of Modernism is not neglected: the central bay of each façade is a recessed glass curtain wall.

To give the AT&T tower a separate identity on the skyline, it is sited at the corner of the block farthest from the Sears Tower. And the glittering pinnacle of the later building places it in sharp contrast to the Sears's ebony silhouette. The central elements on all four sides of the AT&T extend above the flat top—slender granite towers to the east and west, sturdier ramparts to the north and south. The intent, in Ellis's words, is "a silhouette that gets lighter as the building rises with nothing to arrest the eye." A screen of steel and glass rods frames these towers, effectively shielding the mechanical facilities from view. To continue the upward line, a pair of 100-foot spires will in time rise from the center of the rooftop.

AT&T's employees began to move into the building on April 3, 1989, four years after proposals for a corporate center had been requested. The sixty-story skyscraper and its sixteen-story adjunct were phase one of the center. Phase two—a thirty-four-story skyscraper for United States Gypsum—was completed in 1992 (see no. 63). —J.H.C.

Fig. 1. *John Burgee Architects with Philip Johnson. 190 South LaSalle Street, 1983–87*

Fig. 2. *View of the lobby of 190 South LaSalle Street, with the sculpture* Chicago Fugue, *by Anthony Caro*

104. 190 South LaSalle Street, 1983–87

John Burgee Architects with Philip Johnson
Associate architects: Shaw and Associates

The forty-story office tower 190 South LaSalle Street (fig. 1), commissioned by the John Buck Company, is the first building in Chicago by noted architects Philip Johnson (born 1906) and John Burgee (born 1933).

In the spirit of their AT&T Building (begun 1977) in New York, the architects drew on historical sources in the design of the LaSalle Street building. With Alan Ritchie of their firm, they explored sources that ranged from Dutch Renaissance to Art Deco in origin before settling on a masonry structure— facing its five-story base in red granite and cladding the shaft in pink—that bears a conscious relationship to John Wellborn Root's famed Masonic Temple of 1892 (see introduction, fig. 11), as well as the same architect's Rookery Building of 1888 (see no. 2), diagonally across the street. Johnson has said that the "gables and arches [are] from Root," but "the rest is me." Although architecture critic Paul Gapp, in the *Chicago Tribune* (November 8, 1987), called Johnson's self-conscious silhouette "cartoonlike" and "a caricature of Postmodern excess," he found the base "impeccably tasteful" and beautifully detailed, down to its "handsome metal lamps." Gapp also praised the interior, observing that "the lobby of 190 is its showpiece, of course. For sheer richness, it is reminiscent of the extravaganzas carved on the ground floors of 1920s New York office buildings by William Van Alen, Ely Jacques Kahn and that crowd."

The spectacular lobby on LaSalle (fig. 2) is 180 feet long and 40 feet wide, with marble walls and pilasters that support an enormous, gold-leafed barrel vault. The northern end of this luxurious space contains a sculpture by British artist Anthony Caro, whereas the smaller lobby off Adams Street has a tapestry by Helena Hernmarck based on a Jules Guérin rendering for the Plan of Chicago (1909). The result, in Johnson's words, "is surely the most lengthy, high, and dignified lobby in the city." An equally important space is the law library on the top floor, created for the firm of Mayer, Brown, and Platt by Burgee and Johnson. The elevator lobbies were designed by a Chicago firm, Powell-Kleinschmidt.

In all, then, this Chicago building by Burgee and Johnson adds something special to the spaces and skyline of the city. But a New Yorker, architecture critic Paul Goldberger, writing in the *New York Times* (September 11, 1988), may have had the last word: "Of the many post-modern skyscrapers that have tried to allude to the great eclectic skyscrapers of the 20s and 30s, this is one of the few anywhere that actually manages to give us some of the richness, the generosity of space, the sense of solidity, and the sense of connection with the rest of the city that marked the best older buildings." —J.Z.

105. Leo Burnett Building, 1987–89

35 West Wacker Drive
Kevin Roche–John Dinkeloo and Associates

Fig. 1. Kevin Roche–John
Dinkeloo and Associates. Leo
Burnett Building, 35 West
Wacker Drive, 1987–89

Fig. 2. Robert A. M. Stern. Late
entry to the Chicago Tribune Tower
Competition, 1980. The Art
Institute of Chicago

When in 1896 Louis H. Sullivan published his tripartite theory of skyscraper design (that a tall building should be designed like a column, with a distinctive base, elongated shaft, and elaborate top or capital), he was only articulating what he had earlier built in his Schiller Theater of 1892 (see introduction, fig. 12) and his Wainwright Building of the year before in St. Louis. Indeed, his theory of skyscraper design became commonplace at the turn of the century, when many architects adapted it to a variety of styles. But it took the Chicago Tribune Tower Competition of 1922 and an entry by Adolf Loos to bring about a literalization of that popular theory. His controversial entry was shaped like a monumental Doric column (see Chicago Tribune Tower, no. 32). The 1980 exhibition *Late Entries to the Chicago Tribune Tower Competition* brought conceptual responses to Loos's proposal by some of the entrants, most notably New York architect Robert A. M. Stern. Stern reshaped Loos's idea into a pilaster (fig. 2) in order to "retain the shape of the standard office building box." Chicago architect Helmut Jahn of Murphy/Jahn was the first to realize Loos's design in an actual building, the skyscraper at 425 Lexington Avenue (1983–87) in New York, a rectangular, glass variation on a column. East Coast architect Kevin Roche (born 1922), whose firm descends from the office of Eero Saarinen, designed a masonry version of a giant pilaster in this tradition for Morgan Guaranty Trust at 60 Wall Street (1984–88), another New York tower. Roche's Leo Burnett Building in Chicago, commissioned by the John Buck Company, relates to that larger tradition, as well as to Roche's recent past.

The 635-foot-tall tower features a series of colonnades at the ground level, the fifteenth floor, and the top of his fifty-story, steel-frame, granite-covered skyscraper. The green tones of its masonry relate to the color of the Chicago River and to earlier towers such as the Carbide and Carbon Building of 1929 (see no. 47). Whereas the Carbide and Carbon features gold accents throughout, the Leo Burnett achieves color accents by means of its large, profiled mullions, which sparkle throughout the façades. The reflective-glass windows are deeply recessed, reinforcing the substantiality of the masonry façade and reducing competition with the glowing mullions. —J.Z.

106. 225 West Wacker Drive, 1985–89

Kohn Pedersen Fox
Associate architects: Perkins and Will

Few architects have the opportunity to build two skyscrapers side by side and thus achieve a sympathetic relationship between them. The first Chicago high rise by Kohn Pedersen Fox, a New York firm, was 333 Wacker Drive of 1983 (see no. 93). Two years and several high rises later, the same firm—and the same designer, William Pedersen—received the commission for 225 West Wacker Drive (fig. 1) from The Palmer Group.

Pedersen had voiced the hope in 1983 that any building placed next to 333 might be masonry-clad, a pleasing contrast to the taut glass skin of his earlier building; and he was able to grant his own wish. The new, thirty-one-story office tower at 225 West Wacker Drive is sited squarely to the grid and takes its cues from earlier classical masonry structures that line the Chicago River, such as the Builders and Engineering buildings (see nos. 43 and 46) to the east. Just as the focal point of the restored Builders Building is its handsome lobby, the impressive entrance of the Kohn Pedersen Fox tower leads to an apse-shaped lobby capped by a conical ceiling, which is generously illuminated by a large circular window above the entrance.

Neither the river nor the Merchandise Mart of 1931 (see no. 56) on the opposite bank is ignored in this contextual design. As in the Mart, the corners of 225 West Wacker Drive are towers, although rectangular in shape rather than octagonal as in those of the Mart. The pairs of towers at the north and south ends of 225 are tied together by metal bridges that recall those spanning the Chicago River. The final contextual reference is to Pedersen's own earlier building. The three-story arcade at the base directs pedestrians toward the Franklin Street arcade of 333 Wacker Drive, reinforcing that link with the city fabric that marks urbanity at its best.

Whether deliberately intended or not, the skyscrapers by Kohn Pedersen Fox and the Leo Burnett Building (see no. 105) of 1989 by Kevin Roche–John Dinkeloo and Associates, only two blocks apart on Wacker Drive, offer striking resemblances. They bear out architecture historian Robert A. M. Stern's dictum that "classicism is the new modernism."
—J.H.C.

Fig. 1. Kohn Pedersen Fox, with Perkins and Will. 225 West Wacker Drive, 1985–89

Fig. 1. Kohn Pedersen Fox, with
Harwood K. Smith and Partners.
311 South Wacker
Drive, 1986–90

Fig. 2. Plan of 311 South Wacker
Drive, c. 1986.

107. 311 South Wacker Drive, 1986–90

Kohn Pedersen Fox
Associate architect: Harwood K. Smith and Partners

The skyscraper at 311 South Wacker Drive (fig. 1) is one of three projected sixty-five-story buildings designed for the block adjacent to the Sears Tower (see no. 80) on the city's West Side. This fourth Chicago project by the New York firm of Kohn Pedersen Fox (see nos. 93, 101, and 106) is its largest in the city. The main entrance to the complex is a barrel-vaulted winter garden that fronts on Wacker and leads directly into the tower. Glass galleries running to the north- and southeast from the glass-enclosed interior garden will serve as links to the two future towers. A system of underground passages, called Pedways, is planned to connect the winter garden to the Sears Tower and to Union Station on the other side of the river. The developer, Lincoln Property Company, will absorb seventy percent of the cost, and the city and state will fund the remaining amount.

The reinforced-concrete-supported building at 311 South Wacker Drive surpasses Water Tower Place (see no. 81) as the tallest building in the world of this structural type. The unusual polygonal configuration of 311 is determined by the overall site plan (fig. 2). What appears to be an octagonal form when viewed from the side facing Wacker Drive is embedded in a slab—essentially the hypotenuse of a triangle—on the side facing Franklin Street. However, the octagon emerges as a free tower above the fifty-first floor. A glass cylinder at the pinnacle is to be illuminated at night, as will the winter garden at the base. Like the AT&T Corporate Center (see no. 103) to the north of the Sears Tower, 311 relies on Gothic detailing to emphasize its verticality. And also as in the case of the AT&T and such buildings as 225 West Washington Street and 303 West Madison Street (see no. 94), whose most extensive façades are on Franklin, the developer chose the more prestigious address for the tower. On Franklin, the building's base extends to the lot line, offering to the street a dense, layered wall of glass separated by granite spandrels and mullions, but creating a strong relationship that is characteristic of the designs of Kohn Pedersen Fox and of Pedersen in particular.

The ingenious site plan features extensive temporary landscaping—such as a decorative pattern of walkways—and two permanent corner plazas. If towers two and three are constructed, the space above the winter garden will function like a nineteenth-century light well. Nevertheless, if as planned all three towers are equal in height, their angled sides will be dark. For now, the single octagonal tower has become a striking element in the city's changing western skyline, where once the Sears Tower stood alone. —J.H.C.

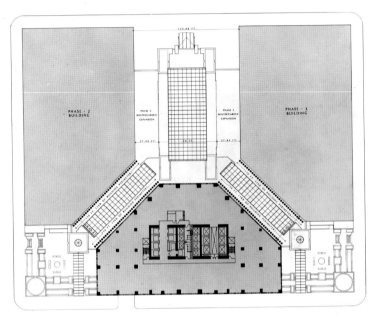

108. PaineWebber Tower, 1986–90

181 West Madison Street
Cesar Pelli and Associates, with Shaw and Associates

When the firm of Miglin-Beitler Developments was choosing an architect for its second major skyscraper in the Loop, it wanted one who had not previously done a building for Chicago. The partners selected the Argentinian-born Cesar Pelli, based on his designs for New York's Museum of Modern Art Tower (1984) and World Financial Center in Battery Park City (1988). Pelli saluted Chicago with a design paying homage to Eliel Saarinen's entry in the Chicago Tribune Tower Competition of 1922 (see no. 32).

Pelli's fifty-story tower of granite and silver-tinted glass shares the unbroken verticality of Saarinen's design. The setbacks are tipped with polished metal finials, detailing evocative of 1920s skyscrapers such as William Van Alen's Chrysler Building (1930) and Hood and Fouilhoux's American Radiator Building (1924) in New York. Interior spaces of the PaineWebber Building are virtually column-free, and the fifty-story tower was designed to function without transfer elevators. A five-story, glass-roofed loggia at street level, said to be inspired by the Uffizi Gallery in Florence, leads to a lobby surrounded by restaurants and retail shops. Two wall sculptures by American artist Frank Stella (born 1936) have been installed in the lobby with particular attention to their siting by the architect.

The tower is located at the southeast corner of Madison and Wells streets, diagonally opposite the 1982 Madison Plaza (see no. 90), also built by Miglin-Beitler. As Madison Plaza represented a revisionist treatment of the glass box in the early 1980s, so the later building was an end-of-the-decade recognition of the Golden Age of the skyscraper. In an even grander statement, in 1990 Miglin-Beitler made plans to erect a third skyscraper, at the southwest corner of the two streets. Also designed by Cesar Pelli, it was proposed to be the tallest building in the world, exceeding in height both the Sears Tower and New York's World Trade Center (see Introduction, fig. 27). This awe-inspiring project was never carried out due to the collapse of the market for tall office buildings that followed the 1987 stock market crash. New owners of the site have developed it with retail shops at street level, topped by a ten-story parking garage. —J.H.C.

Fig. 1. Cesar Pelli and Associates, with Shaw and Associates. Model of PaineWebber Tower, 181 West Madison Street, 1986–90

Epilogue:
Thirteen Projects in
Progress in the 1990s

120 North LaSalle Street,
1988–91

Architect: Murphy/Jahn
Developer: Ahmanson Commerical
Development Corporation

Downtown Chicago grew at an astonishing rate in the 1980s, achieving an entirely new skyline to the west and adding tower after tower of mixed use complexes to North Michigan Avenue. Construction of high-rise buildings virtually ceased in the real estate recession of the early 1990s. Several completed towers languished almost totally empty for three to four years, and many designs such as 150 North Dearborn died on the drawing boards. An ingenious add-on skyscraper completed in 1997 for Blue Cross-Blue Shield (see p. 293) was the first office tower to open in five years.

However, in 1996 developers began announcing conversions of both loft buildings and skyscrapers into residences, and even proposed a new fifty-story tower for the west Loop. Interest revived as well in the renamed River East, the area to the north of the Chicago River and east of Columbus Drive, and in the river's west bank. Retail is still vital on North Michigan Avenue, and the John Buck Company plans two projects: a shopping complex anchored by Nordstroms behind the landmarked façade of the art-deco McGraw-Hill building at 520 North Michigan Avenue (Thielbar and Fugard, 1928–29); and a high- and low-rise project for the two blocks bounded by Grand Avenue and Ohio, State, and Rush Streets. This proposal includes a Hilton Hotel, and retail, entertainment, and residential units. Also on North Michigan, with hotel rooms once more in demand, a deluxe Park Hyatt is rising across from the historic Water Tower with completion announced for 2000. Designed by Lucien Lagrange and Associates, the 67-story tower will include street-level retail, 203 hotel rooms on floors three through nineteen, and condominium residences, developed by LR Development Company, beginning on the twentieth floor.

State Street, which has received a much needed redesign of its public amenities including new lighting, is also due for a new office tower and retail mall to be designed by Cesar Pelli. Developer J. Paul Beitler has acquired the long vacant site at Adams and State, first occupied by the demolished Fair Store (Jenny and Mundie, 1890–91) and then Montgomery Ward.

The late 1990s hold the promise of renewed building; the following selections summarize the fates of thirteen projects announced for the early 1990s.

120 North LaSalle Street

The narrowness of this mid-block site that runs through to Wells Street presented the architects with a problem. They turned this limitation into an asset by extending a curved bay over LaSalle and a stone trellis over the adjoining Court Place, a busy walkway. A curved and recessed loggia at street level, enhanced by a mosaic mural by Roger Brown, adds liveliness to the streetscape. The exterior skin is of stone and glass and when the upper floors rise above the dark brick of neighboring buildings the tower becomes a light and expressive presence on the skyline. The building filled slowly when it opened in 1991, but in 1997 it is surrounded by activity as the adjoining Bismarck Hotel and Palace Theater complex (Rapp and Rapp, 1926) undergoes renovation, utilizing Tax Increment Financing, much favored by Mayor Richard M. Daley to rescue declining areas of the center city.

American Medical Association Building

515 North State Street
Kenzo Tange
Associate architects: Shaw and
Associates
Developers: John Buck Company
and Miller Klutznick Davis Gray
Comapny
Completed 1990

Chicago Bar Association Building

321 South Plymouth Court
Tigerman McCurry
Developer: Miglin-Beitler
Developments
Completed 1990

Chicago Place

700 North Michigan Avenue
Base: Skidmore, Owings and
Merrill
Tower: Solomon Cordwell Buenz
and Associates
Developer: 700 Michigan Tower
Partnership
Completed 1990

Chicago Title and Trust Center

161–71 North Clark Street
Kohn Pederson Fox
Developer: The Linpro Company
One tower and the Center
completed 1993

American Medical Association Building

Chicago Bar Association Building

Rendering of Chicago Place by Rael Slutsky

Chicago Title and Trust Center

Japanese architect Kenzo Tange's first Chicago skyscraper, this sculptural, thirty-story-high office tower of glass and aluminum was designed for a site that is part of the American Medical Association's extensive real estate holdings on the Near North Side. A smaller, twenty-story residential tower is also planned. Plazas will surround both buildings, and passageways linking the buildings to Michigan Avenue will proceed through the existing Marriott Hotel (Harry Weese and Associates, 1976–78), owned by the developers of the American Medical Association Building.

Collegiate Gothic is the prevailing style for the headquarters of the Chicago Bar Association, designed by Tigerman McCurry. The firm's first skyscraper, this sixteen-story tower has limestone cladding, cathedral window detailing, a wood-burning fireplace in the ground-floor lounge, and a cast-aluminum figure of Justice over the entrance. The building is connected to the John Marshall Law School to the north and overlooks the Harold Washington Library Center (Hammond Beeby and Babka, 1990) to the south.

The reconfiguration of upscale shopping on North Michigan Avenue continues with this forty-story development, its eight-story base by Skidmore, Owings and Merrill providing the neighborhood with still another atrium mall (the major tenant: Saks Fifth Avenue). The exterior detailing of the base recalls such D. H. Burnham and Co. buildings as the Railway Exchange (see no. 17). The apartment tower by Solomon Cordwell Buenz and Associates has rippling bays with large windows—which take advantage of the relatively unobscured views above the eleventh floor—and an Art Deco closure.

Chicago Title and Trust Center (above center) and Chicago Title Tower (above right) are phase one of a block-long complex on Clark Street between Randolph and Lake. Part of the city-sponsored North Loop Redevelopment project, the pair of glass and aluminum skyscrapers will be connected by the thirteen-story center and a skylit gallery providing entrances to both towers. The project also had included renovation of the adjacent Harris and Selwyn theaters (C. Howard Crane and Kenneth Franzheim, 1923). Finally, in 1997, Mayor Richard M. Daley and the Goodman Theatre board announced that a totally new Goodman Theatre, incorporating the Harris and Selwyn historic structures, would be completed by 2000, in the heart of a revived Loop theater district.

Chicago Union Station Tower North

501–29 West Adams Street
Lucien Lagrange and Associates
Developer: U.S. Equities Realty
Cancelled project

City Place

676 North Michigan Avenue
Loebl Schlossman and Hackl
Developer: Fifield Development
Corporation
Completed 1990

Morton International Building

100 North Riverside Plaza
Perkins and Will
Developer: Rubloff
Completed 1990

North Loop Redevelopment Block 37

Bounded by State, Washington,
Dearborn, and Randolph Streets
Murphy/Jahn (Helmut Jahn,
assisted by Philip Castillo)
Developers: FJV Ventures, The
Levy Organization, JMB Realty
Corporation, and Metropolitan
Structures
Cancelled project

Rendering of Chicago Union Station Development

Rendering of City Place

Morton International Building

Model of North Loop Redevelopment Block 37

The Chicago Union Station Development project calls for construction to begin in 1990 on the first of two twenty-five-story office towers planned to rise above Union Station (Graham, Burnham and Company, 1913–24), west of the Loop. The station's headhouse, encompassing the grand waiting room and other public facilities of the original passenger concourse, has been granted landmark status and therefore must be preserved. Renovation of the commuter and Amtrak passenger facilities was completed by Lucien Lagrange in 1989 and incorporates new circulation patterns that circumvent the old waiting room, now referred to as the Great Hall. Instead of the new towers, Amtrak in 1998 requested proposals for exterior building renovations and interior remodeling to include a hotel and expanded retail shops.

Located at the corner of North Michigan Avenue and Huron Street, this forty-story tower includes thirteen floors of offices at the top, a twenty-four-story hotel in the middle, and a three-story base occupied by retail stores. Two separate lobby entrances on Huron Street lead to the office tower and hotel, but the retail shops are entered directly from Michigan Avenue. Granite predominates in the base, punched windows define the hotel floors, and ribbon windows those for the offices. The F. W. Woolworth Co. store that had long occupied the site was guaranteed a long lease at a low rent in order to make construction possible. However, instead of moving in, Woolworth's sublet its space to a fashionable retail shop.

The developer obtained air rights over an Amtrak rail line on the river's west bank to construct this thirty-six-story award-winning skyscraper. Designed by a team from Perkins and Will headed by Ralph Johnson, it is patterned on the early Modernist architecture of the Dutch de Stijl movement. The design includes a new two-level river walk, and a small public park as replacement for one demolished during construction.

This mammoth development, occupying almost a full block and intended to help revitalize State Street, has been scrapped. The now infamous Block 37 remains empty, providing a city-sponsored ice-skating rink in the winter and an arts program for inner-city children in the summer, but 1998 may be the last winter for ice skaters. In February it was reported that Macy's was considering the site for its second Midwestern location, a strong indication of renewed life for State Street.

One North Franklin Street

*Skidmore, Owings and Merrill
Developer: Oxford Advisors
Group
Completed 1991*

633 St. Clair Place

*633 North St. Clair Street
Loebl Schlossman and Hackl
Developer: Romanek Properties
Completed 1991*

77 West Wacker Drive

*R. R. Donnelley Center
Ricardo Bofill
Associate architects: DeStefano
and Goettsch
Developer: The Prime Group
Completed 1992*

Blue Cross-Blue Shield Building

*Corner of Randolph and
Columbus Drive
Lohan Associates
Develper: Walsh, Higgins &
Company
Phase-one completed 1997*

Model of One North Franklin Street

Model of 633 St. Clair Place

Perspective view of 77 West Wacker Drive.

Blue Cross-Blue Shield Buildling

This thirty-eight-story office tower, faced in light-colored granite and featuring Chicago windows, is related to its neighbor on the diagonally opposite corner, 303 West Madison Street (see no. 94), also designed by Skidmore, Owings and Merrill. Joseph Gonzalez, head of the design team for both buildings, was assisted on One North Franklin Street by William Drake, partner in charge; Michael Damore, project manager; and Peter Brinckerhoff, studio head.

Responding to the reduced demand for "mixed-use" complexes in the North Michigan Avenue area, this twenty-eight-story tower to the east of the avenue opened as an office building but sat virtually empty until 1997, when Chicago and Texas investors teamed with the Dallas-based Wyndham Hotels and Resorts to begin conversion of the building to a hotel. The three-story granite base relates in scale and character to neighboring low-rise structures. A curtain wall of emerald-green-tinted glass and granite culminates in towers at the center and in each corner.

Chicago's position as a showplace for international design is expanded with the building of the first American skyscraper by the well-known Spanish architect Ricardo Bofill. Said to exemplify "modern classicism," the fifty-story tower has a silver-tinted glass curtain wall with detailing of white-granite columns, chamfered corners, and arches extending above the roofline on each of the four façades. Arched pediments over the doorways on Wacker Drive repeat the classical motif. Underground walkways connect the building with the CTA subway and 203 North LaSalle Street (see no. 97), the transportation building nearby.

When Blue Cross-Blue Shield made the decision in 1993 to build a new corporate head-quarters, there were 20 million square feet of empty office space in downtown Chicago. However, in all that emptiness, buildings with the average 35,000- to 40,000-square-foot floors required by the client did not exist. Lohan Associates' challenge was to create a design that answered that need, and that also allowed for future expansion. Their solution was a two-phase, add-on structure. The thirty-three-story tower seems to stretch horizontally, its interior enhanced by a light-filled atrium. Eventual phase-two construction will reach 57 floors. Below-ground pedway connections link the building with parking and a vast subterannean world of retail shopping in the adjacent Illinois Center (see no. 73). The first Chicago office building to open in five years, the building occupies a prime site facing Grant Park.

Profiles of Chicago Architectural Firms

The architects and offices profiled on the following pages designed some of the landmarks among Chicago skyscrapers of the past century. These brief sketches, arranged chronologically, provide hints of the genius of these practitioners.

William Le Baron Jenney

Dankmar Adler

Louis Henri Sullivan

William Le Baron Jenney

William Le Baron Jenney (1832–1907) was born in Fairhaven, Massachusetts, and was educated at the Lawrence Scientific School of Harvard University in Cambridge, Massachusetts. Between 1853 and 1856, he studied for the diploma at the Ecole Centrale des Arts et Manufactures in Paris. During the Civil War, Jenney earned the rank of major in the Union Army Corps of Engineers, designing fortifications at Shiloh, Corinth, and Vicksburg. He settled in Chicago in 1867 and with Louis Y. Schermerhorn and John Bogart established the partnership of Jenney, Schermerhorn, and Bogart, all three of whom had extensive experience in railroad planning and construction. The firm received commissions to design three urban parks in 1869 and collaborated, as well, with Olmsted, Vaux and Co. of New York in the planning of the suburban community of Riverside, Illinois, in 1868–69.

Jenney left the partnership shortly before Riverside was completed and entered practice with Sanford E. Loring. Together they wrote *The Principles and Practice of Architecture* (1869). This started Jenney, an engineer, on an architectural career as a specialist in large office buildings and stores, such as his Portland Block (1872), First Leiter Store (1879), Home Insurance Building (1885), and Fair Store (1891), all four now demolished. Still standing are his Manhattan Building (see no. 6) and Second Leiter Building (see no. 7), both of 1891.

In designing these and later buildings, Jenney, whose partners subsequently included William Augustus Otis and William Bryce Mundie, developed a reputation as the father of the Chicago skyscraper, as much for his training of young architects as for the buildings he constructed. Daniel H. Burnham, William Holabird, Martin Roche, and Louis H. Sullivan were among those who apprenticed with him. In 1905, Jenney retired and moved to California. He died in Los Angeles two years later.

Adler and Sullivan

One of the most important architectural partnerships in late-nineteenth-century Chicago was that of Adler and Sullivan. Their engineering and design developments would have an impact on modern architecture the world over. Dankmar Adler (1844–1900) was born in Lengsfeld, Germany, and came to the United States with his family in 1854. After working with Augustus Bauer in Chicago, Adler joined the Illinois Light Artillery during the Civil War. Upon his return to Chicago, he worked with several architects before establishing his own firm in 1879. In his first project, the Central Music Hall (1879, demolished 1901), he was so successful in solving the engineering and acoustical problems of theater design that he became known as one of the foremost experts in the field and received numerous theater commissions, including that of acoustics consultant for Carnegie Hall in New York (1891).

Louis Henri Sullivan (1856–1924) was born in Boston and at an early age developed a reverence for nature that would later emerge in the beautiful foliate ornament he designed for his buildings. After studying briefly at the Massachusetts Institute of Technology, in Cambridge, Sullivan worked in the architectural offices of Frank Furness in Philadelphia and William Le Baron Jenney in Chicago. Sullivan then studied architecture at the Ecole des Beaux-Arts in Paris and joined Dankmar Adler's office in 1879. The two men became partners in 1881, and together they were responsible for some of the most important structures in Chicago's great skyscraper period of the 1880s and 1890s.

Adler and Sullivan produced more than two hundred projects, including hotels, office buildings, residences, stores, synagogues, theaters, and warehouses. Among their most prominent works in Chicago were the McVickers Theater (1883), the Auditorium Building (which included a hotel, office building, and a theater; 1887–89, see no. 3), and the Schiller Theater (1891–92), as well as the Transportation Building for the World's Columbian Exposition (1893) and the Chicago Stock Exchange Building (1893–94), of which only the Auditorium remains standing. In these important, early Chicago skyscrapers, Adler generally solved the engineering problems while Sullivan turned to matters of design and ornament—each brilliantly complementing the other with innovative approaches in their respective fields.

Adler and Sullivan's partnership ended in 1895 when a nationwide economic depression left them with few clients. Adler, who went on to work for the Crane Elevator Company, would also design a school and synagogue in Chicago, but his architectural practice was cut short by his death in 1900. Sullivan continued to practice architecture for nearly thirty more years. During this period, he produced some of his most brilliant designs, including the Gage Building (1898–99, see no. 13) and the Schlesinger and Mayer Store (1898–99, 1903–04, now the Carson Pirie Scott and Company Store, see no. 14), both in Chicago. However, Sullivan's work after 1900 consisted mainly of small banks, stores, and churches throughout the Midwest. He is remembered for his influential writings, as well, including *Inspiration* (1886), *The Autobiography of an Idea* (1922), and *A System of Architectural Ornament* (1924).

Daniel Hudson Burnham   *John Wellborn Root*

Burnham and Root

The partnership of Burnham and Root was formed in 1873 by two young architects working in the office of Carter, Drake and Wight, a Chicago firm. The more experienced and better educated of the two was John Wellborn Root (1850–1891). He was born in Lumpkin, Georgia, but when the Civil War broke out, his family fled the South and in 1864 sent Root to school in Liverpool, England. Returning home after the war, Root moved to New York in 1866, entering New York University to study civil engineering and receiving a bachelor's degree three years later. He took a job with architect James Renwick for a year and spent another in the office of John Butler Snook, designer of the first Grand Central Station in New York (1871), where the twenty-one-year-old Root was made supervisor of construction on the great iron-and-glass train shed; it was an experience that surely contributed to the evolution of his design for the light court of the Rookery (see no. 2) in later years. Following the Chicago Fire in 1871, the New York architect Peter B. Wight, like many other members of his profession, took advantage of the need to rebuild the city and moved to Chicago, entering into partnership with Asher Carter and William H. Drake, and invited Root to join them.

Daniel Hudson Burnham (1846–1912) was born in Henderson, New York, and raised in Chicago. An indifferent student, he failed the entrance examinations for both Harvard and Yale universities and decided to forego college. After trying various careers, including politics and prospecting for gold, he became an apprentice in the architecture office of William Le Baron Jenney and Sanford Loring. Burnham soon established his own practice with Gustave Laureau, but the partnership failed. The following year, in 1872, Burnham entered Wight's firm, where he met Root, and the two soon established their own office.

The depression of 1873 was a severe handicap for the two partners, but their fortunes turned with their introduction to the influential John B. Sherman, one of the founders of the Union Stock Yards. The successful completion of Sherman's home and stable on fashionable Prairie Avenue in 1874 launched the architects' practice, which was further cemented by the marriage of Burnham to Sherman's daughter and of Root, in 1879, to the daughter of the general solicitor for the Chicago, Burlington and Quincy Railroad. The building of mansions for Chicago's magnates led to numerous commissions for commercial office buildings and many of their most important designs. The firm of Burnham and Root is credited with over 270 projects for buildings extending from Ohio to California. Especially important was their contribution from 1873 to 1891 to the development of the tall, unadorned commercial structure. Two of their most influential designs survive in Chicago: the Rookery (1885–88, see no. 2) and the Monadnock Building (1884–91, see no. 8).

Both men were active in promoting their profession, and Root frequently contributed to the *Inland Architect* and other journals. Their mutually supportive relationship has been cited as a major factor in their success. Although Root's brilliant career was cut short by his death at the age of forty-one, his legacy to the Chicago School was his remarkable ability to integrate the functional and aesthetic demands of the tall commercial structure.

D. H. Burnham and Company

At the death of John Wellborn Root in January 1891, the firm of Burnham and Root adopted the name of its surviving partner, becoming known as D. H. Burnham and Co. It would design much of Chicago's historic cityscape. The classical buildings that became the Burnham hallmark following the World's Columbian Exposition of 1893 are having renewed influence today as architects turn to earlier forms of expression in the Postmodern era.

The Burnham office, like that of William Le Baron Jenney, not only produced buildings of uniformly high quality but also offered solid training to many young architects, including Peirce Anderson, Charles B. Atwood, Frederick P. Dinkelberg, Ernest R. Graham, Peter J. Weber, and Howard J. White. Burnham's practice evolved as the concept of the large corporation was emerging in the United States, and his own firm began to take on some of the characteristics of the corporate office, with Burnham himself acting as Chief Executive, dividing responsibilities among the many hands.

The design work of this firm fell into two general categories: individual buildings and city planning. Burnham's contributions to both fields were innovative and influential. Capable of building stately, classical office buildings such as the Railway Exchange (1904, see no. 17) and the Peoples Gas Company Building (1911, see no. 17), the firm also produced the skeleton-framed Reliance Building (1895, see no. 5), which, with its white-glazed terra-cotta façade and large expanses of glass, is seen by architectural historians as a precursor of the International Style of the 1920s. Burnham was also a noted designer of major department stores at the turn of the century, beginning with the Marshall Field and Company Store (1892–1914, see no. 9) in Chicago and continuing with elegant examples in Boston, New York, Philadelphia, and even London.

One of the foremost city planners in America, Burnham's first experience in urban design came with the World's Columbian Exposition of 1893. As chief of construction, Burnham helped to build an ideal, well-ordered festival city, which stood in sharp contrast to the chaos of adjacent Chicago. Later called the "White City" for its many white, classical buildings, the fair had a profound influence on architectural design nationwide. Burnham himself was called upon to draw up plans for Washington, D.C. (in concert with others, 1902), as well as for Manila, Cleveland, and San Francisco (all 1905). He and his assistant Edward H. Bennett drafted the celebrated Plan of Chicago (1909), the first comprehensive metropolitan plan in America. Their recommendations had an enormous influence on the development of the city in the 1920s, resulting in the construction of the Michigan Avenue Bridge, the widening and straightening of many streets, and the establishment of new parks and forest preserves. The slow improvement of the banks of the Chicago River, of increasing concern in the 1980s, stems from recommendations in the plan.

As the head of two major architectural firms and a leader in city planning, Burnham occupies a critical position in the history of modern American architecture. Upon his death in 1912, he left a personal legacy to the city of Chicago when he endowed an architectural library at The Art Institute of Chicago that has served many generations of architects and architectural historians.

Ernest R. Graham, Peirce Anderson, Edward Probst, and Howard J. White, 1922

Office of Holabird and Roche, c. 1915

Graham, Anderson, Probst and White

At Daniel Burnham's death in 1912, his architectural practice was one of the most successful in the country, and he left many commissions on the boards. Ernest R. Graham (1868–1936), who had started work as a draftsman for Burnham and Root in 1888, assumed leadership of the successor firm, Graham, Burnham and Company. Graham had received his technical training at Coe College in Cedar Rapids, Iowa, and at Notre Dame University in South Bend, Indiana. When he was just twenty-five, Graham directed the completion of many buildings for the World's Columbian Exposition of 1893. Five years after Burnham's death, Peirce Anderson, Edward Probst, and Howard Judson White, who had all joined Burnham in various capacities, united with Graham in a new firm, Graham, Anderson, Probst and White. Together they designed many major landmarks in Chicago, New York, and elsewhere.

Born in Oswego, New York, Peirce Anderson (1870–1924) graduated from Harvard College in Cambridge, Massachusetts, and later studied electrical engineering at Johns Hopkins University in Baltimore. On the advice of Daniel Burnham, whom he met on a trip to Chicago in 1894, Anderson enrolled in the Ecole des Beaux-Arts in Paris to study architecture. Four years later, he returned to Chicago as Burnham's chief designer. Chicagoan Edward Probst (1870–1942) first received architectural training in the office of Robert Penecost and, over a period of eight years, worked for several other architects before joining D. H. Burnham and Co. Howard J. White (1870–1936) was also born in Chicago. He began his architectural study at the Manual Training School. At the age of eighteen, he entered Burnham's office as a junior draftsman and remained there throughout his career.

Known for its skillful adaptation of classical forms to modern requirements, Graham, Anderson, Probst and White was Chicago's leader in the creation of corporate headquarters throughout the 1920s and early 1930s and an important designer of banks, railway stations, stores, and other major commercial structures across the country. Among its tall Chicago office buildings are the Wrigley (1922, addition 1925, see no. 29), the Straus (1924, see no. 35), the Builders (1927, see no. 43), the Pittsfield (1927, see no. 44), the Chicago Civic Opera (1929, see no. 50), the Merchandise Mart (1923–31, see no. 56), and the Field (1934, see no. 57). Among its Chicago public buildings are the Field Museum of Natural History (c. 1920) and the John G. Shedd Aquarium (1929). Its Chicago banks include the Federal Reserve (1922, see no. 34), the Illinois Merchants (1924, see no. 34) and the Foreman State National (1930, see no. 55).

Graham is remembered for his patronage as well as his architecture. He was the donor of the Hall of Geology at the Field Museum of Natural History and before his death established the Graham Foundation for Advanced Studies in the Fine Arts, particularly devoted to the field of architecture. The office of Graham, Anderson, Probst and White is still active in Chicago, and in 1988 the Chicago Chapter of the American Institute of Architects presented the firm with an award for its restoration of the dome of the Illinois State Capitol in Springfield.

Holabird and Roche and Holabird and Root

The tall office buildings designed by Holabird and Roche were among the most remarkable and original contributions to the evolution of the Chicago School of architecture in the 1880s and 1890s. The firm was established in 1883 by William Holabird (1854–1923) and Martin Roche (1853–1927), who met in the office of Chicago architect and engineer William Le Baron Jenney. In the beginning they designed small apartment and commercial buildings in Chicago and Evanston, Illinois, but the commission for the twelve-story Tacoma office building (1887–89, demolished 1929) in downtown Chicago brought the partners international acclaim. The Tacoma, like many of Holabird and Roche's subsequent buildings, including the south addition to the Monadnock (1892–93, see no. 8), the Old Colony (1893–94, see no. 10), and the Marquette (1893–95, see no. 11), was notable for its iron and steel structure and for the generous expanses of glass that formed its exterior walls.

After the turn of the century, the firm continued to grow in size and stature, designing the distinguished Chicago Savings Bank Building (1903–04, see no. 16) and the Gothic University Club (1908–09, see no. 21). Its commissions ranged from department stores—Mandel Brothers (1900), the Rothschild (1906, 1910), and the Boston Store (1905–17)—to hotels, such as the Stevens (1925–27, see no. 39) and the Palmer House (1925–27, see no. 40). Holabird died in 1923, but the practice continued under the name of Holabird and Roche. With the death of Martin Roche in 1927, however, Holabird's son, John Augur Holabird (1886–1945), and John Wellborn Root, Jr. (1887–1963), son of Burnham's partner, took control of the firm and renamed it Holabird and Root.

The young men enjoyed immediate success, distinguishing themselves with such renowned setback skyscrapers as 333 North Michigan Avenue (1927–28, see no. 41), the Palmolive Building (1927–29, see no. 45), the Daily News Building (1929, see no. 52), and the Chicago Board of Trade Building (1929–30, see no. 53). Their American Modernist designs, based on stripped-down classicism and largely influenced by their formal educations at the Ecole des Beaux-Arts in Paris, are characteristic of the great Art Deco skyscrapers of the 1920s and 1930s.

Both Holabird and Root took part in planning the Century of Progress Exposition of 1933 in Chicago. In 1937 John Holabird was instrumental in recruiting Ludwig Mies van der Rohe to head the School of Architecture at the Illinois Institute of Technology. The death of Holabird in 1945 marked the end of an era for the firm. With the resumption of postwar building in the 1950s, the remaining partner, John Root, increasingly left control of the practice to others.

The office of Holabird and Roche and its successor, Holabird and Root, was one of Chicago's most prolific practices, completing more than 7,500 commissions between 1883 and 1945. The firm was cited by the American Institute of Architects in 1983 for a century of outstanding architectural design: "From its early 'Chicago School' buildings of the 1890s to its most recent award-winning designs, the firm has written some of the most significant pages of America's architectural history."

Ludwig Mies van der Rohe, with a bust of the architect by Marino Marini

Marshall and Fox

Benjamin H. Marshall (1874–1944) and Charles E. Fox (1870–1926) formed a partnership in 1905 and over the next two decades were responsible for a number of exclusive hotels and luxury apartment buildings in Chicago. Marshall, born and educated with the city's elite, had access to clients from this social class, which gave them commissions for elegant Renaissance and classical buildings. These include famous hotels such as the Blackstone (1908, see no. 20), the Drake (1919, see no. 28), and the Edgewater Beach (1923–24); Marshall and Fox also designed sumptuous apartment buildings such as 1550 North State Parkway (1911, see no. 28), which had ten, 8,000-square-foot apartments, or one per floor; as well as the South Shore Country Club (1915) and commercial structures such as the Steger Building at Wabash Avenue and Jackson Street (1909) and the Lake Shore Trust and Savings Bank at Michigan Avenue and Ohio Street (1921). In addition to these and other works, their office received a number of "bread-and-butter" commissions from early-twentieth-century restaurant chains such as Horn and Hardart and Thompson. This output is amazing if one considers that Marshall's career could have been ruined when his Iroquois Theater (1900) was razed by a disastrous fire on December 30, 1903, that killed some 600 people.

But of all the firm's buildings, Marshall's own home and studio in nearby Wilmette, Illinois (1921), seemed to epitomize his extravagant life-style and love of opulence. Built like a Pompeian villa, it incorporated architectural treasures from his travels — a harem screen from Cairo, a Chinese temple room, a fifteenth-century Roman pulpit that housed a movie projector, and a French sedan chair remodeled into a telephone booth. This building also had a work area for forty-five draftsmen. Marshall often held dinners for as many as seventy-five guests, the most famous honoring Edward, Prince of Wales (later crowned Edward VIII of England), and the most notorious involving chorus girls from a Chicago theater. His life-style and buildings belong to the expansive era preceding the Great Depression of the 1930s, which hit Marshall as well. He had to sell his studio in 1936, remodeling it for another family. As C. William Westfall aptly noted in the *Chicago Architectural Journal* (1982): "When he died his entire estate would not have covered a year-and-a-half's maintenance expense for the studio."

Ludwig Mies van der Rohe

Ludwig Mies van der Rohe (1886–1969) was born in Aachen, Germany. He apprenticed as a stonemason in his family's tombstone business and then as a draftsman for a designer of stucco ornament. From 1905 to 1907 he worked as a draftsman for the furniture designer Bruno Paul in Berlin. It was there that he received his first commission: the design of the Riehl House (1907), which, though altered, still stands at 3 Spitzweggasse in Potsdam. Hired by architect Peter Behrens in 1908, Mies worked for him on such buildings as the German Embassy in St. Petersburg (now Leningrad), of 1912, as well as several house projects.

But Mies's career came into its own after the First World War, when a variety of building and furnishing commissions came his way, resulting in two of the masterworks of the Modern movement: the German Pavilion at the International Exposition of 1929 in Barcelona (long demolished, the pavilion was reconstructed there in 1984–86) and the Tugendhat House in Brno, Czechoslovakia (1928–30; renovated c. 1980–87). In 1930 Mies was appointed director of the Bauhaus in Dessau, and when the school was forced to leave that city two years later, moved with it to Berlin, where it was closed by the Nazis in 1933. This event, as well as the lack of commissions owing to the Depression of the 1930s, led Mies to leave Germany for the United States. While he was designing a house for Mrs. Stanley Resor in Jackson Hole, Wyoming, in 1937–38 (unexecuted), he was invited to head the School of Architecture at Chicago's Armour Institute of Technology, then housed in The Art Institute of Chicago. Upon arrival in 1938, he hired new faculty, changed the curriculum, and in the 1940s moved the school — renamed the Illinois Institute of Technology (IIT) — to a new campus of his design on State Street between Thirty-first and Thirty-fifth streets. Crown Hall (1950–56), the home of the School of Architecture, is one of Mies's most famous buildings.

While teaching at IIT, Mies, through the patronage of developer Herbert Greenwald and others, began to design a number of high-rise buildings in Chicago and elsewhere, including 860–880 Lake Shore Drive (1948–52, see no. 58), the Federal Center (begun 1959, see no. 61), and the IBM Building (begun 1966, see no. 74), all in Chicago, and the Seagram Building (1954–58) in New York. Although Mies's work after the Second World War was often characterized as the epitome of high-rise design, he also completed several low-rise buildings of major importance, among them the Farnsworth House in Plano, Illinois (1946–50), and the National Gallery in West Berlin (1962–67). Mies trained a number of young architects at IIT, many of whom later worked in his office, including Daniel Brenner, Jacques Brownson, and George Danforth, as well as Joseph Fujikawa, Bruno Conterato, and Mies's grandson, Dirk Lohan, who were members of the firm at the time of Mies's death on August 19, 1969. The office of Mies van der Rohe remained in operation until 1975, when the partnership of Fujikawa, Conterato, Lohan and Associates was formed. In 1982, Fujikawa left to establish a new firm with Gerald Johnson. In 1986, after Conterato's retirement, Dirk Lohan changed the name to Lohan Associates.

Fazlur Khan and Bruce Graham, with Hancock Center model, 1965

Perkins and Will

The architecture firm of Perkins and Will was founded in 1935 when Lawrence B. Perkins (born 1912) and Philip Will, Jr. (1906–1985), formed a partnership specializing in small commissions, particularly North Shore residences inspired by the Prairie School. From 1936 to 1941 the firm was known as Perkins, Wheeler and Will, when E. Todd Wheeler became a partner. The small practice received national recognition in 1940 for the design of the progressive Crow Island School in Winnetka, Illinois, a Chicago suburb, in collaboration with the renowned Finnish architects Eliel Saarinen and his son Eero. Crow Island pioneered the concept of zoned areas for different age groups and led the architects to specialize in school design in postwar baby-boom America.

By 1950 the firm changed its name to The Perkins and Will Partnership, indicating its growth as the result of many commissions received, primarily for schools; in 1952 the partners opened offices in White Plains, New York, to serve their East Coast clients, in particular to build the Heathcote Elementary School (1954). Eventually they also opened offices in New York City and Washington, D.C. By the mid-1950s the partnership had become a major designer of elementary and high schools in the United States and one of the largest architectural practices in the country. In 1957 Todd Wheeler returned to the practice, specializing in the design of hospitals, which became another mainstay of the firm. Also in 1957, Perkins and Will designed its first high-rise office building, in Minneapolis. By the end of the 1960s, constructing health facilities such as Stamford Hospital in Connecticut (1968) and commercial office buildings such as the United States Gypsum Building in Chicago (1963, see no. 63) were as large a part of the practice as the educational commissions. One of Perkins and Will's best-known designs, the First National Bank Building of Chicago (1964–69, see no. 72), dates from that period.

Beginning in the 1960s and 1970s, the firm radically expanded its geographical boundaries and worked in Belgium, Egypt, Hong Kong, Indonesia, Iran, Iraq, Kuwait, Lebanon, Malaysia, and Saudi Arabia. At the same time, the firm continued to design hospitals, universities, and office buildings across the United States, including the Northern Trust Bank (1974) and the Standard Oil Building (1974, see no. 77), both in Chicago. About this time the name of the firm again became Perkins and Will. In recent years, the large architectural office has continued to design independent projects around the world, including the Chicago office tower 123 Wacker Drive (1988, see no. 99) and has collaborated with other firms on projects such as 333 Wacker Drive (1983, see no. 93), 900 North Michigan Avenue (1989, see no. 101), and 225 West Wacker Drive (1989, see no. 106), all with Kohn Pedersen Fox, a New York firm. Today Perkins and Will remains a large firm with offices in Chicago, New York, and Washington, D.C., and with clients from around the world.

Skidmore, Owings and Merrill

The Century of Progress Exposition opening on Chicago's lakefront in the summer of 1933 provided two young architects and brothers-in-law, Louis Skidmore (1897–1962) and Nathaniel Owings (1903–1984), with their first opportunity to work together. Out of this professional association there grew a partnership, in 1936, and with the addition of John O. Merrill (1896–1975) in 1939 they established the firm of Skidmore, Owings and Merrill.

From the start, the partnership of Skidmore, Owings and Merrill provided complete professional services in the fields of architectural design, planning, and engineering. In fifty and more years of experience, Skidmore has undertaken a variety of projects in the United States and in over forty countries throughout the world, and has been responsible for many important innovations in design and technology. In its corporate organization and broad influence, it may be considered a descendant of the firm of D. H. Burnham and Co.

Skidmore, Owings and Merrill has offices in Chicago, New York, San Francisco, Washington, D.C., Los Angeles, and London. For each of its projects, the office forms a design team composed of a project partner, a design partner, a project manager, and a senior studio architect. The team includes other designers and specialists as needed, and all work closely with an engineering partner. Many of the firm's greatest achievements from the 1960s through the 1980s resulted from the pairing of design partner Bruce Graham with engineering partner Fazlur Khan, most notably on the John Hancock Center (1965–70, see no. 75) and the Sears Tower (1968–74, see no. 80).

The Chicago office of the firm came to prominence when the postwar resurgence of skyscraper construction began in the late 1950s. The influential Inland Steel Building (1954–58, see no. 60) and the first Harris Trust and Savings Bank addition (1954–60, see no. 62) were both products of the decade. Leading design partners over the years include Walter Netsch, who graduated from the Massachusetts Institute of Technology, in Cambridge, served in the United States Army Corps of Engineers, and worked with Lloyd Morgan Yost before joining Skidmore, becoming a general partner in 1955; Bruce Graham, who graduated from the University of Pennsylvania in Philadelphia, worked in the office of Holabird, Root and Burgee in Chicago, and joined Skidmore in 1950, becoming chief of design in 1951; and James R. DeStefano (now practicing with James Goettsch), who joined the firm after graduating from the Illinois Institute of Technology. In addition to Fazlur Khan, Myron Goldsmith, a student of Mies's at the Illinois Institute of Technology, was instrumental in the engineering achievements of the firm (see the Brunswick Building, 1961–65, no. 66). Younger partners whose work began to appear in Chicago in the 1980s include Diane Legge, Adrian Smith, and Joseph Gonzalez. The extraordinary output of this large and complex firm has made an impact on the skyline from Chicago to Bangladesh and continues to do so today.

Harry Weese

Harry Weese and Associates

Architect Harry Weese was born in Evanston, Illinois, in 1915, and studied at Yale University, in New Haven, Connecticut, and at the Massachusetts Institute of Technology, in Cambridge, from which he received his architecture degree in 1938. Also studying city planning under Eliel Saarinen at the Cranbrook Academy of Art in Bloomfield Hills, Michigan, Weese worked for Skidmore, Owings and Merrill both before and after his naval service in the Second World War. He opened his own office in 1947.

Weese has declared that the influences of his formative years were Alvar Aalto, Le Corbusier, and Ludwig Mies van der Rohe. His oeuvre—as eclectic in its variety and styles as in its influences—covers three principal areas of architectural interest: building design, urban planning, and restoration and renovation. Among his Chicago buildings are the Time and Life Building (1968, see no. 70), the Latin School and Seventeenth Church of Christ, Scientist (both 1969), and the William J. Campbell Courthouse Annex (1975, see no. 78); his design for the Metro transit system in Washington, D.C., of 1975, exemplifies his second interest; and among his many projects in the third area are the restoration of the Adler and Sullivan Auditorium Building Theater (in 1967, see no. 3) and his renovation of Orchestra Hall (1966), the Field Museum of Natural History (1978), Fulton House (1979–81, see no. 85), and the Medinah Athletic Club (1988–89, see no. 49). Although Harry Weese and Associates is known particularly for its work in Chicago, the firm's design for the First Baptist Church of Columbus, Indiana (1965), is one of its most poetic achievements.

Weese is known for his visionary plans for the city of Chicago, among them the redevelopment of the riverfront and the building of parks along its length. He has been active on the Mayor's Advisory Council on Architecture and on the Open Lands project. He is a long-term financial supporter of the magazine *Inland Architect*, and his office has trained many fine architects. Weese was appointed to the National Council on the Arts by President Ford.

Helmut Jahn

C. F. Murphy Associates and Murphy/Jahn

C. F. Murphy Associates and its successor firm, Murphy/Jahn, are in many ways extensions of the great architecture practices of D. H. Burnham and Co. and Graham, Anderson, Probst and White, those historic specialists in high-rise construction. Charles F. Murphy, Sr. (1890–1985), founded the firm in 1959. Born in New Jersey and raised in Chicago, he trained at the De La Salle Institute as a stenographer and began his career in Daniel Burnham's office in 1911. After Burnham's death in 1912, Ernest R. Graham became head of the firm, which was renamed Graham, Burnham and Company. Murphy became Graham's administrative right-hand man, a job he retained when Graham left the office to found Graham, Anderson, Probst and White. After Graham's death in 1936, Murphy and two associates from the Graham firm, Alfred P. Shaw and Sigurd Naess, formed the office of Shaw, Naess and Murphy. Shaw withdrew from this firm in 1946, a year later forming the partnership of Shaw, Metz and Dolio.

Naess and Murphy practiced together for thirteen more years, designing the city's first major skyscraper in the postwar era, the Prudential Building (1952–55, see no. 59), as well as the Chicago Sun-Times Building at 401 North Wabash Avenue (1957). At the retirement of Naess in 1959, C. F. Murphy Associates was formed. The firm designed a number of major Chicago buildings, including the Continental Insurance Building (1962), the Chicago Civic Center (1965, see no. 65), and the second large convention center called McCormick Place (1969), as well as the O'Hare International Airport (opened 1963). In forming the design teams for those grand-scale commissions, the firm drew on some former students of Ludwig Mies van der Rohe at the Illinois Institute of Technology (IIT), including Jacques Brownson, who designed the Chicago Civic Center; Gene Summers, who worked on McCormick Place and the Kemper Arena in Kansas City (1973); and Gertrude Lemp Kerbis, who, under Stanley Gladych, designed O'Hare Airport. The firm made history for the Chicago skyscraper in 1967, however, by hiring German-born IIT student Helmut Jahn (born 1940) as an assistant to Gene Summers.

Jahn assumed ever-increasing design responsibility within the firm, and when Summers left in 1973 to enter independent practice in California, Jahn was promoted to executive vice president and director of planning and design. He first made his mark in Chicago with his design of the expressionistic Xerox Centre (1977–80, see no. 83). His subsequent buildings (see Chicago Board of Trade Addition, 1980, no. 53; One South Wacker Drive, 1982, no. 84; the State of Illinois Center, 1985, no. 86; and the Northwestern Atrium, 1987, no. 87), often controversial in their design and materials, draw on the imagery of America's urban past, particularly of the 1920s and 1930s. Yet they also stress today's technology and the traditions of Modernist vocabulary that are Mies's heritage. In 1987, Jahn completed the spectacular United Airlines Terminal at O'Hare International Airport, continuing the work that the Murphy firm began there in the early 1960s. But his influence goes far beyond Chicago, with major skyscrapers in Los Angeles, New York, and Philadelphia, as well as Frankfurt in his native West Germany. In 1981, the name of the firm C. F. Murphy Associates was changed to Murphy/Jahn, and a year later Jahn himself became president.

Acknowledgments

The help received in surveying a century of Chicago skyscrapers necessarily comes from many sources. We would like to thank the architects, building owners, corporation executives, developers, and public relations officers who were so generous in taking the time to respond to our queries, retrieve photographs from their files, and contribute information that greatly enriched our research. Their efforts have played a large part in forming this volume on the Chicago skyscraper.

We must thank in particular individual people who were extremely generous in providing us with research material: Jack Brown, Executive Director of the Ryerson and Burnham Libraries at The Art Institute of Chicago; Wim de Wit and Scott LaFrance of the Architectural Archive at the Chicago Historical Society; and the staff of the Glencoe Public Library, Glencoe, Illinois, who were patient and thorough in their assistance. Lucy Borich and Scott Nathan, interns in the departments of Museum Education and Architecture at The Art Institute of Chicago, were indefatigable in their search for pertinent matter on the earliest buildings on our lists. Professor Sally Chappell of De Paul University, Chicago, generously shared with us her research on the firm of Graham, Anderson, Probst and White. Professor Robert Bruegmann of the University of Illinois at Chicago and Russell Lewis, Director of Publications at the Chicago Historical Society, allowed us access to their unpublished catalogue raisonné of the work of two major architectural firms, Holabird and Roche and Holabird and Root. And Tessa Craib-Cox, Director of Communications at Skidmore, Owings and Merrill, gave us full access to the firm's invaluable archives.

Locating photographs for a book of this size is a monumental task, and we sincerely thank those who assisted us in our search, particularly the many photographers listed in the credits who gave us permission to reproduce their stunning images. We owe a great debt of gratitude to Michael O. Houlihan of Hedrich-Blessing for allowing us to publish so many of his firm's exquisite photographs. And to John Gronkowski, who shot so many of the pictures, often in response to an urgent request, goes a special note of thanks. We are also very grateful to the many people who either provided us with photographs or allowed us to photograph from their rooftops—or both— including Stanley Allen of Harry Weese and Associates; J. Paul Beitler, Deborah Greening, and Mark Jarasek of Miglin-Beitler Developments; Kit Bernardi of the Chicago Hilton and Towers; Darcy Bonner of Himmel Bonner Architects; Laurence Booth of Booth Hansen and Associates; Broadacre Management; John Buck and Joan Campbell of The John Buck Company; John Buenz of Solomon Cordwell Buenz and Associates; Canadian Centre for Architecture in Montreal; The Civic Center for the Performing Arts; Continental Bank; Constance Bea Day of Loebl Schlossman and Hackl; Constance Dickinson of Stein and Co.; William Donnell of the Montauk Company; Deborah Doyle of Doyle and Ohle Architects; Dragonette; Daniel J. Edelman; Fifield Development Corporation; Lonn Frye of Frye Gillan Molinaro; Bertrand Goldberg of Bertrand Goldberg Associates; Golub + Company; Harris Bank; Pat Heatherly of MAREX Properties; Hammond Beeby and Babka; JMB and Urban Investment and Development Company; Kohn Pedersen Fox; Kathy Koster of Koster and Company; Mary Sue Kranstover of Perkins and Will; Linpro Company; Tony Long of A. Epstein and Sons; Margaret V. Mohr of Peoples Gas, Light and Coke Co.; Keith Palmer of Murphy/Jahn; The Prime Group; Deborah Rashman of Fujikawa Johnson and Associates; Bonnie Reuben of the Hotel Inter-Continental; Christopher Rudolph of Rudolph Associates; Santa Fe Southern Pacific Corporation; Dan Shannon of Lincoln Properties; Alice Sinkevich and Laurie McGovern of Holabird and Root; Patrick Shaw of Shaw and Associates; Adrian Smith of Skidmore, Owings and Merrill; Lila Stilson of the University of Texas at Austin; Morris Swibel and Mr. Szymanski of Marina City Management; Tishman-Speyer Properties; U.S. Equities; John Vinci and Ward Miller in The Office of John Vinci; Larry Viscochil of the Department of Photography at the Chicago Historical Society; Dan White of the Civic Opera Building; Mary Woolever of the Ryerson and Burnham Libraries at The Art Institute of Chicago; and Gloria Zylowski of the Merchandise Mart.

The authors are also grateful to Abigail Sturges for her elegant design of this book, to Daniel Waterman for his astute preparation of the captions, and to Milli Payton for typing large portions of the original manuscript. Finally, we express our gratitude to Jane Fluegel, editor of this publication for Rizzoli, for her skill in merging our three voices into a harmonic whole.

John Zukowsky
Pauline A. Saliga
Jane H. Clarke

Photograph Credits

Listed below are the photographers whose splendid images appear on the pages of *The Sky's the Limit*. We are indebted to all who have so generously agreed to the publication of their photographs. The numbers indicate the pages on which those images appear.

Harold Allen 36. Apolinski Photography 217, fig. 3. Orlando R. Cabanban 190, 291. Wayne Cable, Cable Studios 85, fig. 6; 89, fig. 1; 90; 91; 272; back cover. Capes 67. Chicago Aerial Survey Co. 94. Chicago Architectural Photographing Company 56; 80; 84, figs. 3 and 4; 96; 98; 100; 102; 112; 120; 124; 128; 140; 144; 152. Ralph D. Cleveland 49. David Clifton 208, 209, 218. Collection Centre Canadien d'Architecture/Canadian Centre for Architecture, Montreal 41. Detroit Publishing Co. 10, fig. 16. Ron Gordon 37. John Gronkowski Photography Front cover; 23, figs. 2 and 3; 39; 51; 86; 87; 88; 115, figs. 2 and 3; 119, fig. 2; 126; 132; 133, figs. 2 and 3; 134; 142; 145; 158; 159; 167; 172, figs. 3 and 4; 173, fig. 5; 202; 210; 219; 236, fig. 1; 273; 284. Harr for Hedrich-Blessing 207, fig. 2. Hedrich-Blessing 13, fig. 25; 104; 135; 137; 138, fig. 4; 141; 176; 177; 181; 182; 184; 186; 188; 189, fig. 3; 192; 196; 197; 198; 199; 201; 204; 206; 216; 220; 250; 252; 258; 259; 260; 261; 262; 263; 265; 266; 267; 270; 276; 293. Timothy Hursley, The Arkansas Office 215; 227; 242; 243; 244; 245; 264. Howard Kaplan, HNK Architectural Photography 217, fig. 2. Barbara Karant, Karant and Associates 82; 83; 271. George Lambros 179. John McCarthy 189, fig. 2; Bruce Mitzit 113. Gregory Murphey 248; 254; 255, figs. 2 and 3; 256; 257; 268. Murphy/ Jahn 14, fig. 29; 160; 161; 232; 233; 234; 235; 238; 239; 240; 241. Nick Merrick for Hedrich-Blessing 222. Richard Nickel 9, fig. 13; 10, fig. 15; 60, fig. 4. Jock Pottle 274, 275, 286. Cervin Robinson 62. Ezra Stoller © ESTO 13, fig. 23; 180; 193, fig. 3; 212; 213; 223; 224. J. W. Taylor 7, fig. 3; 8, figs. 5–10; 9, figs. 11 and 12; 16; 22; 38; 46; 58; 64; 66; 74; 75, fig. 2; 92; 225. Bob Thall 60, fig. 3; 61. Raymond Trowbridge 166. Philip Turner 194. Nick Wheeler 278. John Zukowsky 123, fig. 2; 149; 163; 200; 211; 247; 282.

Listed below are the architectural firms, archives, museums, developers, building owners, and others who provided photographs from their archives and offices for use in *The Sky's the Limit*. We are most grateful to them for helping us locate the best images possible.

The Art Institute of Chicago, Ryerson and Burnham Libraries 7, figs. 3 and 4; 8, figs. 5–10; 9, figs. 12–15; 10, figs. 16–18; 12, figs. 21 and 22; 13, fig. 24; 16; 18; 20; 22; 26, figs. 1 and 2; 27, figs. 3 and 4; 28, figs. 5 and 6; 29, fig. 7; 30; 32; 33; 38; 43; 44; 45; 46; 48; 49; 50; 52; 53; 56; 57; 58; 59; 64; 66; 67; 70; 72; 73; 74; 75, fig. 2; 76, figs. 1 and 2; 78; 80; 84, figs. 3 and 4; 85, fig. 5; 92; 94; 96; 97; 98; 99; 100; 102; 106, figs. 3 and 4; 107, fig. 5; 108; 110, fig. 3; 112; 116; 118; 120; 122; 124; 128; 129; 130; 131; 138, fig. 3; 139; 140; 144; 146; 148; 155; 157; 164; 168; 170; 193, fig. 2; 205; 225; 236, fig. 2. The Art Institute of Chicago, Department of Architecture 11, fig. 19; 14, figs. 27 and 28; 53; 71, figs. 2 and 3; 105, fig. 2; 162; 171; 207, fig. 3; 283; 294; 295; 297; 299, right. Booth Hansen and Associates 89, figs. 1 and 2; 90; 91; 244; 245; back cover. The John Buck Company 2, 174, 237, 281, 291. Busch-Reisinger Museum, Harvard University, Cambridge, Massachusetts 109, fig. 2; Chicago Hilton and Towers 125. Chicago Historical Society 6; 7, fig. 2; 11, fig. 20; 19; 25; 34; 54; 152; 154; 156; 166; 178; 189, fig. 2; 296. Collection Centre Canadien d'Architecture/Canadian Centre for Architecture, Montreal 41. Continental Illinois National Bank 114. Frye Gillan Molinaro 68; 69; Fujikawa Johnson and Associates 183, 208, 209, 218, 250. Bertrand Goldberg Associates, Inc. 189, fig. 3; 190; 191. Golub + Company 119, fig. 3. Hammond Beeby and Babka 82, 83. Himmel Bonner 143. Historic American Building Survey 10, fig. 15; 24; 36; 60, fig. 4; 62. Holabird and Root 85, fig. 6. Hotel Inter-Continental 150, 151. Kohn Pedersen Fox 274, 275, 286. Lincoln Property Company 287. The Linpro Company 291. Loebl Schlossman and Hackl 179, 228, 229, 292, 293. Lohan Associates 293. Miglin-Beitler Developments 249, 288, 290, 291. Montauk Company 40; 42, figs. 3 and 4. Murphy/Jahn 14, fig. 29; 160; 161; 232; 233; 234; 235; 238; 239; 240; 241; 242; 243; 292. Museum of Finnish Architecture, Helsinki 110, fig. 4. Perkins and Will 123, fig. 3; 186; 206; 230; 231, figs. 2 and 3; 270; 271; 292. The Prime Group 293. The Public Building Commission of Chicago 193, fig. 3. Skidmore, Owings and Merrill 135; 137; 138, fig. 4; 141; 194; 195; 215; 222; 223; 224; 248; 252; 253; 258; 259; 260; 261; 262; 263; 264; 265; 266; 267; 268; 272; 276; 278; 293; 298. Solomon Cordwell Buenz and Associates 216; 217, figs. 2 and 3; 291. U.S. Equities Realty 292. University of Texas at Austin 75, fig. 3. Urban Investments, a Division of JMB Realty 254; 255, figs. 2 and 3; 256; 257. The Office of John Vinci 60, fig. 3; 61. Harry Weese and Associates 13, fig. 26; 147; 220; 299, left.

Index

DATE DUE

Demco, Inc. 38-293